1988

Creative
Play Direction

Creative
Play Direction

Robert Cohen

University of California, Irvine

John Harrop

University of California, Santa Barbara

Prentice-Hall, Inc., Englewood Cliffs, New Jersey

Library of Congress Cataloging in Publication Data

COHEN, ROBERT
    Creative play direction.

    (Prentice-Hall series in theatre and drama)
    Bibliography: p.
    1. Theater—Production and direction.   I. Harrop,
John, joint author.   II. Title.
PN2053.C58   792′.0233   73-9865
ISBN 0-13-190918-5

Prentice-Hall Series in Theatre and Drama
Oscar G. Brockett, Editor

Printed in the United States of America

10   9   8   7   6   5   4   3   2   1

Prentice-Hall International, Inc., *London*
Prentice-Hall of Australia, Pty. Ltd., *Sydney*
Prentice-Hall of Canada, Ltd., *Toronto*
Prentice-Hall of India Private Limited, *New Delhi*
Prentice-Hall of Japan, Inc., *Tokyo*

Contents

II
Interpretation, 21

3   Interpreting the Script, 23

Overall versus Moment-to-Moment Interpretation   Intrinsic versus Extrinsic Interpretation   "Right" versus "Vital" Interpretation   Moral Imperatives in the Director-Actor Relationship   Intrinsic Interpretation—Moment-to-Moment Dramaturgical Analysis   Outside Resources for Study   The Overall Interpretation—Intrinsically Derived   Working Extrinsically   Summary of Interpretation

III
Composition, 47

4   Production Design: The Choice of a Theatre, 49

Basic Theatre Designs and Their Utility   A Director Chooses a Theatre   The Staging Area   Violating the Stage   The Scenery System   Scene Changes The Quality of the Design

5   The Ground Plan, 94

Choosing a Ground Plan

6   Blocking, 110

Terms   Called-for Stage Actions   The Chosen Actions   Blocking Creates Clarity   Blocking Creates Focus   Blocking Establishes Credibility   Blocking Establishes and Heightens the Inner Action   Blocking Creates Behavior   Blocking Creates Special Effects   Blocking Creates Aesthetic Effects   Blocking Creates Variety   Blocking Creates Abstract Effects and Symbolic Patterns   The Director's Blocking Tools   Blocking Terms   Working Out the Blocking   Recording the Blocking

7   Lighting, 147

Lighting Instruments   Lighting Control   Effects of Lighting   Lighting the Action   The Effects of Controlled Lighting   The Director Works on Lighting the Play

8   Audial Composition, 154

Rhythm   Pace   Music   Sound Effects   Integration of Sounds and Sights

IV
Acting, 167

9   Directing Actors, 169

The Actor-Director Relationship   General Directorial Methods   Directing in the Nineteenth Century   The Stanislavski System and Naturalism   Later Naturalistic Techniques   Antinaturalism Techniques   Gordon Craig: The Actor as Über-Marionette   Vsevolod Meyerhold: The Physical Actor and Space   Jacques Copeau: The Spiritual Ensemble   Antonin Artaud: A Theatre of Cruelty   Peter Brook and Jerzy Grotowski   Alienation: Bertolt Brecht's System   Game Theory and Acting   Improvisation   Auditions and Casting   Summary: Working with Actors

V
Style, 217

10   Styling the Play, 219

Intrinsic Style   Extrinsic Style   Creating Style   Style Informs the Whole Production   Historical Styles   Contemporizing the Play   Setting the Play in an Arbitrary Period   Aesthetic Styles   The "Isms"   Example: *Lysistrata* The New Theatre   Realism and Naturalism   Summary

Appendix, 271

11   Directing the Play, 273

A Production Model   The Proposal Phase   The Preproduction Phase   The Production Phase   Rehearsal Timetable

Selected Bibliography, 297

Index, 301

Preface

This book examines and illuminates the art and process of play direct-ing, not as performed by any single director or school of directors, but from a creative approach, with an eye to a wide variety of options. We believe that directing is a creative rather than an imitative act, and that suggestions which open up the field are more valuable to the student than prescriptions which narrow it down. The quality of the director is ultimately determined by the choices he makes, not by the precepts he follows.

The book is divided into an introduction, an appendix, and four central parts, which deal in turn with interpretation, composition, acting, and style. Although these may be distinguished as the four central concerns of play directing, no academic organization should obscure their total interdepen-dence. The order in which topics are discussed is customary, but certainly not sacred.

For ease of identification we have tried to cite only well-known dramatic classics, which we support with additional information necessary to make our directorial points. We have leaned somewhat heavily on Shakespeare, and particularly on *Hamlet,* because of its great familiarity and ability to sustain, over the years, hundreds of valid interpretations and production styles.

Finally, while both authors of this book are responsible for generating every word herein, the sections on interpretation and composition were first drafted by Robert Cohen, and those on acting and style by John Harrop.

Our thanks to Dr. Theodore Hatlen of the University of California at Santa Barbara for assistance with photographic research, and to those students of the School of Fine Arts, University of California at Irvine, who appear in the workshop photographs.

Creative
Play Direction

I
Introduction

1

The Development
of the Director

Contemporary play directing is a creative art. Today top play directors are lionized in national publications, featured on late night television talk shows, given billing above the title of the plays they direct, and offered salaries and profit percentages which would astound their nineteenth century counterparts. Today drama students study the work of directors (from a literature developed to assist that study) in the same way that earlier students studied writers, painters, and composers. Whether this is a splendid or sorry state of affairs is debatable; that it is true is beyond question.

The "Emergence of the Director"[1] is one of the most astonishing developments of theatre history. Until relatively recent times—say the last ninety years of a history that reaches back twenty-five centuries—directing

---

[1] The title of an excellent essay by Helen Krich Chinoy, in *Directors on Directing*, rev. ed., ed. T. Cole and H. K. Chinoy (Indianapolis: The Bobbs-Merrill Co., Inc., 1963).

3

was unknown, undescribed, and unconsidered as a theatrical art. Little was recorded of the nature of stages, staging, and the overall mise-en-scène. Historians inquiring into the specifics of the fifth century B.C. Athenian theatre or a sixteenth century London public playhouse are forced to conjecture on the basis of a few fragmentary, accidentally preserved pieces of information. The physical theatre and its uses was long considered uninteresting; classical historians and critics paid no more attention to theatre practice than a modern literary analyst does to the nature of linotype machines. The "art" of the theatre was generally considered to lie in the dramatic literature written for it, or in the actors' interpretation of that literature, rather than in the totality of the medium, the modern director's concern.

Pre-nineteenth century direction was not remarked upon because it was not asked to be remarkable. That is not to say that it was carried out by dull or untalented people, but that neither the theatre artists nor audiences required or appreciated the originality of approach that is a director's hallmark today. On the contrary, earlier dramatic periods developed a firm set of conventions that "directed the director," and no óne could tamper with stage conventions except at great peril. In the simplest, most common form of direction, the playwright simply chose his actors, met with them and read the script aloud as he expected them to speak it, and explained how, when, and where they should move about the stage. This done, brief rehearsals were held and the play was performed. Imagine, for example, the probable rehearsal schedule for the 1601 premiere of *Hamlet*. Shakespeare already knew what kind of theatre he would play in (the Globe), what kind of scenery and props were at his disposal (most had been in use since the Middle Ages), what actors would play the parts (the parts had been written with specific actors in mind), and what kind of acting style the play would require (the style of the Lord Chamberlain's Men). There were no extended discussions about interpretation, because the playwright obviously knew what the play was about, nor were there any elaborate rehearsal techniques, because the actors were presumed to know how to act. A season which saw over fifty premieres allowed little time for experimentation. So it is no wonder that hardly half a dozen facts and anecdotes survive about Elizabethan play directing, or for that matter, about directing in any period before the past century; directing was not remarkable in the sense that no one at the time thought it a particularly interesting subject on which to remark.

Thus the history of directing, which might be spread over twenty-five centuries, is in fact confined to one, with the period before about 1850[2]

[2] It is impossible to date precisely the beginning of modern directing, as the "revolution" occurred in different minds and different cultures at different times.

relegated to the prehistory of the directorial art. To be sure, this generalization glosses over some significant exceptions, but to ignore it would be to ignore a fundamental shift in the nature of the creation of theatrical art. For while the conventional theatre of Sophocles, Shakespeare, Calderon, and Molière is hardly to be considered primitive, the conventions that governed it are no longer prescriptive. The director has arisen to take their place.

The Prehistory of Directing

Before about 1850, directing consisted largely of instruction. The ancient Greek director was called a *Didaskalos*, an "instructor." Instruction implies a generally accepted set of rules and established goals; for example, we expect a French instructor to teach us the accepted usage and grammar of his language, not to create lyric poetry. The early director, like the French instructor, had a functional rather than creative purpose: to convey to his actors, designers, and technicians the production "plan" that everyone knew was correct. Presumably the director's plan was more subtle, sophisticated, artful, or even bold than the average spectator's would have been, and presumably he had gifts for explaining that plan and helping his colleagues realize it; but essentially his duty was to see that a predetermined norm was realized successfully. To the early director, "correctness" was the highest compliment. To understand the impact of the revolution in aesthetic judgment, we need only note that "unexceptional" was used as a word of *praise* in nineteenth century American dramatic criticism. Applied to an actor's performance, it meant that he made no exceptions to the "correct" method of playing the role.

The few exceptions to the ancient concept of the director's role constitute what little directorial history we now possess. Aeschylus, skilled in choreography, made choral movement an intrinsic part of his productions. From an ancient biography we learn that with his wildly disordered entrance of the Furies in *The Eumenides*, Aeschylus "so terrified the crowd that children died and women suffered miscarriage."[3] Sophocles, who employed scene painting and introduced the use of a third actor, wrought on theatre convention permanent changes which were as much directorial as literary. Charles Macklin, an eighteenth century actor-manager, made such striking changes in the interpretation of Shylock in Shakespeare's *The Merchant of Venice* that he won the immediate hostility of literary critics. But these exceptions were indeed exceptions. More

---

[3] A. M. Nagler, *A Source Book in Theatrical History* (New York: Dover Publications, Inc., 1959), p. 5.

than any other artists, theatre directors until modern times have been exceedingly conservative.

The model "prehistoric" director could be Sophocles at the Theatre of Apollo, Cynat[4] at the Lucerne Weinmarkt, Shakespeare at the Globe, Molière at the Palais Royal, Goethe at Weimar, or any of the hundreds of anonymous or barely known stage directors in the theatre capitals of the world before modern times. This model director might also be the playwright; if not, he believed that he knew exactly what the playwright intended. He knew his theatre intimately, and his actors were for the most part regulars. He knew how each role was to be played and was adept at conveying that information to the actors. He arranged them about the stage in a conventional manner so that the right actors could be seen at the right times, and he made sure that the dialogue was properly spoken. Finally, he assured a correct and if possible lavish investiture of scenery and costumes. He would not be asked to examine the roles in the play, or the features of the theatre building, for alternate options of interpretation or staging. He never tried to call attention to himself through originality or creativity. His name was never listed on any program.[5] He gained his knowledge by a lifetime of apprenticeship and observation and passed it on to his successors with refinements, never overhauls. We have no monuments to the work of these anonymous directors, for unlike the silent architects of the Middle Ages they have bequeathed us no Chartres Cathedrals. They are best described by their medieval appellation, *maîtres de jeu,* or playmasters: they organized the ceremony, rather than creating its impact.

The Beginning of the "Modern Age" of Directing

Directing developed as an independent art as it grew from an instructional process to a creative one. This gradual development, related to simultaneous changes in society, philosophy, and the other arts, came about during the latter part of the nineteeth century, although it had been quietly building up for almost a century. The names associated with it are Darwin, Freud, and Nietzsche, as well as Saxe-Meiningen, Gordon Craig, and Stanislavski.

The total change in thinking that occurred toward the end of the

---

[4] Stager of a medieval passion play.

[5] Printed programs are recent additions to the theatre. Even when they became widely used, directors' names were rarely included. Frequently a star's name would appear on the program in a directing capacity; the nineteenth century American actor Edwin Booth often did this. However, research reveals that the productions "directed by Edwin Booth" were in fact directed by his stage manager, D. W. Waller.

last century involved the overthrow of the concept of the ultimate norm, as it had been understood since the time of Aristotle. Man's authority over the universe had been shaken first by the Copernican astronomers who had told him that he was not the center of the universe. The onslaught of the late nineteenth century was begun by Darwin, who explained that man was biologically an animal, and by Freud, who added that he was spiritually an animal as well, and that his perceptions and actions were motivated and deflected by unconscious processes. Nietzsche and the atheistic philosophers argued that man acted in the absence of godly ordinances, and Einstein furthered man's disorientation by explaining that energy and matter were simply different forms of the same substance, and that matter, energy, time, and motion were all laced into a bewildering nexus of relativity.

These new ideas toppled man from his rational pedestal into an alien and ultimately unknowable universe. The principle of uncertainty, a law of modern physics, says that the more closely we examine anything, the less possible it is to see what it is. While this principle is meant to refer to a subatomic level, where the light necessary to "see" an electron would so alter it that it could not be seen, or understood, it may be applied metaphorically as well. Science has given up the quest to "understand" the universe, and has limited its task to relating and explicating phenomena.

Philosophically this has led to a general acceptance of phenomenology, the modern way of looking at things. Phenomenology requires that the observer continually realize that he is not seeing "the whole picture"; that there *is* no objective "whole picture." The phenomenologist knows that he is looking at individual phenomena which form his individual point of view. There is no universal point of view, nor any total summation to be derived from synthesizing phenomenological observations: as Camus says, "Aspects cannot be added up."

The impact on the arts of phenomenological thinking has been enormous. In the visual arts it became evident for the first time in French impressionism, a style which was given that name after a showing in 1874. The principal aesthetic approach of the impressionists was to demonstrate that there were an infinite number of ways of "seeing" a scene. Claude Monet painted water lilies again and again to show how variable their image was when filtered through ever varying light conditions and the states of consciousness of the viewer and the artist. Technically, the impressionists sought to portray the "aspects" of color and light, rather than their synthesis, which occurs beyond the retina of the eye. They painted splashes rather than areas, points instead of lines. This particular movement reached a climax with the development of "pointillism," in which the canvas was covered with thousands of miniscule points of painted color to give an impression, rather than a recreation, of a scene. The visual arts have now gone much beyond impressionism, until we have reached a point of total creativity and nonreliance on models or masters. Today there is neither norm nor "correctness" in painting and sculpture.

As painters broke away from the conventional and rational models, so did poets, and about the same time. That a poet could write a treatise on "How to Write Poetry," as did Boileau and many others in the seventeenth and eighteenth centuries, became ludicrous in an age which admired Whitman, and appalling in the time of Eliot, Pound, Cummings, and Lawrence. The standard form was broken, along with the concept that there was to be a standard form—and they have never been reestablished.

Theatre has moved in the same direction as the other arts, albeit more conservatively, largely because theatre is collaborative, involving a great investment of money, time, and people. A painter may decide one day to throw out canvas and oils and restock with zinc, tin, and a welding iron; the theatre manager cannot do this so simply and inexpensively. Even so, the theatre has moved, and directors have moved it.

The Modern Director as Artist

The prototypes of the modern director were the men who ran the seventeenth and eighteenth century playhouses of London and the rest of Europe. Their duties were diversified by the development of representational scenery and by the need to perform revivals of older plays. The use on stage of wings, drops, borders, and traps meant that someone had to arrange the furniture and the actors, so that the actors would not trip over each other. The frequent production of revivals of the works of dead playwrights created a need for someone to explain to the actors what their lines meant and to negotiate differences of opinion. In London these early directors were also the star actors; hence they were called actor-managers.

If the actor-managers had a common goal, it was to achieve a unified and correct scenic style. Lacking philosophical or aesthetic guidelines, they opted for a unifying motif: historical authenticity. During the nineteenth century Samuel Phelps and Charles Kean in England and Edwin Booth in America produced huge Shakespearean revivals which attempted to create in absolutely accurate detail the world of eleventh century Denmark or the Rome of the Caesars. Their industry was remarkable: great sums were spent on historical research, authorities were consulted to ensure the authenticity of costumes and properties, and theatre programs frequently included twenty-page inserts describing and annotating each

Victoria & Albert Museum

Figure 1. *Nineteenth century staging.* Shakespeare's *Henry VIII*, staged by Charles Kean at the Princess Theatre, London, in 1855. Notice the extraordinary attention to historical detail within the formal pictorial composition.

property seen in the production. The actor-managers were also interested in transmitting "correct" interpretations of the plays, and Edwin Booth was invited by the scholar H. H. Furnival to add several hundred footnotes to the Variorum editions of *Othello* and *The Merchant of Venice*.

However, the actor-managers were stars, basically, and their concern for production integrity, though entirely sincere, was star-centered. Booth's great scholarship and research on *The Merchant of Venice*, for example, ended with his exit (as Shylock) in the fourth act—Shakespeare's fifth act was eliminated from Booth's production. Without exception, the actor-managers stopped producing when they stopped acting; they had no interest in pursuing directing as an independent enterprise. It fell to others to wrench directing away from its adjunct status and to practice it as a creative act.

First to pursue directing on its own was a German nobleman with a provincial repertory troupe. He is usually referred to as Saxe-Meiningen, although his full title was George II, Duke of Saxe-Meiningen. His work

Figure 2. *Nineteenth century staging.* Trial scene from Shakespeare's *A Winter's Tale*, produced by American actor-manager Edwin Booth at Booth's Theatre, New York, in 1871. Elaborate historical realism was achieved by an artful combination of painted figures and live actors. Striking as the scene may have been, it was unoriginal, copied to the letter from Kean's 1856 British production. This was typical of the times.

came to prominence when his company left the Duchy and appeared in Berlin in 1874; coincidentally, the year that brought impressionism to Paris brought what might be considered its theatrical equivalent to Berlin.

The concept of total integration of subordinate units was what Saxe-Meiningen, not an actor himself, brought to the stage. His company consisted of repertory performers, who rotated between starring roles and "bit" parts. His crowd scenes were staged not in rank and file fashion the day before opening night, as they had been in the past, but with attention to every person and artifact on stage. His scenery, still in the tradition of historical authenticity, was designed to be used by the actors instead of as a backdrop for them. Stage movement was fluid, involving carefully

Theatermuseum, Munich

Figure 3.   Sketch by the Duke of Saxe-Meiningen for the blocking of a crowd scene in *Julius Caesar*, about 1870.

plotted individual "blocking" for every actor, not just the leading characters. While the actor-managers had been able to stage spectacular crowd tableaux, these tableaux had remained static. Saxe-Meiningen, however, managed to create a highly dynamic harmony which set a model for future stage productions.

With the discoveries of Saxe-Meiningen, directing entered its modern phase. Step by step, the director asserted his importance and authority. Quickly the ideal of historical authenticity—which even Saxe-Meiningen had more or less accepted—became a thing of the past. Directorial movements in various European countries shaped a modern dramatic art which was as unlike its predecessor as Van Gogh was unlike Gainsborough. In France, beginning in 1887, André Antoine promoted the ideal of naturalism. Championing the plays and philosophies of Émile Zola, Antoine tried to make his stage a scientific laboratory for the study of society. Actors coughed, snickered, or hiccuped their way through turgid, aimless scripts in an effort to recreate real life in a real setting. For a play about butchers, Antoine built a real butcher shop of real wood, with real counters and real meat hanging from real hooks, around which buzzed real flies. The theatre of Antoine (*le théâtre libre*) ran so counter to the old school of acting and directing (where the lead actor always stood center and faced front) that it became known as "the theatre of Antoine's back." Konstantin Stanislavski, in his Moscow Art Theatre, formed in 1898, also promoted naturalism in acting and directing and tried to merge it into a newer, more poetic form.

In Germany expressionism took a foothold, and directors strove to communicate the spiritual meanings of their plays through the scenery, the style, and the entire mise-en-scène as well as the text. For example, Fritz Erler, a precursor of expressionism, in his 1908 production of Goethe's *Faust* replaced the old stock scenery with huge grey screens which turned red upon the entrance of Mephistopheles, indicating the passions creeping into Faust's consciousness. Expressionism in theatre is similar to its counterpart in painting; it basically assumes that the medium is *part of* the message, not a neutral vehicle for its transmission. Thus the advent of expressionism made the director at least coequal with the playwright, and indicated that the mise-en-scène, the director's creation, was at least as important as the text. Virtually the entire stream of contemporary theatre has been, in this sense, expressionistic.

Elsewhere in Europe, the Swiss designer Adolphe Appia enlarged the director's palette with his revolutionary designs and discoveries in the use of stage lighting. In the days of the actor-manager, when artificial lighting first became known to the theatre, lighting had remained functional, purely to illuminate the action and help the audience to their seats. Lighting effects were simple: colored lights to indicate a time of day, "calcium" spotlights to create a moonlight effect, and modest dimming for nighttime scenes. But Appia, aided by the invention of incandescence, discovered the powerful theatrical effects of spotlights, shadows, dimouts, blackouts, and backlighting. In 1911 Gordon Craig, whose name is often associated with Appia's and whose thought certainly owes much to Appia, gave the new age international recognition with the celebrated publication of his book, *On the Art of the Theatre.* Craig promoted the director as artist, as the complete creator of theatrical art. "I have contempt for any man who fails in the whole duty of the stage director," declared Craig, who shocked contemporaries by claiming the director's total right to disregard the playwright's stage directions, scene descriptions, and other supportive material. Indeed, Craig demanded that the director be an absolute dictator over every portion of theatrical performance, and that "until discipline is understood in a theatre to be willing and reliant obedience to the director . . . no supreme achievement can be accomplished." Craig anticipated a renaissance in theatre, brought about by supreme directors exercising their creative powers over the concept and total execution of a theatrical production.

Craig's renaissance has arrived. The twentieth century has been the era of the director: Max Reinhardt, Jacques Copeau, Elia Kazan, Jean-Louis Barrault, Louis Jouvet, Bertolt Brecht, Peter Brook have influenced the theatre as much as virtually any playwright. The shape of much great contemporary theatre has been created by directors and playwrights in conjunction: Elia Kazan working the multilevel time-place structure into Arthur Miller's *Death of a Salesman,* or shaping the balance of empathy in the plays of Tennessee Williams; Jouvet giving elegance and theatrical poetry to the plays of Jean Giraudoux; Bertolt Brecht, the theoretician of the theatre, directing political "sense" into the plays of, among others, Bertolt Brecht.

The day of the anonymous director/stage manager was past. Even such bastions of directorial anonymity as the Comédie Française broke down and in 1937 listed directors on its programs coequal with the playwrights. For the Comédie, which took this step belatedly, it was the first official recognition of the director in more than 250 years of continuous theatrical history.

Although, like every revolution, the emergence of the director has had bitter critics, it is a fact of our time. No student of directing can nor should ignore it, for in his present position as artist, the director has opportunities and responsibilities that were unknown fifty years ago. And they must be fulfilled: mere competence in directing is no longer enough. In every arena—community, college, or professional—the director must fulfill his new obligation: to find in his production that which is unique, exceptional, profound, theatrical, exciting. In short, he must create.

The Contemporary Creative Director

Modern directing, which has developed from the explosion of the values, icons, and conventions of the past, is by nature unconventional and unique. No serious director in America or England today follows the fixed precepts of any standard directing "textbook," nor are there any inviolable basic rules of directing. Among leading directors there would be disputation rather than consensus on "correct" methods of casting, blocking, interpreting, and creating effects. Most directors insist on the freedom to change their methods with every play they direct, every new actor, every new discovery. The director's only "given" is the command to create a vivid and original theatrical experience. How he implements that command depends on his talent, his technique, and his creative imagination.

2

The Director's Function

What is the director's function? Is he simply the man who tells the actors where to enter the stage and what to do there? Is he primarily responsible for pacing the production, as most provincial play reviewers seem to think? We shall avoid being too prescriptive, and simply answer that, in the broadest terms, *the director himself determines what his functions shall be.* Ideally the director decides what needs to be done, who shall do it, and how.

For example, consider the assumption of directorial functions by Louis Jouvet. Jouvet was France's great director during the interwar period. He presented the original premieres of the plays of, among others, Jules Romains, Jean Giraudoux, Jean Paul Sartre, and Jean Genêt. Jouvet considered himself "un homme du théâtre," and personally undertook the following tasks in a typical production which he directed:

1. He chose the play.

2. He collaborated with the author in revisions.
3. He cast the play.
4. He interpreted the play to the cast and the audience, publishing his interpretation in newspaper articles and books.
5. He contracted for a theatre.
6. He hired all design and staff personnel.
7. He arranged for financing.
8. He staged the play.
9. He designed the scenery, sets, costumes, and lighting.
10. He worked in the shop building the sets, actually inventing lighting instruments for the performance.
11. He wrote the theatre program.
12. He advertised the production.
13. He acted a leading role.
14. He coached the other actors.
15. He supervised the company performance and morale during the run.

Jouvet did not assume all the functions in all his productions or even in a majority of them, but he was capable of any or all of them as the case required. The point is, there is no limit on the amount of a director's involvement in his production. Staging the play is only one of the many directorial functions involved in play production, and not necessarily the main one. The extent to which he assumes these functions largely determines the breadth of his creative options.

The director acquires specific functions by a combination of circumstance and personal choice. He delegates functions because it is in his interest to do so, or because he finds himself forced to do so; he collaborates with persons he chooses or who have been forced upon him. The director must balance carefully between the arrogation of authority and the delegation of responsibility; missteps in either direction can lead to disaster.

The Director Assumes His Functions

To determine how a director assumes directorial functions we must begin with a clean slate: no play, no theatre, no actors, no assistants. The director usually begins by choosing a play or a piece of theatrical material. In film parlance and occasionally in professional theatre this is called the "property." It need not be a conventional play at all; it could be a "nudie" review such as *Oh! Calcutta!,* an improvised guerrilla theatre or infiltration theatre piece, a revival of *South Pacific,* or a reading of *Medea* in the original Greek. The concept of what constitutes a play must be creatively redefined. Richard Schechner defines a "theatrical event" so broadly as to include happenings, the 1967 march on the Pentagon, and the beer party which brought together cast and audience at the Minneapolis Firehouse Theatre's production of Euripides' *Iphigenia at Aulis.* "The theatrical event," says Schechner, "includes audience, performers, text (in most cases), sensory stimuli, architectural enclosure (or lack of it), production equipment, technicians, and house personnel (when used). It ranges from nonmatrixed performance to highly formalized traditional theatre; from chance events and intermedia to the 'production of plays.' A continuum of theatrical events blends one form into the next."[1]

Shortly after the selection of a play, or even at the time of its selection, the director will probably make two other major decisions: who will be in the play and where it will be staged. He will decide to produce (or to propose to his possible backers) *Peer Gynt* in Central Park, *As You Like It* with an all male cast, *King Lear* with Laurence Olivier, *Barefoot in the Park* on Broadway, or *Gammer Gurton's Needle* in the local high school. It is important to realize that *when these selections have been made, a great portion of the directorial function is complete.*

In practice, directors frequently do not choose the play, the actors, or the theatre. Television directors, for example, are usually hired after all these decisions are made; the director of a single television episode may be handed a script a day or two before it is to be televised or taped, and told which actors will play which parts. His directorial options are almost entirely restricted to the staging of the material. But most theatre directors at least have a hand in these first three functions and proceed to assume several more, particularly interpreting, coaching, staging, and determining the overall design of the production. The most important and creative contemporary directing is performed by men and women on and off Broadway and in regional, college, and community theatres who have extensive artistic control over their productions. That is the type of directing we shall discuss in this book.

A Collaborative Art

A complementary directorial obligation is to decide which functions should be delegated to collaborators. The success of any theatrical enterprise is always in some measure the success of the collaborating artists. Jouvet's tremendous assumption of responsibilities was an exception, and it is worth noting that as his career progressed, he delegated more and more of the operation to others.

[1] "Six Axioms for Environmental Theatre," *Tulane Drama Review,* XII, No. 3 (Spring 1969), p. 41.

The director behaves differently as collaborator from his behavior as a performer in his own right; he must be, in addition to an original and imaginative thinker/doer, a highly sensitive artist/administrator. A willing collaborator recognizes and uses fully the talents and creativity of his co-workers. If the director is a frustrated actor or designer, he may find it difficult to inspire actors or designers working in his production, since he really has little faith in anyone but himself. On the other hand, the director does need to retain authority over collaborators. Imagine a production of *Hamlet* in which the scene designer produces a series of abstract gray stone steps spilling out from a gray and white cyclorama, the costume designer clothes the actors in authentic fourteenth century Danish garb, the prop master decides that all props should be made out of yellow and red plastic, Hamlet models his readings on the Olivier album, Ophelia is a refugee from six years of environmental improvisation, and the lighting designer figures that followspots and red striplights best enhance the play's inner action. None of these ideas is necessarily awful in itself, but together they spell a catastrophe, and although the case is exaggerated, similar instances of directorial intimidation are all too frequent. The director need not presume to be smarter or more talented than anyone else on his staff, cast, or crew. He must simply organize and unify the disparate elements of his production into a consistent whole that makes a significant contemporary statement.

It is helpful to the director that his production team is deployed in a fairly formal collaborative hierarchy. At the top of this organization is the producer, who may be one man (like David Merrick), a community board of trustees, a university drama department, or a commercial partnership formed strictly for the purpose of presenting a particular play.[2] The producer arranges for the financing of the production, and as such (it seems to matter not at all whether the production takes place in a capitalist or communist culture) ranks above the director, who is ultimately responsible to him. While the producer's responsibility is for the financial soundness of the enterprise, the director remains the artistic head. Subordinate to him, ordinarily, are the designers and the actors.[3] Subordinate to the producer are the business manager and his staff, but the director

[2] To confuse matters a bit, until the last twenty years the British used the word *producer* as we do *director*.

[3] There are, of course, exceptions. If the designer is more experienced and highly paid than the director, or if one of the actors is a star and/or has financed the production, the director may find his authority challenged. Subordination is rarely a matter of tyrannical control, either. "The theoretic hierarchy could never be made to work without the lubrication of common sense and tact," says Tyrone Guthrie (*A Life in the Theatre* [New York: McGraw-Hill Book Company, 1959], p. 134).

must be consulted about (if he does not initiate) specific working methods for everyone involved in the artistic nature of the production.

The director is a leader. This is really his first function, and also the reason why it is virtually impossible to begin a career in the theatre as a working director. The production team might number three or four people, as for a college production of *Krapp's Last Tape,* or several hundred for a Broadway musical; the director must ensure that all these people are working together toward the same artistic goals. His hierarchic position, though well established on an organizational chart, must be earned by the trust and respect he engenders among his co-workers. He leads many diverse people, frequently of independent temperaments, almost always under the pressure of deadlines. He must be able to communicate, delegate, decide, and command under both normal and crisis conditions. He must be able to bolster, teach, protect, charm, and inspire his co-workers, without the overbearing attitude which could destroy effective collaboration. These personal attributes are the necessary entrance requirements for the profession of directing; without them the most brilliant, original, artistic, and sensitive would-be director is relegated to directing himself in a one-man show.

The Four Concerns of Play Directing

Let us assume that the embryonic director is a person of sensitivity, artistry, and originality. He is capable of leadership in a vital artistic collaboration. He is anxious to direct, and qualified people are similarly anxious to help him by acting, designing, working technically, and finding financing for his production. This ideal embryonic director still needs four tools with which to create the theatrical experience he wants to communicate to his audience: *interpretation, composition,* both visual and aural, *acting,* and *style.* When the director has examined all his options in these areas and has made and implemented his choices, he has directed the play. How he deals with the choices defines what kind of director he is. These four areas—and the examination and implementation of the director's choices—are the central concern of this book.

II
Interpretation

3

Interpreting the Script

It is a common assumption that script interpretation is the director's first responsibility, because all other directorial decisions, such as questions of stage composition, can be answered only in terms of a preformulated interpretation. In practice this is not always true. At times many directors candidly admit that they have no interpretation of the play as they begin rehearsals and none when the play opens, and plays produced in such a manner have occasionally succeeded enormously. It is hard to believe that an interpretation is needed for most Broadway sex comedies or Scribian farces, for example, since the single object of these plays is to entertain the audience continually.

Yet it is also fair to state that most plays are approached from a directorial interpretation, even if such an interpretation is unarticulated. The director's interpretation is a set of ideas, images, and feelings that express what the director wants his play to communicate to the audience. This set of ideas includes the director's conception of the play's meaning, and whatever additional meanings he plans to infuse into the production (or burden the production with, depending on his success at blending interpretations).

For simplicity, let us divide the director's interpretational function into two categories—*overall interpretation* and *moment-to-moment interpretation*—and into two sources—*intrinsic interpretation* and *extrinsic interpretation*.

Overall versus Moment-to-Moment Interpretation

Overall interpretation is the director's concept of the meaning of the entire play. *"Hamlet* is a play about a man who thinks too much"; *"The Three Sisters* is a play about the coming of the Communist Revolution"; *"Othello* is a play about Elizabethan racism and homosexuality." These are three controversial overall interpretations which the director might try to convey to the audience through the implementation of the production. Moment-to-moment interpretation is the director's analysis of the beat-by-beat inner action of the play, what is happening at every moment of every scene in each character. Moment-to-moment interpretation is diagrammatic understanding of motivations, objectives, inner monologues, and psychological understandings, even in nonrealistic plays.

Whether overall interpretation is derived from moment-to-moment analysis or vice versa is an open question. Directors frequently begin production with a firm overall idea and seek to make every moment in the play conform to that overriding interpretation. Or they may begin with only a few scenes visualized and work studiously through rehearsals to deduce an overall interpretation from the bits of evidence conveyed by those scenes. Most productions noted for highly original interpretation are inductive; that is, the director begins rehearsals with a carefully conceived overall interpretation. Ellis Rabb's *Merchant of Venice* at the American Conservatory Theatre (1971) is a case in point. Rabb decided at the outset that the play concerned a homosexual elitist society in Venice, with Antonio its chief patron and Bassanio a young man opting (with difficulty) for a bourgeois heterosexual marriage. Rabb's interpretation meant that the most dramatic trial scene occurred not in Act IV (the trial of Shylock), but in Act V (the "trial" of Bassanio), and thus made sense of the last act of Shakespeare's play, long considered difficult to bring off successfully. It also added new and poignant meanings to many moments in the play, such as Antonio's recantation during Shylock's trial: "I am a tainted wether of the flock, Meetest for death: the weakest kind of fruit . . . ." On the other hand, strikingly original interpretations occasionally call attention to themselves and away from the excellence of the script and the actors' performances. A traditional interpretation has usually become traditional because it receives little resistance from the text; productions celebrated for their naturalism and fine acting usually result from a greater emphasis on moment-to-moment script interpretation than from a strikingly original overall concept. But there is no reason why this is necessarily the case.

Intrinsic versus Extrinsic Interpretation

A director's two basic sources of interpretative decisions are the text and himself. The extent to which he uses the one rather than the other determines whether his interpretation is basically intrinsic or extrinsic.

Intrinsic interpretation comes precisely from the text and from materials that illuminate the text. Such materials include explanatory remarks by the author, critical remarks about the author and his play, biographical and historical data, and material concerning the play's critical and theatrical history. Intrinsic interpretation seeks to recreate the playwright's world and his play as a part of that world.

Extrinsic interpretation comes from the world of the director and the world of his audience. Whereas intrinsic interpretation attempts to define precisely what the play "means," extrinsic interpretation involves what, in the present production, the director wishes the play to "say." For that reason, extrinsic interpretation is often considered "reinterpretation" or "updating."

We need not justify extrinsic interpretation on the basis that the author really intended these meanings; his script is simply deep and elastic enough both to suggest and to permit them. For example, *Othello* has been produced with implications of American racism, *Hamlet* with a bow to Freudian (Oedipal) theories; and *King Lear* as a paean to existential alienation; such productions can be justified by their dramatic vitality, but not by their exact replication of the author's original intentions. Because of their frequent production and consequent overfamiliarity, and their profundity and universality, classics are obviously most subject to extrinsic interpretation.

Critics and even directors frequently assail extrinsic interpretation. The generation of directors after Jacques Copeau followed his maxim "le texte seul compte" (only the text counts); thus our generation of directors was preceded by one which asserted that the director's sole function was to elucidate the pure meaning of the text as created by its author. To be sure, Copeau's maxim was honored more in the breach than in stage practice, as any examination of his production books shows, but the maxim remains in theoretical service to this day. It is unrealistic theory, however.

Director Peter Brook says, "When I hear a director speaking glibly of letting a play speak for itself, my suspicions are aroused, because this is the hardest job of all. If you just let a play speak, it may not make a sound. If what you want is for the play to be heard, then you must conjure its sound from it."[1]

"Right" versus "Vital" Interpretation

The transition from intrinsic to extrinsic interpretation, from the director's finding what the playwright "meant" to his expressing what the play "says" to him, is largely unconscious, crossing an undefinable line at a hidden point. Certainly we have reached an existential age in which there is no such thing as a right or wrong interpretation. Of course, there are historically correct interpretations, such as the D'Oyly Carte presentations of Gilbert and Sullivan operettas which have been produced intact since their original premieres in the last century, and there are productions which are authorized or certified by the playwright and even directed by him, which have some claim to "correctness." But the vitality of the theatre depends on the fact that as times and people change, attitudes do also, and play productions must adjust to those changes if genuine communication is to occur. Because *The Trojan Women, A Midsummer Night's Dream, Hamlet,* and *King Lear* permit reinterpretation throughout the centuries, their impact is as immediate today it was when they were written.

No director—and no critic, for that matter—can "see" a play exactly as the author intended; directors or critics who assume that they can are guilty of an arrogant lack of perspective. The exactly "correct" production never existed: our perception is limited by restrictions on our imagination and ability to determine the author's intent, and altered by the ideas and imaginative leaps of our sensory apparatus and intelligence. A Hindu parable tells of eight blind men who felt and then described an elephant. The first felt the tail and exclaimed that an elephant was like a rope, the second felt the animal's hide and insisted that an elephant was like a wall, and so on. In the same way, reality appears different to different people. No single view is exclusively "correct," not even the author's.

The director's aim, then, is a vital interpretation, rather than a "correct" one. Tyrone Guithrie said,

> An interpretive artist can only make his own comment upon the work
> which he endeavors to interpret, and . . . to do so humbly is the only pos-

---

[1] *The Empty Space: A Book About Theatre—Deadly, Holy, Rough, Immediate* (New York: Atheneum Publishers, 1968), p. 25.

sible attitude to the "creator" (or, more truly, the expressor) of the "original" idea. Throughout my own career I have been criticized for impertinently attempting to express my own subjective, and admittedly limited, comment upon the masterpieces which I have been privileged to direct. I consider such criticism misplaced. I know perfectly well that my comment upon *Oedipus Rex, Hamlet* or *All's Well That Ends Well* is not the final, any more than it is the first, interpretation of these works. My collaborators and I have merely added one more comment to the vast corpus of criticism, admiration, revulsion, reverence, love, and so on, with which a masterpiece of human expression is rightly surrounded.[2]

This situation should not alarm the dramatic author. Theatre is a collaborative art, most vital when that collaboration is healthy and flexible. Nowhere is there more potential for greatness than in the director-author relationship, even when the author is no longer alive. Some author-director combinations have produced dynamic fusions of talent, such as the long-lasting partnerships of Tennessee Williams and Elia Kazan, Jean Giraudoux and Louis Jouvet, Paul Claudel and Jean-Louis Barrault, and Anton Chekhov and Konstantin Stanislavski. Such collaboration, even if stormy, can be a factor in scaling the greatest heights to which the theatre artist can aspire.

Moral Imperatives in the Director-Author Relationship

Interpretation always comes from both intrinsic and extrinsic sources, that is, from the play and from the director. The ideal is the best of both, the worst of neither. The director is neither an automaton who helps the author technically transform his play from page to stage, nor a tyrant who arbitrarily hacks the play to pieces in the act of creating his own.

In collaboration with living authors, the director must be guided by ethical considerations. The Dramatist's Guild, which is involved in all contracts for new plays being professionally produced, insists that the author have veto power over the selection of the director, and the right to insist on or veto script changes. Beyond the law, a director should treat the playwright as a collaborative artist (presumably the most important one) on his production team.

However, the artistic director of the production has the right to interpret his play as he chooses, even if the playwright screams, the actors curse, the producer cuts the budget, and the critics yelp like mad dogs. The theatre today seeks vision, vitality, and excitement, and the director

[2] *A Life in the Theatre* (New York: McGraw-Hill Book Company, 1959), p. 139.

has been elected to elicit them. If the playwright wants a production of absolute fidelity, he can direct it himself; Arthur Miller took over the direction of his play *The Price* partly for this reason. The final criterion for measuring play interpretation is that it make a production work, engendering what we recall (or fantasize) about a great theatrical experience: catharsis, empathy, understanding, astonishment, hilarity, awe—feelings that can be powerfully communicated from the stage to the audience. If a play works, no one will complain about the director's reinterpretation of the text; if it fails to work, no amount of critical commentary by the director in his program note can persuade the audience not to remain indifferent. Propriety and nicety have never been very helpful in theatrical interpretation. They certainly are not now.

Intrinsic Interpretation, Moment-to-Moment

Although no firm line separates intrinsic and extrinsic interpretation, it is clear that the director can analyze either intrinsically or extrinsically; that is, he can approach the play from these two vantages (not necessarily simultaneously) with an eye toward their coalescing in the final interpretation. Ordinarily the director begins by thinking intrinsically, because only when he has a firm grasp on the play's intrinsic moment-to-moment action and overall theme can he seriously begin to apply externally derived interpretive ideas. (For example, it would be impossible for a director to decide to produce a Marxist *Hamlet* if he had not read the play.) We will follow the director's normal method of organizing his sources of information to arrive at an interpretation.

STUDY OF THE TEXT

A first quick reading of any play reveals only a fraction of the action occurring within it. Even in a simple play the inner action is complex; the changing interrelationships of characters and situations are found only through several readings, each from a somewhat different point of view. The director's familiarity with the inner action, which is ordinarily at the heart of his overall interpretation, must be developed in painstaking detail. This is easily overlooked. Examine, for example, the opening scene in *Hamlet* (I. i. 1-15).

> *Enter Bernardo and Francisco, two sentinels.*
> BERNARDO. Who's there?
> FRANCISCO. Nay, answer me: stand, and unfold yourself.
> BERNARDO. Long live the King!
> FRANCISCO. Bernardo?

BERNARDO. He.
FRANCISCO. You come most carefully upon your hour.
BERNARDO. 'Tis now struck twelve; get thee to bed, Francisco.
FRANCISCO. For this relief much thanks; 'tis bitter cold,
    And I am sick at heart.
BERNARDO. Have you had quiet guard?
FRANCISCO. Not a mouse stirring.
BERNARDO. Well, good night.
    If you do meet Horatio and Marcellus,
    The rivals of my watch, bid them make haste.
FRANCISCO. I think I hear them. Stand, ho! Who is there?

The scene looks simple, but appearance is deceptive. We recognize that Bernardo is replacing Francisco at the sentry post, that Francisco has had a quiet guard, and that others are coming, but there is much more to the scene. Follow the example of scene interpretation closely to see the level of detail which must be pursued.

"Enter Bernardo and Francisco." Shakespeare (or the editor) fails to say from where the characters enter, but it is obvious that they do not enter at the same time or place. In a modern production, with lights and/or a curtain, Francisco can be "discovered" at the rise of the curtain. Nor need the dialogue or Bernardo's entrance follow immediately. The director may wish to indicate mood, time, action, or character by inventing business for Francisco as he awaits his replacement. Francisco might be pacing out his sentry duty, sleeping against a post, warming his hands against a fire, reading a book, even relieving himself behind the battlements.

"BERNARDO. Who's there?" This is a highly uncharacteristic line which must be carefully interpreted. Ordinarily the on-duty guard challenges the newcomer, not vice versa. A few lines later Francisco does his job correctly, hearing Horatio approach and challenging him immediately. But here Francisco apparently does not hear Bernardo before he arrives on stage. Moreover, Bernardo's question is unusual: he knows he is to replace Francisco at this place and time, and would ordinarily have no doubts as to whom he was seeing.

Uncharacteristic dialogue should alert the director that a between-the-lines explanation is needed; in interpreting a moment in a play he must not only find out what is happening, but what is *not* happening, why a character says something unexpected. A possible interpretation and staging of Bernardo's opening line follows.

> Bernardo, arriving alone for guard duty, is aware of the possibility of the ghost's appearance, and is therefore in a highly alert and frightened state. Francisco, on the other hand, has not been told of the ghost's appearance the previous night. (Later in the play it becomes clear that only

Horatio, Marcellus, and Bernardo know of the ghost, and Francisco does
not reappear in the play after this scene). Francisco is therefore carrying
out his guard duty perfunctorily. At the end of his long tour at the sentry
position he is sitting against the battlement wall, huddled in his blanket,
tending a fire. Bernardo, tiptoeing to his post, does not see Francisco at first,
and Francisco is so enclosed by his blanket that he does not hear Bernardo.
Suddenly Francisco rises to poke the fire. Bernardo sees the blanket move
and in his agitated state is alarmed at the prospect of seeing a ghost. He
nervously cries "Who's there?"

"FRANCISCO. Nay, answer me: stand and unfold yourself." This
should have been Francisco's immediate response: to challenge the arriv-
ing guard. He is embarrassed at having been caught derelict in his duty
and speaks brusquely to cover his embarrassment.

"BERNARDO. Long live the King." Possibly a prearranged password,
although Horatio does not use it later. Bernardo must recover his composure quickly, or Francisco will think something is the matter. Bernardo,
it is now understood, wishes to prevent Francisco from knowing about the
ghost of Hamlet.

"FRANCISCO. Bernardo?" This confirms Bernardo's earlier uncharacteristic behavior. Since he was expected, and since he comes "most carefully upon his hour," Francisco should ordinarily be expected to recognize
him immediately, without further questioning. That he does not reflects
his puzzlement at Bernardo's original alarm.

"BERNARDO. He." Bernardo confirms his identity, probably with a
gesture, handshake, or embrace.

"BERNARDO. 'Tis now struck twelve; get thee to bed, Francisco." The
first of three subtle and not so subtle admonitions that Francisco leave before the ghost arrives. That it is twelve the director might wish to confirm
by the tolling of a bell in the distance.

"FRANCISCO. For this relief much thanks; 'tis bitter cold and I am
sick at heart." An atmospheric line which is all the more poignant when
we realize that Francisco knows nothing of the ghost, and senses a dread
presence merely from the air itself. The line also establishes the physical
cold of the surroundings, which the director could confirm by stage business.

"BERNARDO. Have you had quiet guard?" Bernardo is fishing for information without revealing what he knows. Had Francisco known about
the ghost, Bernardo would probably have asked him, "Has this thing appeared again tonight?"—which Marcellus asks Bernardo a few moments
later. But Bernardo asks a neutral, nonrevealing question and receives a
neutral answer: "Not a mouse stirring." Again, we can discover what is
happening by examining what is *not* happening.

"BERNARDO. Well, good night." The second admonition for Francisco to leave, perhaps uttered more directly. Why is Francisco lingering? Perhaps to gather up his blanket and other accouterments.

"BERNARDO. If you do meet Horatio and Marcellus/The rivals of my watch, bid them make haste." Bernardo does not want to be left alone with a ghost nearby. Francisco has just served his tour alone, and Bernardo's concern for his companions can be justified only by the particulars of the situation.

"FRANCISCO. I think I hear them. Stand, ho! Who is there?" Francisco calls out as he should, demonstrating that his original behavior toward Bernardo derived from unusual circumstances.

Our interpretation of the first fifteen lines of *Hamlet* is intrinsic—deduced from the lines of the play rather than from any external theory. However, the interpretation is neither exhaustive nor unarguable. Directors with different insights would discover inner actions not suggested above, even contradictory to the preceding analysis. Even if our interpretation were followed explicitly, there would be countless ways of implementing it. The point is that the inner action must be studied with extraordinary attention to detail. If the actors performed the opening lines without considering the questions raised by this discussion, the play would open flatly and without definition. True, it is not absolutely vital that the audience involve themselves in whether Bernardo is acting strangely or whether Francisco has been let in on the ghost's appearance; unless they are very familiar with the play they will not even know that they have missed anything by not answering these questions. But without close interpretation and performance, the scene will lack texture, meaning, and definition. And obviously, if that is true of the first fifteen lines of *Hamlet,* it is true of the rest of *Hamlet* and of every other play besides.

FINDING THE INNER ACTION

The examination of the text for inner action, or subtext, involves probing the intentions, motivations, and inner monologue of each character during the scene in question. Even a thousand readings by the director could not explain every moment of every character's performance; that is why much moment-to-moment interpretation occurs not in the director's study but in rehearsal. The actor's task is to present a consistent and thoughtful characterization that makes sense to him (the character/actor). Francisco can hardly memorize his lines without wondering how much he is supposed to know about the ghost. A good actor will spend a great deal of time questioning his character's behavior. Directors aid their actors' work in this matter by being ready to answer and initiate questions. "Why are you doing this? What are you thinking about now? What do you want from him?" are the kinds of questions directors frequently ask during rehearsal. The director may not have a ready answer, but trusts the actor to come up with something, perhaps through discussion. The important thing is that questions are asked.

Moment-to-moment interpretation takes time. Stanislavski rehearsed plays for over a thousand hours at his Moscow Art Theatre—about eight hours per playing minute—and much if not most of that time was discussion of intentions and motivations. Directors who brag that they can "bring in" a production with just fifty or sixty hours of rehearsal probably "see" only about 5 percent of the subtext of the play. They may win plaudits in the hinterlands, but their work usually dissolves if exposed to intense critical analysis.

Dramaturgical Analysis

Moment-to-moment analysis is not simply an accumulation of unrelated events. Plays are carefully organized presentations of experiences, and the technical name for that organization is *dramaturgy,* the art of dramatic composition. Dramaturgy is the process by which a playwright presents a series of acts, inner actions, revelations, attitude changes, and thought processes so as to create climaxes and reliefs. In this, the theatre differs markedly from everyday life. Arguments in real life are irregular and sporadic; rarely do they rationally come to a satisfying climax. Theatre, even in our existential world, rarely permits that sort of frustrating experience. The elements of dramaturgy are usually present in every scene of a play: exposition, inciting action, rising action, climax, and resolution.

Exposition is the introduction or exposure of relevant material. The audience is informed about the individuals who will soon experience a conflict. They are also informed, ordinarily, of the prior conditions which bear on the conflict.

Inciting action is the introduction of a source of conflict among the characters or within a single character. In melodrama, a pure dramaturgical art, the classic inciting action is the detective's entrance to assert, "Dr. Jones did not commit suicide, he was murdered. And someone in this room is the murderer."

Rising action is the detailed struggle of the characters to overcome the conflict. The conflict cannot be easily overcome, and frustration, rage, and fear may grow. The source of conflict becomes more insistently irritating, and the characters grow more desperate to rid themselves of the irritant.

Climax is the identification and exorcism of the irritant through violence, argument, hilarity, or some other means. In melodrama the detective discovers the murderer and kills him in a shoot-out. In Aristotelian terms the climax of a tragedy is said to provoke in the audience a *catharsis,* a purging of the emotions and an enlightening of the spirit.

Resolution is the reestablishment of the sense of order and calm that existed before the inciting action. In many Shakespearean tragedies, for example, the last lines are spoken not by the principal characters, but by fairly neutral characters whose speeches set the house back in order—a new order, not a reversion to the old one.

Directorial interpretation uses the dramaturgical devices throughout a production, by the moment-to-moment clarification of conflict and inciting actions, the sensitive projection of subtext during rising action, and the induction of catharsis during a well-wrought climax and resolution. Let us examine the opening scene (after a monologue) from Tennessee Williams' modern classic, *The Glass Menagerie.*[3]

> (*Amanda and Laura are seated at a drop leaf table.*)
> AMANDA (*calling*). Tom?
> TOM. Yes, Mother.
> AMANDA. We can't say grace until you come to the table!
> TOM. Coming, mother. (*He . . . takes his place at the table.*)
> AMANDA (*to her son*). Honey, don't *push* with your *fingers.* If you have to push with something, the thing to push with is a crust of bread. And chew—chew! Animals have secretions in their stomachs which enable them to digest food without mastication, but human beings are supposed to chew their food before they swallow it down. Eat food leisurely, son, and really enjoy it. A well-cooked meal has lots of delicate flavors that have to be held in the mouth for appreciation. So chew your food and give your salivary glands a chance to function!
> (*Tom deliberately lays his . . . fork down and pushes his chair back from the table.*)
> TOM. I haven't enjoyed one bite of this dinner because of your constant directions on how to eat it. It's you that make me rush through meals with your hawk-like attention to every bite I take. Sickening—spoils my appetite,—all this discussion of animals' secretion—salivary glands—mastication!
> AMANDA (*lightly*). Temperament like a Metropolitan star! (*He rises and crosses downstage.*) You're not excused from the table.
> TOM. I'm getting a cigarette.
> AMANDA. You smoke too much.
> (*Laura rises.*)
> LAURA. I'll bring in the blanc mange.

This short scene contains all the classical dramaturgical attributes of a longer play. The exposition, aside from Tom's opening monologue

[3] Reprinted from Tennessee Williams, *The Glass Menagerie,* © Random House, Inc., by permission of the publisher.

before this scene, is clear simply from the exchange in the first two lines, in which Amanda names Tom, and he replies to her as "Mother," revealing the essential characteristic of their relationship, which is to be explored. The inciting action is twofold: Amanda chides Tom for not coming to the table and for his unrefined eating habits. The situation is not unusual; the audience can respond to the introduction of an obvious irritant in the mother–son relationship.

In the rising action both Amanda and Tom try to justify their points of view, Amanda begging Tom to eat leisurely to better enjoy his meal, Tom begging to be left alone to eat as he wants to. Yet we understand from this simple exchange that Amanda is really disturbed at far deeper aspects of Tom's personality than his eating habits; her harping shows us her insistence on babying a grown-up son and her refusal to see the new reality which threatens to engulf her. Tom is irritated not so much at his mother's specific remarks, but at his inability to counter them successfully. His frustration intensifies her anxiety, and her anxiety intensifies his frustration, causing a spiraling buildup of dynamic energy that demands release.

The climax of this scenelet is modest: Tom leaves the table without finishing his dinner and lights a cigarette. Amanda's "You smoke too much" is a climactic line which really means "You are not what I had hoped for in a son." The minor climax of this scene prefigures more unrestrained ones to follow; this climax delays the dramaturgical process, allowing the rising action to begin again, and again, and again until the final climax of the play is achieved. The resolution of this scene is also specific: Laura rises to bring in the blanc mange (the very name of the dessert connotes a cooling off), reestablishing the illusion of harmony which existed before the inciting action occurred. The resolution, like the climax, is not complete, and this is a pattern for scenes and subscenes during the course of the moment-to-moment interpretation. If every scene ended with Oedipus gouging out his eyes, the theatre would become very boring.

There is nothing arbitrary about the ordinary dramaturgical process, neither is it restricted to plays. A bullfight follows much the same pattern, with exposition (the procession), inciting action (entrance of the bull), rising action (series of passes, each closer than the last), climax (killing the bull), and resolution (ridding the arena of the bull's carcass, and cheers for the matador). Perhaps the dramaturgical process imitates the act of sexual congress, which has been described by modern physiologists as consisting of inciting action (erotic stimulation), rising levels of action (plateaus of excitement), climax (climax, or orgasm), and resolution (detumescence).

The director uses dramaturgical principles by examining his script for incitements to action, climaxes, and resolutions. He examines the rising action to discover at what points the argument climaxes: where Tom feels like continuing his line of reasoning, and where he decides to peak and cut it off. He recognizes Amanda's "You smoke too much" as a climactic line and directs the actors accordingly. He analyzes Laura's "I'll bring in the blanc mange" as a premature attempt at resolution. A play that produces an integrated series of incitements, rising actions, climaxes, and resolutions becomes a meaningful communicative experience. One that simply presents the audience with a series of arbitrarily organized phenomena is as dense as a treatise written in a foreign language.

Outside Resources for Study

The director often needs resources in addition to his intellect and imagination to understand the intrinsic meanings of a text. This is particularly true of noncontemporary and foreign plays, but even a local, contemporary playwright may use allusions and references unknown to the director or anyone else on the production staff. Difficulties in intrinsic interpretation call for the use of external resources, many of which are easily available.

DICTIONARIES

Obviously the director must know the meaning of every word in the play. Most modern American plays present little problem, at least to a modern American director, but in foreign plays or revivals words can frequently be a stumbling block. The plays of Shakespeare, for example, are filled with words that have no present meaning or whose present meanings differ from the ones Shakespeare intended. Most editions of Shakespeare include footnotes and/or glossaries that give the sixteenth century meaning of disputed words, but even these footnotes may be open to question. A helpful resource for the complete understanding of old English words is the *Oxford English Dictionary,* which not only defines every word in the English language, but also gives the entire history of each word, tracing its usage from earliest times through Shakespeare's to our own.

One common misconception of a Shakespearean line is Juliet's famous plaint, "Romeo, Romeo, wherefore art thou Romeo?" Incredibly, this line is frequently read with *wherefore* misapprehended as *where,* so that countless young actresses have leaned over the balcony crying, "Wherefore *art* thou Romeo?" as though they were calling a dog home for dinner. Of course, *wherefore* meant (and means, although the word is now generally obsolete) *why,* not *where,* and the line should be read "Wherefore art thou *Romeo?"* Occasionally Shakespeare uses a word that is found absolutely nowhere else, such as *exsufflicate,* in *Othello,* and a meaning must be imaginatively attributed, either through etymological research or by context analysis.

VARIANT EDITIONS

Older plays often face the director with the problem of differing versions. Most plays in the Shakespearean canon were printed in Quarto editions as well as in the First Folio, and in many cases variant readings exist which editors have tried to collate into an "official" text. One famous variation is Hamlet's line, "Oh that this too too solid flesh should melt," which in two of the three printed versions of the play reads "sallied flesh." To compound the problem, editors throughout the years not only have chosen among variant readings but have often suggested their own on the grounds that all printings are wrong; one such emendation of the word in question is "sullied flesh." Obviously the interpretation of this key speech will differ depending on whether Hamlet complains about his "sullied," "solid," or "sallied" flesh. The director must be careful in selecting edition and editor, if he does not enter the field of Shakespearean bibliography himself.

From time to time the words of modern plays also need outside elucidation. A production of William Saroyan's *The Time of Your Life* was foundering during rehearsal of a scene in which characters spoke of going "down to the Sunset," until someone explained to the East Coast director that "the Sunset" is a district in San Francisco, the locale of the play. References in the plays of Sean O'Casey and Brendan Behan are unintelligible unless Easter Week and the IRA are explained to the cast. Highly poetic plays like those of T. S. Eliot and Samuel Beckett frequently require use of dictionaries and encyclopedias if the director is to understand even the surface meaning of the lines. Among the insults Vladimir and Estragon hurl at each other in *Waiting for Godot* are such epithets as "morpion," "curate," "gonococchus," "spirochete," and "cretin." In the same play, Lucky speaks of "a personal god, quaquaquaqua, with divine apathia, divine athambia, divine aphasia. . . ." Unless the director's vocabulary equals Beckett's, he will have to look up these words and fit their meanings into the context of the play.

TRANSLATIONS

In directing translated plays, the director can usually choose from several scripts, translate the play himself, or commission someone to

translate it for him. He can even choose to collate several different translations and use the readings that he prefers from each. Collation may result
in an uneven and jerky script, but it has frequently proven worthwhile.

Some translations severely alter the text and subtext of the play.
The first American translations of Giraudoux, for example, so changed
the content of his plays that they should instead have been called adaptations: whole characters and scenes were omitted and added; names and
ages of the characters, dates, places, language, and meaning were arbitrarily changed. The same is true of many other plays. If the director can read
the original, he obviously should, and also incorporate translated versions
of disputed passages into his production.[4]

Even if accuracy is not in question, translations should be carefully
examined for the nature of the inner action their words transmit as well
as for the flavor of the dialogue and poetry. Just as a director collaborates with an author, so does a translator, and though the translator's express purpose can be to transmit the play with total accuracy, he may be
psychologically unable to keep his mind and personality out of his work.
There is no totally accurate translation of a work of art. Changing one
language into another presents a variety of options in every line; a simultaneous examination of two "accurate" translations of any play will produce hardly a single identical line. Translators try to convey not only the
meaning of the text, but the diction, rhythm, poetry, and intangible feeling. Some famous translations sound awkward on stage, and some that
appear feeble in print achieve great heights in performance. Very few
translators—particularly of Greek plays—have much if any experience
with the theatre, and their translations sometimes prove entirely unactable in the hands of modern actors and directors.

HISTORICAL SOURCES

When producing plays of a bygone age, directors frequently find it
invaluable to acquaint themselves and then their actors with the historical perspective of the plays. Trevor Nunn, artistic director of the Royal
Shakespeare Company, frequently begins his rehearsal for a Shakespearean play with a lecture on the world of the play, covering Shakespeare, the
country in which the play is set, and the music, customs, language, and
political situation of the times. Nunn also brings to his first rehearsals
voluminous visual materials, pictures not only of the set and costumes,
but also of the people of the age and their civilization. Nunn's practice is
common and usually helpful. Some directors steep themselves in the his-

---

[4] Commissioning translations or tampering with extant ones may raise questions
of royalty payments and infringements of rights, if the play or the translation is protected by copyright.

tory of the period, giving their actors books that pertain to it. Actors who play historical characters (for example, Thomas More, Marat) may benefit from reading biographies of their characters, even if the literal biography does not correspond to the central topic of the play. The director should read these books first to determine their pertinence and to incorporate them in his interpretation. Many lines in historical plays, and much of their inner action, can be more clearly defined by consulting the sources (or their equivalents) the playwright had when he wrote the play.

The word *historical* need not apply only to plays of past centuries. It would be difficult for a director to evolve an excellent production of John Osborne's *The Entertainer* (1957) if he were not familiar with the events leading up to the Suez crisis, the disintegration of the British Empire, the effect of the nuclear bomb on British domestic culture and policies, and the effects of aristocracy and class division in England.

CRITICAL SOURCES

Dramatic literature includes a large body of written criticism. Only when directing an utterly original play is the director devoid of critical and descriptive material. If possible, the first critical source a director should consult is the author's own words. Published plays frequently include an author's preface, which may give skillful interpretive suggestions; occasionally (as with the plays of Eugene O'Neill) a wealth of critical commentary is written into the stage directions. Most modern playwrights have also written dramatic criticism, at least of their own work; for example, excellent essays on the theatre have been written by Tennessee Williams, Arthur Miller, Luigi Pirandello, George Bernard Shaw, John Osborne, John Arden, Anton Chekhov, Friedrich Dürrenmatt, Jean Giraudoux, Jean Anouilh, Samuel Beckett, Eugene Ionesco, Bertolt Brecht, Edward Albee, Eugene O'Neill, Jean Genet, Jean-Paul Sartre, William Inge, Rolf Hochhuth, and Peter Weiss. The *New York Times* solicits dramatic opinions from playwrights on the eve of their successes in New York, and various journals and books also feature interviews with and statements from playwrights on their craft and their intentions in any given play.

A second critical source is the works of criticism that have been published about most dramatic authors. Published mainly by university presses, these are available in any major college library. The literature on any established playwright, of course, is voluminous; the material on Shakespeare alone could hardly be digested in a lifetime. Experience leads to judicious selection of helpful material. The worlds of literary criticism and theatre practice are all too often remote from each other, and critics, who seldom have to test their points in performance, often tend to be overly prescriptive in their interpretations. Criticism can be of enormous value to the director, but it must be auxiliary—it cannot determine the creation of the stage life of a play.

OTHER PRODUCTIONS OF THE PLAY

Seeing an earlier production of the play is of questionable value to the director. Sometimes it is unavoidable, as when the director is asked to direct a play he has seen, acted in, or even directed before. Max Reinhardt directed *A Midsummer Night's Dream* many times during his long career in the theatre, and each production was different from the last, as he drew on his increasing knowledge of the play. But earlier productions directed by someone else may actually inhibit certain directors' creative powers by subliminally suggesting interpretations, blocking, and business that will come off as borrowed rather than created, part of an earlier plan, not the director's new one.

Directors who feel secure enough to examine the ideas of other directors facing their material can watch prior productions of the plays they are working on. If seeing the production is impossible, the director can study the prompt book, examine photographs, read local reviews, and talk to persons who have seen or worked on the play. The earlier director might be happy to answer interpretational questions. Reviews by New York theatre critics are published biweekly in looseleaf segments which are also bound together at the end of each season, and reviews in the national press can be located in periodical indexes. All such sources may suggest answers to moment-to-moment interpretational questions.

It is often helpful to examine the original production of the play, particularly if the playwright was involved in supervising, advising, or even directing that production. Bertolt Brecht's productions at the Berliner Ensemble are detailed in his *Modellbücher,* which record with text and photographs the blocking, business, settings, properties, and virtually every word of the author-playwright to his actors during rehearsals. Some of Brecht's "model books" are available in published abridgments; others can be had only in East Berlin. But all plays produced since the eighteenth century have some stage history available in libraries, theatre collections, and various personal files, and all these premiere production records can further illuminate the intrinsic meaning or interpretation of a script.

The Overall Interpretation—Intrinsically Derived

When the director has read his text a number of times and has carefully studied the meanings of individual words, the moment-to-mo-

ment development of character relationships, and the world created by
the playwright out of his own psyche, political and social interests, and
physical environment, the director may want to create an overall interpretation for his production. This is not simply the sum of the play's
moment-to-moment aspects. A play never shows a simultaneous existence,
but a temporal existence that differs from exposition to climax to denouement. Overall interpretation synthesizes moment-to-moment meanings but
also supercedes and is wholly different from them.

It is never absolutely necessary to formulate an overall interpretation, of course. Plays vary in obviousness. The director of a nineteenth
century melodrama may simply forgo considerations of overall interpretation ("This play is about a murder and who did it") and work directly
on developing moment-to-moment action and characterization. Or the
complexity of a play may elude the director, who unconsciously chooses a
simplistic interpretational approach.

Some plays, however, are complex even on the surface. It is difficult
to read *Hamlet,* for example, or Molière's *The Misanthrope* without ap-
preciating their apparent ambiguity of approach. We are never entirely
certain how seriously to take Hamlet or Arnolphe at any moment, or how
we should expect to think of them at the end of the play.

An overall interpretation gives a philosophical direction to the presentation of a complex play. It is not enough that the director and the
scholar know what a play is "about"; it is also important that the audience, who see the play only once, leave the theatre with some concrete
ideas about what they have seen. They need not perceive a "message" or a
coherent philosophical "position"; the transmission of interpretation may
be simply a series of vivid images and feelings, ineffable but highly memorable. In his valuable book, *The Directorial Image,* Frank McMullan
suggests that directors interpret plays via imagery rather than ideas, and
transmit those images intact (visually, sonically, and ideologically) as
their "interpretation." Perhaps we can clarify by giving examples of interpretational questions a director might ask of major classic plays.

Hamlet. Is Hamlet really feigning his madness (he claims to put his
"antic disposition" on, as if it were a mask), or is he insane? Does he love
Ophelia? How old is he? Why does he delay his assassination of Claudius?
(The last question is the most answered in the history of dramatic criticism, and all the answers are different.)

Othello. Is Othello a black or an Asian Moor? Does racial prejudice
fit into the subtextual character relationships of the play? Why does Iago
behave the way he does? Why is Othello so susceptible to Iago's questions?
Why does Desdemona so foolishly pursue Cassio's reinstatement? Why
does Emilia steal the handkerchief, admitting her guilt only after the
damage is done?

A Streetcar Named Desire (Tennessee Williams). With whom are we supposed to sympathize? Should we feel protective toward the frail, neurotic Blanche, or toward the "normal" married couple, Stanley and Stella? Why does Stanley rape Blanche? Why does Blanche lie to Mitch? What should we feel about these characters and their behavior?

All these questions will lead to an overall interpretation which is well beyond the mere moment-to-moment happenings. If Hamlet is played as mad, the play is one of madness, and the fruits of madness run rampant in a corrupt court. If he is sixteen the play's meaning differs from that if he is thirty. If he fails to kill Claudius because of deep psychological fixations, the play is very different from what it would be if he fails because the opportunity never presents itself.

The overall interpretation should take into consideration the feelings of the audience. Plays can be weighted toward a certain character; for example, Sophocles' *Antigone* has been interpreted to make Creon a noble hero and Antigone a spoiled brat, and one production of Williams's *Cat on a Hot Tin Roof* shows Maggie as heroic and Brick, rotten. Shylock, in Shakespeare's *The Merchant of Venice,* has been played for both sympathy and ridicule, sometimes in simultaneously competing productions. At the level of overall interpretation the director decides how he will present his characters to the audience, and what kind of feelings he will try to engender. When the play is over, the audience will have a patchwork of ideas, images, feelings, and questions. These, in composite, are the interpretations he has transmitted to them.

OVERALL INTERPRETATION AS EMPHASIS

Overall interpretation is not just a matter of making yes or no decisions. A more subtle area of overall interpretation is generally much more important than specific decisions about a character's behavior or motivation. This is the matter of *emphasis.* Any complex play has hundreds of themes, subthemes, plots, subplots, character relationships, and character revelations, all of which cannot be equally promoted to the audience. The director selects themes that seem important to him and sets them off emphatically to the audience. Other themes he underplays or avoids.

The process of emphasis parallels the compositional process of achieving focus. Just as the director focuses the audience's attention on a given actor, so he focuses their intellectual attention on a certain theme. *Hamlet* has many related themes, but the director who tried to bring out even a few would find himself in difficulty. Audiences seek clarity. It can be argued that they attend the theatre to escape the chaos of mundane existence. The theatrical experience is a programmed one: the director is the programmer. He employs exposition, conflict, climax, and resolution. At every stage the audience is moving through an elaborate maze of magic, emotion, ideas, and theatrical devices. When these become confused, the way is lost; despite the excitement of the individual moments, they seem to be going nowhere and the audience grows irritated, then bored. The director cannot say, "That's like life!" when accused of presenting an unfocused and meandering play; life doesn't charge $7.50 a seat.

Directorial emphasis usually falls on one or more lines from the play which can be isolated and used to clarify and intensify the overall interpretation. For example, in Arthur Miller's *Death of a Salesman* Biff Loman says of his father, "He didn't know who he was." Willie's wife, Linda, exclaims, "He's only a little boat, looking for a harbor." Willy himself says, "You know, I feel sort of temporary about myself." King Lear discovers that, like all other men, he is only a "bare, forked animal." Vladimir, in Samuel Beckett's *Waiting for Godot,* cries, "I can't go on!" and then does.

Lines like these are selected as consonant with the overall interpretation and then emphasized through the use of compositional and audial focus. They can be isolated, surrounded by silence (the "pregnant pause"), elevated physically to a position of maximum attention. They stand as a focal point for all the action of the play; such a line is prepared for, and when made, confirmed so that it lingers in memory after the play. A well-directed play communicates its points in small bursts of intelligence that combine the spatial, the sensual, the intellectual, and the emotional. The spectator makes his own highly personal synthesis of the bursts, sometimes days, weeks, or months after the actual performance.

Working intrinsically, the director at best becomes his own literary critic. Some directors, like Peter Brook, write excellent dramatic criticism, and some dramatic critics, like Eric Bentley, make excellent directors. Though the person equally skilled in both areas is rare, it is apparent that one skill complements the other. A director who can find nothing to say with a script can hardly direct, and a critic who has no theatrical sense can hardly analyze a play's dramatic (as opposed to literary) content. A director's intrinsic interpretation is seen best in his production, and although he may wish to write a note about the play for the program or for the local papers, it is on stage that his interpretation must be clear to be successful.

Working Extrinsically

Extrinsic interpretation involves the director's desire to create a *specific* interpretational effect on his audience. The operational question for extrinsic interpretation, in contrast to "What does this play mean," is "What *can* this play mean."

Working extrinsically means working inductively, from a basic interpretation down to precise particulars. The director tailors the moments of the play to cohere with his overall extrinsic interpretation. "Tailoring" the play is a delicate operation. Traditionally, plays are "cut" in the pre-production period. Cutting is the elimination of dialogue, ordinarily because the dialogue is nonessential, time-wasting, or, in the director's opinion, simply poor theatre. Few plays reach performance with all the words from the original manuscript intact.

Besides reducing a play to manageable proportions, cutting offers the director an opportunity to delete lines that are superfluous to his interpretation. In his "existential" production of *King Lear,* Peter Brook purposely eliminated all signs of Edmund's final recantation and the servant's explanation of how he treated Gloucester's sore eye sockets. More optimistic productions of *Lear* have retained those rather human moments and cut the lines (or even the whole scene) regarding Gloucester's blinding. More dramatic tailoring of script—most critics would call it tampering, not tailoring—is evident in the Joseph Papp production of *Hamlet* (1968), sometimes referred to as "The Naked Hamlet." Thus does Hamlet meet the ghost:

> *Hamlet sits in his coffin-bed, turns on his radio, and begins reading. The radio offers ghostly wailing instead of music, and Hamlet tries to adjust it.*
>
> *A long, green, rubber hand emerges from the bed-clothes and starts to feel its way across the sheets to Hamlet.*
>
> *Audience laughs and gasps. Hamlet looks up and asks the audience what is the matter. The hand touches Hamlet on the shoulder. He leaps out of his coffin and begins flailing with his pillow at the figure which emerges from the bed-clothes.*
>
> HAMLET. Angels and ministers of grace defend us! (*general laughter*)
> GHOST. Mark me.
> HAMLET. I will.
>
> GHOST. I am thy father's spirit—(*Hamlet cheers and runs like a scared rabbit out into the audience. He stays there for some time hiding and cheering*) . . . Now, Hamlet, hear. 'Tis given out, that sleeping in my orchard the lightning struck me. (*The Ghost produces a newspaper with the banner headline*: KING STRUCK BY LIGHTING. . . .)[5]

Extrinsic interpretation and script tampering need not go so far as

[5] Reprinted from Joseph Papp and Ted Cornell, *William Shakespeare's "Naked" Hamlet: A Do-It-Yourself Handbook,* Copyright © 1969 by The Macmillan Company. Used by permission.

Mr. Papp's, nor need they be so sedate as Brook's selective cutting. Yet even though critics complain that Shakespeare is "rolling over in his grave," it is hard to see that anything but an abstract and outmoded commandment has been offended; rather, new generations of audiences have been exposed to valuable dramatic material, and directors have found themselves able (and audiences willing) to excite new issues with reference to the older ones. Few directors today believe in ghosts, and few fear to add their imprimatur to the dramatic material they prepare for their audiences.

WORKING WITH AN EXTRINSIC INTERPRETATION

The sources for extrinsic interpretation cannot be listed in any book, because they are the director's personal sources. Extrinsic interpretation may come from his experience of political events, philosophy, psychological discovery, religion, science, or any other human area. A creative play director is not a craftsman working in isolation from his world; he is not so devoted to the theatre that he brings nothing with him *to* the theatre. Although theatre is not a substitute for polemical argument, the artist in the theatre (or in any other medium) must ultimately have something to say besides the implicit statement, "I am an artist." His statement need not be verbal, scholarly, unique, or even profound, but if he is a great artist it is invariably *there*. Most successful directors today are involved, at least emotionally, in the cultural concerns of their times, in politics, in the sociology of life and art, and in philosophizing about the quality and destiny of human life. Without this involvement, they would be hard put to appreciate, much less direct, the great plays. Though they might be able to "spin out" a passable community theatre production of a Broadway sex comedy, they could hardly tackle a play of even moderate complexity, nor could they hope to direct creatively in any way.

The actual working with the extrinsic interpretation occurs on both conscious and unconscious levels. The director unconsciously projects (or introjects) his personality and/or subjective ideology into his play. If, for example, he is especially sensitive to racist intimidation, he will emphasize such incidents as he sees them in the script when coaching the actors and staging the scenes. As a fish is unaware of the current in which it swims, a director is usually unaware of his special prejudices and sensitivities; he may be shocked when critics praise or damn his "unique interpretation," when all along he felt that he was doing the play "straight." Since the unconscious level is always at work, there is no such thing as a "straight" interpretation of a play with any degree of complexity.

At the conscious level, the director may choose a governing idea for his production which, though latent in the material, is beyond the immediately revealed intentions of the author. This governing idea should be general enough to create a universal theme and specific enough to be applied to moments in the playing of the text. It would be folly to produce *Hamlet* as a plea for racial integration unless relevant lines could be found; it would also be foolish to present it as an appeal for a particular city council candidate in a coming election.

Summary of Interpretation

The director works with interpretation by focusing the audience's attention first on the moment-to-moment action of the play (its story) and finally on an overall concept, feeling, or theme. In this discussion it has been hard to avoid the theatre's only curse word, *message* ("If they want a message, send them to Western Union" is a classic Rialto remark), but it is undeniable that a play presents its audience with something more than a random story of random people. It gives them something with shape, a final meaning, and a set of impressions which, because they are organized, make a lasting mark on the mind and memory. We do not remember ordinary experiences; most of us cannot even recall our behavior during a given hour yesterday. But a superbly organized and interpreted play gives us a concise vision of reality which, properly conceived and transmitted, can leave an indelible mark upon us. Whether the interpretive material comes directly from the playwright's imagination and is simply elucidated, clarified, and intensified by the director, or whether it springs wholly from the director's imagination, struck off like a billiard ball from the playwright's cuestick, matters little in the last analysis: the successful production. Interpretation of a play, in one form or another, is a vital and absolute function of the director, and his achievement will be measured in that final integration of form with meaning which is the art of dramatic production.

III

Composition

The term *composition,* as used in this book, refers to the articulation and orchestration of all the sights and sounds of a theatrical presentation. Stage composition is the visual arrangement (placement and movement) of the actors vis-à-vis the scenery and the audience; audial composition[1] is the rhythmic or arythmic flow of sounds that reaches the audience's ears.

Historically, stage composition is the first area in which directors began to assert themselves, and even today there are directors who still consider that there is little else to the director's art. The reason for the director's relatively quick assumption of the compositional function is obvious: he was the "outsider" in rehearsals who sat back and represented the audience, previewing what they would see. He immediately saw

---

[1] *Audial composition* is not a term in regular usage, though we hope it becomes so. See Chapter 8.

the need to arrange the production as he would like to see it if he were in fact in the live audience.

The goals of stage composition range from the modest ones of orderliness, clarity, and attractiveness to the more theatrically vital ends of achieving dramatic impact, beauty, spectacle, and emotional catharsis. Directors have frequently used compositional techniques to create great emotional climaxes for plays with rather mundane conclusions. Director Peter Hunt, for example, fashioned a successful climax to the musical play *1776* by presenting a tableau showing the signing of the Declaration of Independence, backlit behind a scrim showing the Declaration itself. This arresting, affective composition brilliantly closed the play and engendered a strong emotional response from the audience which the text alone proved unable to do.

There are four major steps in stage composition: the overall *design* of the entire show, the *ground plan* of the individual settings, the *blocking* of the action, and the *business* of the characters. These are discussed separately, as is *audial composition*. These aspects of composition are, however, interdependent, and all involve various levels of collaboration among the director and other staff members. The design of the production and the ground plan involves collaboration with the designer; blocking and business involve collaboration with the actors; and the audial composition involves collaboration with the music director and/or technicians and engineers. The nature of the collaborations, of course, depends entirely on the wishes, talents, and personalities of the persons involved, but because the director remains responsible for the decisions taken in every area, he must be more than simply familiar with the problems and possibilities available in each.

4

Production Design: The Choice of a Theatre

The design of a production is the totality of visual and plastic elements which engage the attention of the audience. The first of these elements, and the one which is too often taken for granted, is the theatre itself. Too often directors choose a theatre building without taking into account that this particular "medium" of theatre is as significant to its "message" as anything that goes on inside the building. The design of a play begins with the theatre in which it is performed, and the artistic nature of the play is affected by the size of the theatre and its location, format, seating arrangement, physical equipment, personnel, regular audience, and local environment, insofar as all of these may affect the feelings and thoughts of the audience. A director can choose a theatre which meets his requirements and desires just as he can cast actors and appoint designers who similarly answer his needs.

49

Basic Theatre Designs and Their Utility

In most theatrical periods, one or two theatre designs account for
virtually all stage productions. In classical Greece a massive outdoor theatre was the home for tragedy and comedy. In Elizabethan times the public
theatres—the Globe, the Fortune, and the Swan—were relatively similar
to each other, imposing their particular spatial gifts and limitations on the
plays of Shakespeare, Ben Jonson, and John Webster. But there were also
private theatres, indoors and intimate, such as the Blackfriars, as well as
stages set up in royal palaces, in which the directors produced their shows.

American and European theatres today exhibit one predominant
form of working architecture: the *proscenium stage*. Basically this is a rec-
tangular building with the audience at one end and a stage at the other,
the division between them marked by a proscenium arch through which
the audience observes the action of the play. Prosceniums vary in width
from eight feet (The Cabaret Theatre, New Orleans) to a hundred feet

Courtesy of Radio City Music Hall

Figure 4. *Proscenium stage: spectacular.* The massive proscenium of Radio
City Music Hall, New York. The proscenium opening is 60 feet high and
100 feet wide—enough to accommodate a straight-across chorus line of 36
Rockettes. The Music Hall, used for variety shows and films, seats 6000.

D. J. Benit

Figure 5. *Proscenium stage: intimate.* In the tiny proscenium of the Cabaret Theatre, New Orleans, an intimate satirical review, *Fudgeripple Follies*, plays within arm's length of the spectators. Proscenium width is less than 8 feet, but the arrangement of scenery, actors, and audience is not fundamentally different from the Music Hall.

(Radio City Music Hall, New York) and in height from eight feet to over seventy. Audiences vary from a handful to several thousand. Ordinarily a curtain divides the audience from the stage between acts, and occasionally a forestage extends beyond the curtain for certain special effects. Virtually all Broadway and commercial European theatres have proscenium stages, with an audience capacity of a thousand plus and a proscenium width of about forty or fifty feet. Most university theatre plants feature a proscenium stage theatre with similar dimensions. While the proscenium stage is an outgrowth of theatre architecture of the sixteenth and seventeenth centuries, and while it had its absolute peak in the nineteenth century, it is in no way outdated as a theatre form, and new proscenium theatres are built each year with exquisite refinements including hydraulic pit lifts, flexible prosceniums, computerized rigging systems, and turntable stages.

The chief characteristic of the proscenium stage is that it presents to the audience (and to the director) a highly controllable stage picture. The proscenium arch acts as a frame which looks roughly similar from all parts of the auditorium. Since the audience is located on only one side of the action, looking in one direction all the time, scenery can be highly illusionistic or realistic. In the proscenium theatres of the seventeenth, eighteenth, and nineteenth centuries, two-dimensional painted scenery had its heyday, and the naturalistic sets of the late nineteenth and early twentieth centuries were ideally suited to proscenium presentation. The box set, with its real walls, ceilings, light fixtures, and furniture, is possible only on a proscenium stage. Scenery in this type of theatre can be effectively hidden from the audience between scenes either backstage or in the flies, brought on at will either behind a closed curtain or in sight of the audience. Stage tableaux can be effectively created, as can effects which depend on the entire audience's seeing a certain actor's eyes or lips at a given moment.

The Guthrie Theater

Figure 6. *Thrust staging.* Chekhov's *The Three Sisters*, staged by Sir Tyrone Guthrie at The Guthrie Theater, Minneapolis, 1963. The action is almost entirely projected into the midst of the audience. The dark patch right center is a vomitorium access to the stage.

A second form of theatre presently in wide use is the *thrust stage,* also called open stage, platform stage, or three-sided arena stage. The stage is a square, round, or trapezoidal platform surrounded on three sides by audience—usually sitting in a highly raked (angled) area—and backed by occasional scenery pieces or a permanent architectural structure. The thrust stage theatre ordinarily has no hanging scenery, and what scenery it does have must be fairly limited. Thrust stages are aided immeasurably by the use of *vomitoria,* entrances through and under the audience (see illustration on page 52). Newer regional North American theatres rely ex-

Center Theatre Group

Figure 7. *Modified thrust staging.* Ben Jonson's *Volpone,* staged (and contemporized) by Edward Parone at the Mark Taper Forum Theatre, Los Angeles, 1972. The thrust does not extend so far into the audience as at The Guthrie Theater, and many scenic and blocking elements are meant to be viewed frontally, as in a proscenium theatre.

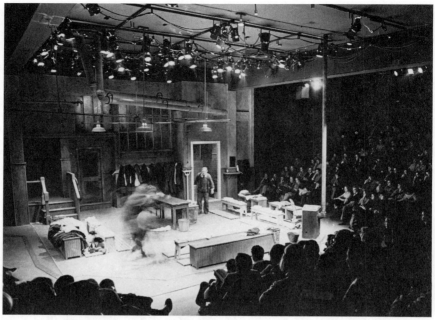

Long Wharf Theatre

Figure 8. *Three-sided arena staging.* An extreme thrust stage with the audience arranged in a "U"-shaped arena around the action, which need not be separated by a raised stage as at The Guthrie. Shown here is the celebrated 1971 production of David Storey's *The Changing Room*, directed by Michael Rudman at the Long Wharf Theatre, New Haven, Connecticut.

tensively on thrust stages; notable among them are the Mark Taper Forum in Los Angeles, The Guthrie Theater in Minneapolis, the Stratford Shakespeare Festival Theatre of Ontario, the Long Wharf Theatre in New Haven, Connecticut, and the Pacific Institute for the Performing Arts theatre in Santa Maria, California. Many universities have built thrust stage theatres to supplement their proscenium stages, and many community and off-Broadway theatres use the thrust stage as their only theatre.

The chief characteristic of the thrust stage is that it "thrusts" the performer into the midst of the audience, emphasizing him and his performance rather than the scenery around him. The Elizabethan public theatre (for example, the Globe) was basically a thrust stage, and it is not surprising that many of the first thrust stages built in the United States were constructed for Shakespearean revivals. By virtue of having a back wall the thrust stage also retains some of the illusionistic possibilities of the proscenium stage, especially because the audience members are all

Theatermuseum, Munich

Figure 9. *Classic thrust stage.* The Globe Theatre of London (1599) in a hypothetical reconstruction by Richard Southern.

able to see a projection or a set located there. A not inconsiderable feature of the thrust stage is that, since less scenery is required or expected, productions can ordinarily be mounted at lower cost.

A form of theatre architecture which has been much propounded but rarely used is the *arena* theatre, or theatre in the round. The action occurs in the middle of an arena surrounded by the audience, and the actors enter down the aisles. The Arena Stage in Washington, D. C., has had great success with this form, but it has not grown in popularity relative to its older sibling, the thrust stage.

Arena staging focuses even more on the performer and almost totally eliminates the possibility of solid scenery, since anything over two or three feet high would block the view of the actors from various points in the audience. Arena staging limits the possibilities of spectacle, eliminates linear composition (since everyone in the audience has a different perspec-

Arena Stage

Figure 10. *Four-sided arena staging.* The Arena Stage, Washington, D.C., pioneered in the professional use of "in the round" staging, as this format is occasionally called. Characteristically, scenery is held to a minimum.

tive), eliminates tableaux in the ordinary sense, and forces every actor to have his back to at least some of the spectators at all times. The benefits of arena staging, on the other hand, are intimacy and a frequently extraordinary intensity, with the audience involved almost in a participatory fashion with the drama. In the 1950s and 60s, huge arena-style tent theatres or music tents opened throughout the United States, to stage high-budget productions, mostly musicals. Few of these arena stages have outlasted their novelty, however, and the arena form has not reached the widespread potential its adherents anticipated.

Outdoor theatres, or amphitheatres, are probably modeled on the theatres of ancient Greece and Rome. Some are huge permanent structures with stone seats (softened by pillows) and architectural stages, occasionally using buildings as backdrops, as does the Mary Rippon Theatre in Boulder, Colorado. Others are carved out of natural formations—pits, quarries, chasms, and so forth—and seat great numbers of patrons, for example the Red Rocks Amphitheatre in Denver and the Quarry Theatre at the University of California at Santa Cruz. The Hearst Theatre in Berkeley, California, is a replica of a fourth century B.C. Greek stage. Modified bandstands such as the Hollywood Bowl and the Carter Barron

Arena Stage

Figure 11. A wall-less but otherwise realistic interior setting at the Arena Stage.

Amphitheatre in Washington, D. C., can be used for staging plays, and in New York City a bankside in Central Park was the original home of the New York Shakespeare Festival. These giant amphitheatres have proven values for all but the most intimate of plays. European directors, particularly Firmin Gemier, Jean Vilar, and Max Reinhardt, have maximized their possibilities. Huge audiences can be accommodated inexpensively, and spectacular stage effects can be achieved. Some productions have become extremely popular: *Aïda* at the Roman Baths of Caracalla, the Théâtre Nationale Populaire productions in a medieval palace in Avignon, France, and the Jones Beach Musicals on Long Island all draw thousands of spectators, creating unusual artistic opportunities for the director.

Yet outdoor theatres need not be large. Small *trestle stages,* carried sometimes in a truck and sometimes by hand, can be set up quickly by street theatre groups like the San Francisco Mime Troupe or the New York Shakespeare Festival touring company, and in an instant we can have Goldoni in Golden Gate Park or *Romeo y Juliette* in Spanish Harlem. Ben Jonson, after all, declared that the theatre was no more than

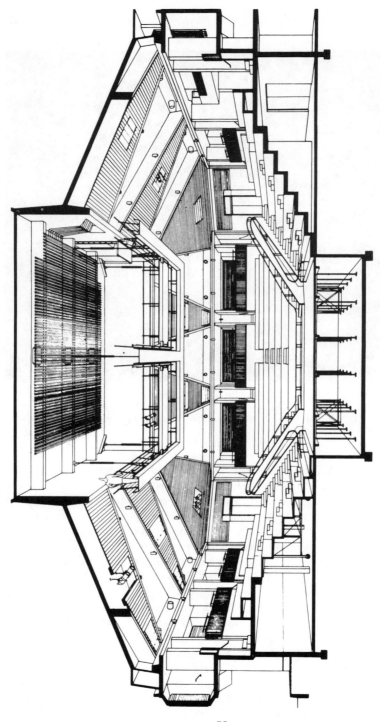

Arena Stage

Figure 12. Sectional drawing of the Arena Stage, showing the vomitoria, stage, audience seating, and lighting positions.

Centro Campesino Cultural Inc.

Figure 13.   *Street theatre.* El Teatro Campesino of California, in a politically-oriented outdoor presentation.

"two boards and a passion," and many producer-directors have proved him correct. Guerrilla theatre companies often stage plays in shopping centers, using the shops as scenery and the customers as audience. In this practice the theatre returns to a form widely popular in the Middle Ages and dormant for centuries.

Finally, *specific* theatres are frequently erected for a single play or style of play. The Old Globe Theatre in San Diego is roughly a reconstruction of an Elizabethan playhouse, and so is the Oregon Shakespeare Festival Theatre in Ashland, Oregon. The Asolo Theatre in Sarasota, Florida, is a restoration of an eighteenth century theatre, and the Goodspeed Opera House in East Haddam, Connecticut, and Ford's Theatre in Washington, D. C., are both reconstructions of working nineteenth century theatres. Most of these theatres prove hospitable to contemporary plays as well.

But no list of forms could exhaust the possibilities of theatres. "I can take any empty space," declares Peter Brook, "and call it a bare stage."[1]

[1] Peter Brook, *Empty Space: A Book About Theatre—Deadly, Holy, Rough, Immediate* (New York: Atheneum Publishers, 1968), p. 9.

Oregon Shakespearean Festival, Ashland. Photo by Hank Kranzler.

Figure 14. *Outdoor Elizabethan replica theatre.* The Oregon Shakespeare Festival Theatre, with a facade modeled after the Fortune Theatre of London (1600), and a seating bowl derived from nineteenth century chautauqua open-air assembly grounds.

Asolo, The State Theater Company of Florida

Figure 15. *Replica court theatre.* The Asolo State Theater, Sarasota, Florida, a transplanted eighteenth century court theatre. Pictured here, from behind, a 1971 production of *Charley's Aunt.*

Jerzy Gurawski, architect. Courtesy of Jerzy Grotowski.

Figure 16. *Uniquely designed theatres.* Director Jerzy Grotowski of the Polish Laboratory Theatre designs specific theatrical environments for each of his productions. This illustrates the scenic action for *Kordian,* by Slowacki. Spectators, in white, become fellow patients in a mental hospital with the actors, in black.

Jerzy Gurawski, architect. Courtesy of Jerzy Grotowski.

Figure 17. The staging area for Adam Mickiewicz's *Forefathers' Eve,* also directed by Grotowski, with spectators surrounding and occupying islands within the freeform stage.

Photo by Raeanne Rubenstein. Courtesy of Richard Schechner.

Figure 18. *Environmental theatre.* Richard Schechner, collaborating with Jerry N. Rojo, the "environmentalist," has directed a series of productions in the Performance Garage, a Manhattan garage fitted out with carpeted scaffolding to serve both as audience and staging area as desired. This is *Dionysus in 69.* Bare-chested actors at top and bottom interact amid four tiers of spectators.

Photo by Elizabeth Le Compte. Courtesy of Richard Schechner.

Figure 19.   A corner of the Performance Garage deployed for *Commune*, 1970. Most of the action occurred in the center.

The theatre is where you stage your play, and it can be designed, or modified, as the director and his staff wish. Polish director Jerzy Grotowski creates a new theatre for each play. For *Dr. Faustus* the audience sits around a "banquet" table and the action occurs on the tabletop. For *The Constant Prince* the audience peers over a five foot wall into a deep pit in which the action takes place. In *Forefathers' Eve* the audience is seated in chairs scattered carefully about an otherwise vacant room, and the action occurs in their midst. To employ the possibilities that Grotowski's staging suggests, directors are asking for, and architects are supplying, "bare room" theatres, or theatre laboratories, consisting of little more than a big room, a grid for lights, and some platforms for seats and/or stages. Richard Schechner took his New York "Performance Group" far from the off-Broadway district, into a warehouse district in lower Manhattan, and produced his *Dionysus in 69* in a vacant garage, where three-tiered carpeted platforms served for stage and "house" alike, and the audience was invited to locate themselves wherever they chose. Schechner

Photo by Frederick Eberstadt. Courtesy of Richard Schechner.

Figure 20. The audience leans over the scaffold in a scene from *Commune*. The environmental situation necessitates frequent audience shifting and even discomfort in search of greater immediacy and impact.

calls this an *environmental theatre,* a phrase which has entered the contemporary stage vocabulary. There is no limit to the possibilities in creating theatre: the only rule is that the theatre must be successful in housing both audience and play in a vital relationship with each other.

A Director Chooses a Theatre

A director does choose, or create, a theatre, even if by merely accepting the theatre offered to him. By agreeing to direct a Broadway play, the director chooses a proscenium style theatre; by accepting a guest show at a regional or community theatre the director is more or less required to use the existing premises. Frequently the "choice" of a theatre is obvious; practical considerations are so overwhelming that there is no conceivable

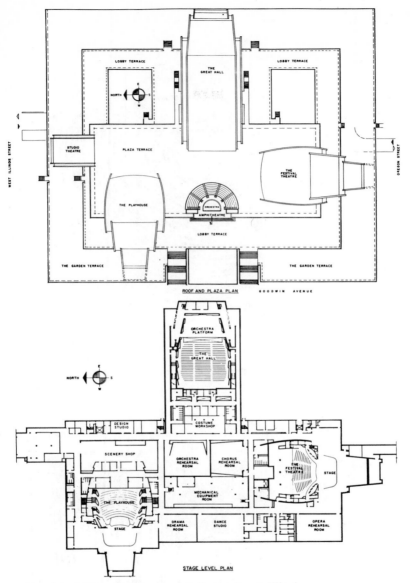

Courtesy of Max Abramowitz and University of Illinois

Figures 21 and 22. *Multiple theatre complex.* The Krannert Center, University of Illinois, allows the director to choose any of five theatres. Above, the three proscenium theatres are separated by a flexible studio theatre and an outdoor amphitheatre, as well as by plazas and terraces. Below, the five theatres share common backstage facilities. Stages are located at the extremities of the complex to minimize interference and provide the audience with a common lobby area.

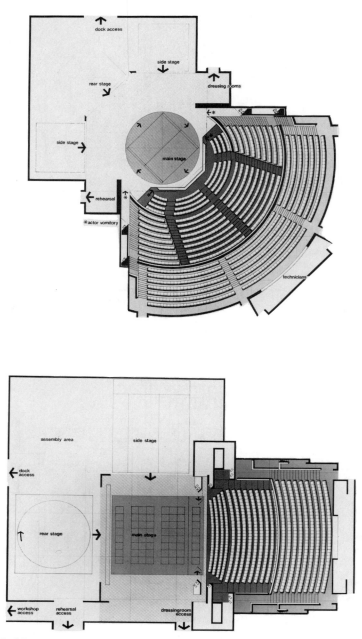

Architects: Denys Lasdun and Partners

Figures 23 and 24. *New National Theatre complex.* The combination of an open stage (above) and a proscenium theatre (below) was adopted by the National Theatre of Great Britain for their new, 1975 premises.

alternative to the "obvious" house. But this section of the book is designed to make a director aware of the possibilities that may be worth exploring.

Most new theatre plants house different styles of performing areas. The Krannert Center at the University of Illinois contains four theatres, and most new college plants include three. There are always nearby amphitheatres, either fabricated or natural, and the outdoors holds great potential. Where there seems to be no choice of theatres, the director, working with his production staff, need not take his facilities as he finds them. A proscenium stage can be made into a thrust by removing some seats and building a platform. A large theatre can be made more intimate by closing off areas, either by drawing a curtain or installing a partition or by isolating the audience. The set and the audience might both be put up on the stage and the auditorium area converted to a maze through which the audience walk to reach their seats. A modern theatre may be "antiqued" by hanging gas lamps and old theatre posters in the house, as, for example, for a music-hall production of Behan's *The Hostage*. The walls of the theatre can be painted, covered, or decorated to make the audience feel part of another era, as was done in the Actors' Studio production of *Marathon 33*. Theatre walls, layouts, prosceniums, lobby displays, programs, and the costumes (and attitudes) of the ushers are not necessarily fixed, and can be modified or redesigned as part of the play's overall composition. A director should avoid the natural tendency to consider the theatre as an unchangeable vehicle for his play: he should consider it *part* of his play, and part of his overall concern.

In choosing, creating, or dressing up a theatre, a director might ask himself the following questions:

1. How will the play look and sound in the theatre? How will the play act, feel, and project? How can the theatre be best arranged to convey what I have in mind? Do I want the audience to be aware of each other, or aware of the building? How can I make them more (or less) aware of each other? Of where they are sitting? Of the outside world?

2. Where does the audience I desire for this play live? Where do they go to the theatre, if they go at all? Without patrons, theatre does not exist; without the right kind of patrons, a specific play might not succeed. *Little Murders* was a failure on Broadway but a success in Greenwich Village; conversely, *Hair* was only modestly successful in the Village but was a bonanza on Broadway. Some plays, such as the productions of Grotowski, are meant for a small coterie of theatre sophisticates (Grotowski hand-selects his audience before every performance). Others depend on a wealthy cultural elite—the Metropolitan Opera, for example. Others, such as street theatre, have to be brought, free of charge, to audiences that are unaccustomed to going to them.

3. How big an audience do I want? How many can I get? It is folly to put

on a play in a huge auditorium when audiences of fifty to a hundred are all that can be expected; the audience feels adrift in a sea of empty seats. It is also artistic folly to present a delicate, intimate play in a giant theatre even if the audience will come, unless measures are taken to ensure that the intimacy of the action is properly conveyed to the far reaches of the house.

The Staging Area

The staging area is where the play takes place: ordinarily on the stage of the theatre. But the staging area need not be the stage, nor must a theatre have a defined stage.

Richard Schechner's Performance Garage has virtually no stage to define. Many environmental theatres go to this extreme, with the action occurring anywhere on the premises. Other productions feature a defined stage but include other areas of the building in the staging area. The Broadway production of *Hair,* for example, featured actors entering and moving through the audience, down the aisles, and across the rows, hanging from ropes and swinging out over the audience, stepping across the arm rests of the auditorium chairs, and sitting in vacant seats (where there were any) or even on the laps of members of the audience! Though by no means an innovation, this created much of the electric theatricality of that production.

Entrances down the theatre aisles are now common, even in proscenium theatres. (That practice, and other, similar ones, are often referred to as "breaking the proscenium arch.") In the Berliner Ensemble production of Brecht's *Das Kleine Mahagonny,* the orchestra sat in a theatre box above the audience, drinking beer when they were not playing. In the New York Public Theatre production of *Stomp,* the staging area included a catwalk around the audience, and a "stage" amid them; during the course of the play, the actors demanded that part of the audience leave their seats and sit on the "stage," while the actors moved into the space originally reserved for the audience.

Violating the Stage

When there is a defined stage and the action occurs outside it, we might say that the accepted stage space has been violated (a more general term than "breaking the proscenium arch"). Violating the stage space may be done for technical reasons: a director may simply want to gain more space for entrances and exits, or, similarly, he may wish to fill or clear the stage with sudden rapidity. He may, however, violate the accepted stage for aesthetic, theatrical reasons as well—and he will accomplish these ends whether he wishes to or not. For violation of the stage creates a different form of audience involvement than does nonviolation, an involvement that the director must reckon with and try to turn to his (and the play's) advantage.

Productions which use a defined nonviolated stage and a defined audience area work within the audience's preconceived expectations, and demand greater audience concentration *on* the play, as opposed to their participation *in* it. This is virtually essential for illusionistic theatre, where the director's intention is to make the audience oblivious to their surroundings and to engulf them with the situations and characters of the play itself. In illusionistic theatre the audience is clearly segregated from the action and generally ignored by the actors. Most naturalistic and romantic plays are produced in this manner, the audience viewing the action much as if they were seeing it through a one-way mirror. Naturalistic proscenium staging is often called "the theatre of the fourth wall removed," meaning that the audience is examining apparently random behavior inside a room whose fourth wall is imaginary. There are many advantages to working in illusionistic styles. The audience is secure and comfortable; their privacy is not violated, they do not feel compelled to take a position or form a judgment, and they are not "on the spot." They can simply relax and enjoy the play they paid to see. Lulled into a state of secure voyeurism, they can become involved in the story and empathize with the characters to their hearts' content. They can laugh, cry, grow angry, and be charmed without having to account for their emotions— they can fall prey to the magic of the theatre. This is an altogether satisfying way of working, and probably 75 percent of play productions in America are basically illusionistic.

Productions which use an undefined or violated staging area (and frequently an undefined audience area thereby) involve the audience in a different way, which we may call participatory. Participation theatre seeks to involve the audience and the actors in a joint experience. The motto of the South Coast Repertory Company (Costa Mesa, California) is "the fourth wall is behind the audience." This is the theme of participatory theatre, which takes the audience on stage, the actors off stage, and gives the audience more to concentrate on than a story and some characters. Participatory theatre asks the audience to be aware of many disparate things: the actors as people, the actors as entertainers, the political themes of the material, the nature of contemporary society, the elegance of wit and poetry. Bertolt Brecht, the great German playwright and director, wrote and directed plays meant to be seen as nonillusionistic. Brecht believed that theatre must rid itself of "magic," creating instead intense political reaction and discussion among its patrons. His theatre of "Verfrem-

Figure 25. *Modified proscenium.* The St. James Theatre, New York, altered by the addition of a runway for *Hello, Dolly!*, directed by Gower Champion. Pearl Bailey as Dolly.

dungseffekt" (distancing) sought to force his audience to consider the moral, not the story, of his plays. To do this he continually violated the romantic concept of an audience segregated from the actors and propelled the action into the house at every opportunity.

Nonillusionistic theatre, however, is not merely political in nature. The classic Greek theatre, which used masks, dances, song, and extraordinary stage effects, was nonillusionistic, as was the Elizabethan, and as is most musical comedy, fantasy, and historical tragedy. There are many reasons why a director may wish to address his audience directly (participation) rather than indirectly (through illusion). Some examples of nonillusionistic theatre using violated stages follow.

Marathon 33, produced by the Actors Studio at the ANTA theatre in New York, made the audience believe that they were spectators at a marathon dance contest in 1933. The entire auditorium was decorated as a dance arena, and while the action occurred mainly on the theatre stage, which was the dance platform, entrances were made through the aisles, the audience was addressed and commented upon directly by the actors, and entertainment specialties were directed to the "dance" audience.

In *Hello, Dolly* a runway, dressed with footlights, projects into the audience so that the star—played in New York by famous entertainers Carol Channing, Ginger Rogers, Mary Martin, Phyllis Diller, Ethel Merman, and Pearl Bailey—can come right into and over the audience and belt out the title song like a night club number. Pearl Bailey as Dolly even sang some of her own night club routines, which had nothing to do with the show, to a madly cheering audience.

The James Joyce Liquid Memorial Theatre, produced by the Company Theatre in Los Angeles and New York, blindfolds the audience and leads them through a maze in which they are touched, kissed, brushed, and given things to smell, eat, and drink—a "sense bath."

In the 1968 New York production of *Tom Paine,* the cast broke the story of the play and entered the audience to engage spectators in a political discussion ranging far from the points of the play's text.

These examples demonstrate the range of nonillusionistic theatre and violated staging areas, though not their limits, which extend as far as a director's imagination can take them.

A word of caution: In discussing directorial options for selection of theatre and definition of a defined, undefined, or "violated" staging area, we have concentrated on the unconventional. By way of reminder, let us state here that most American theatre productions take place in a "normal" proscenium theatre, where the action is confined to the stage and the audience to their seats. We are not exploring departures from this conventional arrangement to suggest that they are improvements. Departures are only possibilities which can be explored; nothing that is creative in the

Company Theatre Foundation

Figure 26. *The audience area as the stage.* The Company Theatre production of *James Joyce Liquid Memorial Theatre,* in which the audience intermingled with the actors and the "stage" disappeared completely. Los Angeles, 1970.

theatre should be taken for granted, or simply handed down as tradition. In the last analysis the director should be able to defend his choice of theatre and staging area on the basis of the play he is directing and the effects he is trying to achieve. He should not simply accept them unthinkingly.

The Scenery System

The nature of the scenery vitally concerns the director's composition. In this field the designer's voice is powerful, but directorial initiative and agreement are absolutely essential. Almost all scenery systems can be included among the following categories (and the overlapping categories between them):

1. A single realistic set (representing a real environment, even abstractly)
2. A single abstract set (representing no real environment)

3. Multiple sets, realistic or abstract
4. No set

Frequently the play strongly suggests (one can almost say requires) one form or another. A single realistic set is virtually essential for many modern American plays, such as *The Boys in the Band, Two for the Seesaw,* or *Born Yesterday.* Multiple sets are invariably called for in musical comedies *(Oklahoma!, Little Mary Sunshine, My Fair Lady)* and two-, three-, or four-set realistic plays *(Heartbreak House, Intimate Relations, The Three Sisters).* Abstract sets seem to be unavoidable in certain more modern plays *(Endgame, The Chairs).* But there is great freedom of choice among the possibilities, and in working out the variations of the possibilities, for nearly all theatre productions.

We can examine the possibilities that have opened up in designing scenery systems by looking at the history of English Shakespearean revivals. Seventeenth, eighteenth, and nineteenth century revivals of Shakespearean plays were staged on a series of "realistic" sets. *Hamlet* used first a representation of battlements, then a throne room, then battlements again, then a room in the palace, then the king's study, then the queen's closet, and so forth (although the texts of the plays were frequently rearranged for the convenience of the designer and the scene shifters). It was discovered late in the nineteenth century, however, that this was contrary to the original Globe staging for which Shakespeare wrote, and in the "Shakespearean Revival" that occurred around the turn of the century, Shakespeare's plays were performed on a permanent architectural, nonscenic setting that seemed to be an accurate re-creation of the original stage. Now we witness complete variety of methods of staging Shakespeare. Both the nineteenth century series of realistic sets and the Shakespearean revival staging are used (though the former is increasingly rare). Single abstract settings are also used, as in Peter Brook's *King Lear,* played against two giant sand-colored panels and three hanging thundersheets.[2] Multiple abstract sets with turntables, flying walls and banners, elevator stages, wagon stages, and actor-bringing-on-the-set staging patterns are often used. Every known scenery system has been used for Shakespearean revivals in our day, and the end is not in sight. For most plays a director can now choose from a number of scenery system possibilities. His directing should be consistent with the nature of the scenery he selects: this is one of his earliest choices in terms of how he does the play. Staging in the Forest of Arden will vary depending on whether the trees simulate real trees or are hanging ropes, magically rising cylinders, or steel sculptures.

[2] London, 1962. See also Brook's set for *A Midsummer Night's Dream,* page 76.

A SINGLE REALISTIC SET

Does the play seem to require, or does the director desire, a single realistic set? If so, certain considerations should be worked out with the designer at an early stage of production: How realistic? Is the scenery to be heavy, with platforms, doors that slam convincingly, bookshelves with real books, bannisters that can be sat upon, windows that open, steps that can be ascended? Or is it to be fragmentary and airy, a room delineated by a few hints of walls, indications of corners, openings for doorways, and fragile, stylized furniture? The audience will accept either, but each will lead to a different kind of composition, and thus of production.

Realistic scenery is obviously associated primarily with naturalistic plays. In the early days of naturalism, "authentic" settings were de rigueur. David Belasco, an American producer of the early twentieth century, was greatly admired for having a dining room at Childs Restaurant (including walls and fixtures) precisely copied down to the last detail of furniture,

Friedman-Abeles

Figure 27. *A single realistic set.* The interior setting used in Frank Gilroy's modern, realistic play, *The Subject Was Roses,* directed on Broadway by Ulu Grosbard. The illusion of day-to-day reality is total; the photo appears to be a candid snapshot of a family at breakfast, rather than of actors on a Broadway stage.

linens, china, and tableware. Realistic scenery in a proscenium theatre creates the strongest possible illusion of scenic naturalism.

A second attribute of realistic scenery is that it allows an actor to relate physically to the scenic artifacts in a way difficult or impossible to achieve on other sets. Some productions depend at least in part on the actors' ability to leap bannister rails, pound or bang into walls, slam doors, and throw furniture. The director may wish to leave the specific activity uncharted in rehearsal, and even in performance. (This may be an unwise decision, but he should have the right to make it.) The only way he can do so freely, of course, is to assure himself beforehand that the scenery can take it.

A set can still be considered realistic even when the actual scenery is somewhat stylized or simplified. Audiences are trained to theatrical conventions, and they will accept many modifications of actuality without even thinking about them. Walls may be built of muslin, bookcases and books may be painted, furniture arrangements may be realistically unorthodox, but the setting still appears realistic. It is even possible, within this general context, simply to indicate the walls with line structures, overhead beams,

Photo by Photo Pic, Paris

Figure 28. *A single abstract set.* The setting for Samuel Beckett's *Waiting for Godot* in its original 1953 Paris production, directed by Roger Blin.

or cardboard cutouts. This must be done in arena staging, and is the usual practice on a thrust stage, where walls would entirely block the view of the stage. The audience's imagination will fill in the rest.

There is a frequent cost advantage in simplifying scenery, but the major difference is aesthetic. Simplified scenery tends to make its point and be forgotten; the audience does not linger over the many details of a natural setting, but focuses on the actors and the action instead. Further, the stylization of scenery may be enchanting, moody, lively, vibrant, and so on without breaking completely away from simplified realism. The designer can be wildly creative, emphasizing the elements of or in the setting which he feels are worth an added touch. A wall can be made out of plastic, a tree of concrete, a crown of rusted spoons, yet the basic arrangement will still be only a modification of a realistic one. The basic decision concerning the single realistic set—how real it is to be—must be made early in the production planning.

Joe Cocks Studio

Figure 29. *A single abstract set used for multiple scenes.* Sally Jacob's setting for Peter Brook's celebrated 1970 production of *A Midsummer Night's Dream.* Three white walls, two doors, a catwalk, some swings, ladders, and aluminum coils were used in various combinations to suggest the palace or the forest. Here, the mechanicals rehearse while Titania swings overhead.

Center Theatre Group

Figure 30.   *A more concrete multiple set.* Director Gordon Davidson used a single multi-level environment in his 1972 production of Shakespeare's *Henry IV*, Part I at the Mark Taper Forum in Los Angeles. Lighting changes define action in various areas of the stage for interior scenes, or over the entire stage area for the battle scene shown here.

THE ABSTRACT SET

Many plays call for an abstract or unlocalized setting. Samuel Beckett's plays, for example, are set in locales which cannot be considered interiors or exteriors; they are more like stage sculptures. August Strindberg's fantasies, Alfred Jarry's *Ubu Roi,* and Jean Cocteau's *Orphée* require, according to their authors, scenery which is unlike anything appearing in the everyday world.

Many plays for which realistic scenery could be used have been successfully, even brilliantly, produced on abstract sets. Peter Brook's *Midsummer Night's Dream* and *King Lear* have already been mentioned. John Gielgud's production of *Hamlet* was performed on a gray-black stage with several platforms, black flats, and drapes scattered about in a seemingly aimless arrangement. Paul Sill's *Story Theatre* takes place on a painted but otherwise bare stage, in front of a screen onto which are projected colorful abstract designs. Michael Cacoyannis's *The Devils* was performed on scaffoldings erected in front of a dark amber cyclorama.

Unlocalized sets are not a modern creation. All ancient theatre was performed on what we would today call abstract settings, since realistic scenery is a relatively modern innovation. Ancient Greek dramas were performed in front of a permanent scene building, the *skene,* which represented interior and exterior locales with a minimum of literalness. Medieval pageant plays and mystery plays were performed in and about stage areas that were only modestly defined in terms of naturalistic detail. The Elizabethan theatre was an architectural masterpiece which permitted interior and exterior scenes to flow rapidly without extensive scenery or scene changes. In all these theatres the stage itself was the setting, and the setting was a stage; there was no attempt to define the literal location in detail. Sometimes symbolic indications would be employed: it has been conjectured that the Elizabethan stage used banners and signs to indicate place or country, and revolving triangular prisms (*periaktoi*) on either side of the stage effected changes of situation in Greek plays. Indeed, Oriental theatre has been purely symbolic throughout its long history and has developed beautiful and poetic stage symbols such as a waving piece of cloth for a river.

The development of realistic scenery can be traced to the court stages of the Italian Renaissance, when for a period the theatre became a form of living pictorial art, used by architects and painters to amuse and amaze the nobility with their realistic copies of everyday physical surroundings. The English theatre of the Restoration period saw the development of painted and architectured realism, and by the nineteenth century most plays were performed in front of elaborately painted two-dimensional sets.

Naturalism brought with it the box set and the "real" set in the late nineteenth and early twentieth century, so that any director requesting abstract settings from his designer today does so by choice. Today's abstract sets are intentionally, not traditionally, abstract. They may borrow from traditions—for example, Shakespearean stage replicas, or Brecht's use of Oriental staging conventions—or they may create new traditions.

The movement toward intentionally abstract settings began in the late nineteenth century in response to the rigidity and "nonartistry" of realism. In 1890 Paul Fort developed in Paris his "Theatre of Art" (Théâtre

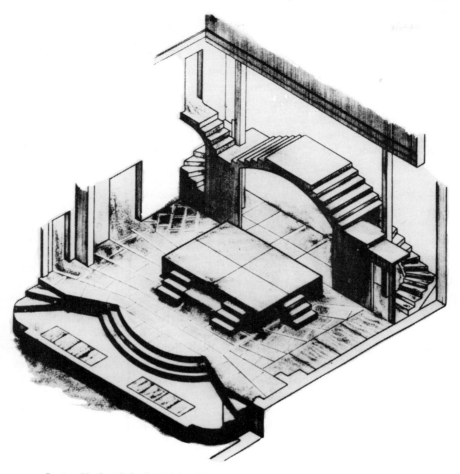

Centre National de la Récherche Scientifique

Figure 31. *The "naked stage."* Jacques Copeau's design for the Théâtre du Vieux-Colombier in Paris (1913) featured an architectural arrangement which, by the occasional addition of curtains and masking units, could be used for the productions of many plays of differing periods.

d'Art) to compete with Antoine's naturalistic Théâtre Libre. Fort performed his plays in front of abstract designs by friends of his: Pierre Bonnard, Odillon Redon, Maurice Denise, the leading impressionists of the day. He also performed plays in front of settings made from wrapping paper and indifferent collages of scrap materials. Later the coming of expressionism led to a greater sophistication of such abstract settings.

In Paris, in the second decade of the twentieth century, Jacques Co-

peau created his Théâtre du Vieux-Colombier, a neo-Elizabethan architec-
tutural stage, to present the poetic plays of Middleton, Shakespeare, and
Claudel, which he considered the only true theatre. All over Europe, the
designs of Adolphe Appia, Gordon Craig, and Leopold Jessner, relying on
giant sprawling staircases, rotating neutral screens, and great geometrical
patterns, revolutionized scenery. Even American designers did not ignore
this movement, and Broadway audiences of the 1920s were familiarizing
themselves with the radical new abstract settings of Lee Simonson and
Robert Edmond Jones, which featured sharply angulated and broken
walls, deep shadowy recesses, unorthodox bolts of light. Theatrical vir-
tuosity was the order of the day.

The effect of an abstract setting today, since it is obviously the product of the director's and designer's choice, is to announce to the audience
that "there is more than just a story here." Abstract sets emphasize the theatricality of the theatre: that it is an art form as well as a form of direct
communication and not merely the depiction of ordinary events calculated to create an empathetic response. Abstract settings state, "The specifics
of locale, period, and time of day are not important here." They lend a
feeling of universality and broad relevance.

Abstract settings have enormous appeal to directors and designers.
For designers the appeal is a chance to transcend the simple depiction of
reality, to make a personal statement about the theme of the play. It is a
chance to create a genuine stage sculpture, as opposed to a simple piece of
interior design. For the director, an abstract setting offers the immediate
opportunity to have his play appreciated as a major creative effort.

However, these appealing factors can accompany enormous liabilities. Direction must be consistent with the entire production plan; the director must use his setting as imaginatively as the designer has drawn it.
A misused abstract set can easily come off as pretentious, even shabby if it
seems to be a substitute for something more difficult to make. Without a
clear sense of its effect in terms of the play's statement, a director would
be foolhardy to agree to an abstract setting for a play which does not intrinsically support one.

Multiple Sets

Today most plays are presented on multiple sets, by which we mean
any setting which contains or presents numerous locations, either simultaneously or in sequence. The most conventional format of multiple set
productions is a series of sets brought in during intermissions in the action. But multiple sets can be created organically, in a single setting,
either by simple juxtaposition or by *a vista* (not concealed) scene changes.

Sequential settings became the norm with the development of wing

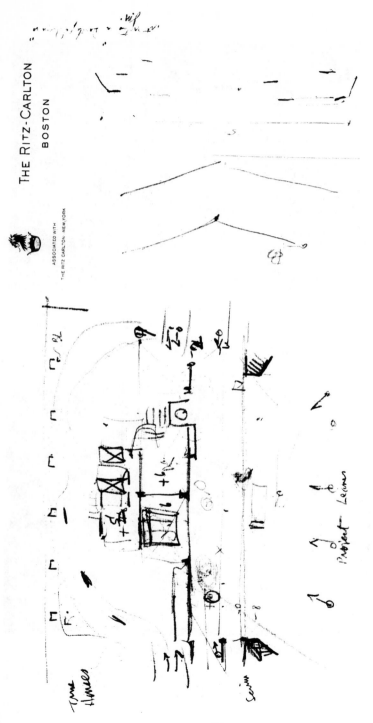

Courtesy of Jo Mielziner

Figure 32. Mielziner's original sketches, on hotel stationery, made for and during conferences with the director of the Broadway production of *Death of a Salesman.*

Photo by Peter A. Juley & Son. Courtesy of Jo Mielziner.

Figure 33. The Jo Mielziner setting for the original Broadway production of Arthur Miller's *Death of a Salesman,* directed by Elia Kazan (1949). Here, the basic setting with all rooms visible simultaneously.

Photo by Peter A. Juley & Son. Courtesy of Jo Mielziner.

Figure 34. A memory scene from *Death of a Salesman,* created by lighting projections (also designed by Mielziner) on a translucent backdrop.

and drop proscenium theatres in the seventeenth century. Sets were created from flat painted scenery brought in on grooves in the stage floor. Scenery was shifted by sliding one set of wings and backflats out and another set in. Modern proscenium houses modify this with elaborate variations. Huge turntables can hold three completely different sets for a three act show, and can change them in a matter of seconds. Fly galleries can hold vast stores of flat scenery which can be whisked in or out in a second or two. "Wagons" transport whole sets on from the side, or fragmentary set pieces from any direction. These wholesale scene changes permit the use of any form of scenery, realistic or abstract, limited only by the facilities of the particular theatre.

Sequential settings have many advantages. They allow for rapid change of mood as well as locale, and can create great audience excitement. Cecil Beaton's *My Fair Lady* settings drew gasps and bravos from the audience as one beautiful scene followed another on the stage. For spectacular musical productions like *My Fair Lady* a series of lavish settings is ordinarily de rigueur. While sequential sets are important in realistic plays to convey vital plot points, they may also convey a symbolic point. In Anton Chekhov's *The Three Sisters,* the action occurs first in the salon, then in Irina's bedroom, and finally in front of the house, demonstrating the sisters' expulsion from their family home.

Organically multiple settings are more difficult to work out than sequential settings, but they may be superior for many plays. The most common form of an organically multiple set is the *simultaneous setting,* akin to those used in medieval European plays, where several locations coexist on the same stage, with most or all of the action occurring on one part of the set at a time. Action in *The Good Woman of Setzuan* occurs in a tobacco shop, a woman's house, a hut, a tobacco factory, a barber shop, a street, and in front of several doors, yet a striking design once combined all these locations on a single multiple set less than thirty feet across. Parts of the set were illuminated only as needed, and the theatricality of the playscript allowed the audience to accept the conventions of the setting. A superb simultaneous set was designed by Jo Mielziner in collaboration with director Elia Kazan for the Arthur Miller classic, *Death of a Salesman*. Kazan, Miller, and mainly Mielziner created a two-story house, with a couple of side stages for Willie's office and Charley's home, allowing the play to take place, in Miller's words, "in a mobile concurrency of past and present." Miller had originally conceived the play as staged with sequential, realistic settings; the simultaneous set of Mielziner allowed Willy to putter about the kitchen while his sons talked about him above; it gave the play a cohesive style which undoubtedly added to its success.

Simultaneous sets give the audience the entire picture of the play at first glance, although portions can be partially withheld by selective light-

Joe Cocks Studio

Figures 35 and 36. *Evolving sets.* Two scenes from Trevor Nunn's 1972 Royal Shakespeare Company production of *Coriolanus* at Stratford-on-Avon. Huge moving blocks, electronically operated, move in and out to define walls, up and down to create staircases and platforms. Above, the Romans and the Volscians (with headdresses) battle before the gates of Corioli. Below, Menenius addresses the plebeians.

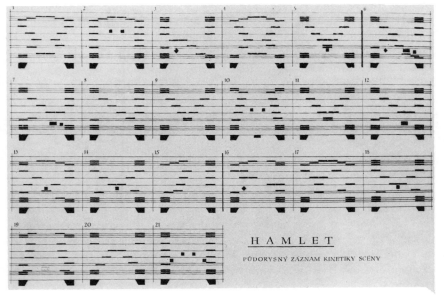

H A M L E T

PŮDORYSNÝ ZÁZNAM KINETIKY SCÉNY

Art Centrum, Prague

Figures 37 and 38. *Evolving sets.* Josef Svoboda's design for a 1959 Czech production of *Hamlet,* using highly polished vertical screens which move mechanically to 21 different positions, each defining a different staging space. Above, configuration number 11, viewed from the audience. Below, the different configurations of screens, shown in ground plan.

ing. There are few if any scenic surprises. The simultaneous set seems to have great effect in preordained tragedies, especially such self-admitted ones as Anouilh's *Antigone,* since the setting itself discloses a certain preordained fatality. Simultaneous sets also allow "dormant" characters to remain on stage, their mute behavior observable by the audience and by other characters.

A final type of organically multiple set is *evolving sets.* One set, by the addition, rotation, or elimination of certain parts, becomes another in full view of the audience. One example is the Christopher Morley set for Trevor Nunn's Royal Shakespeare production of *The Taming of the Shrew.* In that production the curtain opened on the exterior of a tavern. When Christopher Sly was revived by the Lord he was brought into the tavern, which, mounted on two turntables, opened its inside out, revealing the entire cast reveling and dancing inside. The the "play" began.

Turntables, stage wagons, and fly galleries are the most common elaborations of evolving scenery. Typically there is a basic set, with a backdrop which remains permanent and some set wings or side scenery. Other elements drift in and out, turn around, come up from traps or down from the flies. In the Joe Layton production of *No Strings* the scenery was mainly an assortment of wheeled colored screens which whizzed in and out, flipped end over end, and defined whatever setting was necessary to the text. Ming Cho Lee's set for the New York Shakespeare Festival *Peer Gynt* was a huge turntable containing a mammoth scaffolding arrangement. With a simple turn of the table, entirely different arrangements of steps and open spaces faced the audience. Director Gerald Freedman took great advantage of this feature, painstakingly rehearsing his cast to enter the turntable in mid-rotation and arrive simultaneously at their positions as the set turned.

Evolving sets allow for changes without intermissions or lost time. More than any other staging form, they reveal the theatricality of the medium, as the audience actually watches the machinery of the theatre produce the changing illusion. They can unify a production by showing that each scene in a play is integral to the whole. They require enormous advance planning, since every prop and furniture piece must somehow be accounted for at every moment, but for many productions the fluidity, fascination, and stylistic excitement of evolving scenery is well worth the trouble.

The final choice open to the director is *no scenery.* Many plays dictate this; others can be performed that way. Frequently stage directions merely request "bare stage." *Six Characters in Search of an Author* is one of the most famous of these; *Our Town, The Serpent,* and *Impromptu* are others. *Six Characters* and *Impromptu* are set in theatres, so the theatre itself may act as the "set." *Our Town* occurs in a small town, but the author, to indicate the play's universality, decided to let the actors create the scenery with the aid of a few ladders and properties. Shakespearean plays are frequently done on Elizabethan replica stages with no additional scenery, and some suggest that this is how they were originally performed.[3] Many plays are successfully produced without scenery in low-budget theatres and workshops, before audiences willing to go along with them.

The liabilities of bare stage producing are obvious. The audience may grow tired of the bleakness of the bare walls. A conventional audience may miss the opulence they are accustomed to. They may become confused about the time, place, and period of the play, and they may resent the stinginess of the management vis-à-vis their visual entertainment. The absence of scenery can confuse actors as well, and if the bare stage design is not intrinsic to the particular play and production, it may have a harmful effect on their performance. It is not beyond an actor's ability to imagine the door he is supposed to be going through, but he cannot get the feeling from slamming an imaginary door behind him that he would from a real door or even a stage door. Bare stage directing takes skill; it can rarely be accomplished simply by informing the actor that he is to "pretend" the scenery.

But there are considerable assets to bare stage producing; in fact, it is becoming more common in the 1970s than it has been for a long time. First, bare staging relies explicitly on the actor and the text. It was to emphasize the actor that Copeau designed his architectural Théâtre du Vieux-Colombier in Paris with its "tréteau nu" (naked platform). Bare stage designing merely carries this concept to its conclusion. *The Emergence,* produced by the Company Theatre of Los Angeles, is a superb example of the theatricality that can be achieved on a bare stage; in that production, which featured only a few unpainted blocks on an otherwise naked stage, masks, costumes, lighting effects, music, ensemble acting, dancing, and extravagant special effects made scenery, for the time being, unnecessary. The eyes always could return to a naked stage to realize that the "magic" of the theatre was being created by living actors (see page 79).

Bare stage producing also indicates universality, the frank admission that the performance is occurring on a stage and has relevance to life. It uses the stage as a neutral platform for the presentation of a theatrical experience. It also candidly drives home the point that the production is not expensive and must therefore be appreciated for values other than lavish effects. The same approach was used in the 1950s and '60s by film producers who made their "artistic" films in black and white, even though they could easily have afforded color. Some feel that the use of bare stage

[3] There are also suggestions to the contrary. For a summary of opinions see Alois M. Nagler, *Shakespeare's Stage* (New Haven, Conn.: Yale University Press, 1958).

creates an increased receptivity on the part of the audience for poetry, art, and philosophy. It is worth noting, however, that filmmakers have almost entirely abandoned black and white in the 1970s, and this justification for bare stage producing may also have reached its limit. There seems to be no intrinsic reason why a bare stage should call for more "artistic" appreciation. It is the manner in which staging artifacts are used that will determine their impact.

The director should be involved in the matter of selecting a scenery system. He may be forced to accept a theatre and a stage, but he should never be forced to accept a scenery system he does not want. The director can never put his head in the sand at the design stage and expect to have any control over the composition of his production. The scenery system is a primary factor in stage composition, therefore its conception is largely a directorial responsibility.

Scene Changes

Integral with the scenery system is *how* the scenery is to change. In a conventional play using a single set or series of sets divided by intermissions, the scenery and properties are changed by stagehands behind a drawn curtain, or during a blackout if there is no curtain. In the case of multiple organic scenery the settings are changed *a vista,* and they must be planned. *A vista* scene changes are ordinarily accomplished in one of three ways: by stagehands, by actors, or by hidden mechanical means.

Stagehands are persons qualified to move scenery. They can be costumed however the director chooses, and rehearsed like actors to move scenery quickly, efficiently, and on cue. They need not worry about getting their costumes dirty, being out of breath in their next scene, or breaking character. Needless to say, if stagehands are used to move scenery in front of the audience, they become actors, albeit mute ones. They must be costumed; they cannot wear whatever is at hand unless that is the desired effect. Some plays make explicit use of neutral stagehands. *The Fantasticks* uses a mute actor to distribute properties, move set pieces, and act as a wall between two characters. *Muzeeka* is performed with four stagehands who impersonate telephones, carry identifying signs, move set units, and occasionally take a part in the action. Oriental theatre, such as the Nō and Kabuki theatres of Japan, uses such devices extensively.

The use of actors to change scenery is a frequent practice. Actors playing speaking characters set and remove scenery pieces between or during scenes, bringing their chairs on with them, moving flats around, and so on. The obvious liabilities are implied above: actors are concerned with much more than scene changes and are not always happy to move scenery before their big scenes. They may not do it very well, nor are they dressed properly for it. In addition, the effect of an actor concluding an emotional scene and then stooping to strike a chair can destroy the mood of the scene. Complete stage blackouts are difficult if not impossible to achieve, as obligatory fire exit signs, aisle lights, shoe squeaks, and actor noise conspire to let the audience know what is happening on stage as the scenery is shifted.

The use of actors as stagehands, however, has some important virtues. Like evolving scenery, the practice helps to unify a production. It emphasizes that the actors are actors—stage people, not just "characters." It is fully in the spirit of most improvisational theatre, comedia dell' arte, Shakespearean comedy, and modern "theatricalist" productions. It communicates from the actors to the audience a feeling that "we are putting on a show for you," which is frequently desirable. *The Emergence,* mentioned above, used actor stagehands in this way with excellent results.

Frequently the moving of scenery systems can be justified realistically, by having actors who play waiters move the dining table and chairs, butlers move furniture, and other characters naturally pick up a chair from one side of the stage and bring it to another, to seat themselves there. This method might cover awkward scene shifting situations. More often, the actors move the scenery with no realistic justification, merely to serve a theatrical purpose. The audience is generally willing to accept this, as long as it is done with sureness and is consistent with the scenic style.

Mechanical scene shifting can be stunning and need not be enormously expensive. Scenery that evolves *a vista* by hidden means can create electric audience response. This is not because the audience is fooled by magical effects—ordinarily the mechanical means to move scenery are quite obvious. But the effortless shifting of sets with actors simultaneously moving over them and action occurring as they shift creates a fluid cinematographic effect which is lively and enchanting. Though engaged, the audience is never distracted by the nature of the scene shifts; their concentration on the play and its characters can be uninterrupted. Mechanical scene shifting is as old as the theatre: the ancient Greek *exostra, ekkyklema, periaktoi,* and *mechane* operated grandly to reveal new scenes and tableaux to the audience.

New variations of mechanical shifting are explored every day. There is no limit to the possibilities for a skilled technician and an imaginative designer or director.

While we shy away from drawing "rules" for directing, two principles may be safely established concerning scene shifting. First, whatever method that is employed should look intentional. If the actors are to change sets and props, they must look as if they know exactly what they

Art Centrum, Prague

Figure 39. *Quality of design.* A portfolio of contemporary stage designs by Josef Svoboda, showing technological constructions which create striking qualities. Here, mirrored hexagonal surfaces reflect the actors and sculptural scenery in Karel Capek's *The Insect Play.*

Art Centrum, Prague. Design by Josef Svoboda.

Figure 40. Down lights and step levels used in John Dexter's 1969 Berlin production of Verdi's *Sicilian Vespers.*

Art Centrum, Prague. Design by Josef Svoboda.

Figure 41. Textured cubistic construction for Otomar Krejca's 1965 Brussels production of *Hamlet*.

Art Centrum, Prague. Design by Josef Svoboda.

Figure 42. Platforms, projections, and abstract hangings for a 1970 Prague production of *As You Like It*, directed by J. Pheskot.

are doing, and the director must make the shift completely consistent with the total composition and style of the production. All *a vista* scene changing must be rehearsed to absolute perfection, or it can be a worse disaster than actors going dry on their lines. Nothing in the staging of a play for which an audience pays admission should look makeshift simply because no one had the imagination or the time to devise something better.

Second, the director must recognize that scene changing is a vital part of the scenery system. His decision on scene shifting must be made at the time he agrees on the scenery. It is not a last minute decision, but a fundamental one. If he leaves it until the last minute and then decides to have scenery changed in view of the audience, he faces a mishmash.

The Quality of the Design

In collaborating on the play's basic design, the director must be concerned with its quality. If he likes and trusts the designer, a few words are often sufficient. He wants the set light and airy, dark and damp, constricted, cluttered, towering, rustic, ethereal, pop/op, futuristic, spiral, naturalistic, shallow, antique, or whatever. The designer will expect him to describe what he wants with words, images, references, and sometimes with details. Set quality has to do with style as well as composition, of course, but it is central to composing a stage picture. The quality of the design is, after all, what the audience will see on stage, apart from the actors, and the movement and placement of the actors must be related to the nature of the set design.

The quality of design is also seen in the design of costumes and properties. While these are ordinarily not as crucial to the director as the design of the scenery (as they do not determine his spatial patterns), they do play an important role in the overall composition. First, simply by color and shape, costumes, props, and accessories form elements in the stage picture which may be by design harmonious, contrasting, dramatic, awkward, or arbitrary. Certain directorial compositions may require specific color combinations or contrasts which must be envisioned and planned at the design stage, not midway through rehearsals. Second, the style, shape, design, and fit of costumes and properties can (and presumably should) affect stage movement. The same costuming that makes for breathtaking entrances may not be suitable for falling over sofas; and a Louis XVI sofa may not be suitable for falling over! Staging effectiveness depends on everything that is on the stage.

Some directors design their own scenery. Franco Zeffirelli's *Romeo and Juliet,* though controversial, was certainly a masterfully consistent Shakespearean production. Zeffirelli's designs were meant for his blocking and his blocking for his designs, and the effects were astonishing. Small wonder that directors often team up for years with designers whom they find sympathetic. Trevor Nunn and Christopher Morley are one team, Tyrone Guthrie and Tanya Mosievitch another. Like all other artistic collaborations, the director-designer relationship can be delicate, and sympathetic teamwork based on concrete artistic goals is essential to the successful production.

5

The Ground Plan

Technically the ground plan is part of the production design, but it is such a key part from the director's point of view that it rates special consideration. Frequently the director has ground plans in mind before the scenery is designed; often a basic ground plan inspires a design built around it.

The ground plan, also called floor plan, is the stage and set as seen from above. More literally, it is a draftsman's illustration of the set as it intersects the floor of the stage. Its importance is enormous insofar as it determines the visual shape of the play's action, specifically the movement (blocking) of the actors. A character cannot enter upstage center if the doorway is downstage right, and a bedside assault cannot occur downstage right if the bed is upstage left. Create a good ground plan, and the action can almost block itself; create a bad one, which will soon be made permanent in the shop, and the blocking genius of a Tyrone Guthrie could not save the performance.

For this reason, the design or selection of a ground plan is a task in which the director's primary participation is essential. Directors often design their ground plans before the designer has been chosen or hired, and then present the directorial ground plan as the first input of the director-designer collaboration. This is not, of course, to belittle the designer, who may be equally as—perhaps even more—alert to the overall shape of the action as the director; rather it indicates the need for directorial input and final judgment on the specific structure of the setting upon which he will be directing.

Collaboration with the designer, assuming there is a separate designer who has independent artistic prerogatives, is probably most delicate at the ground plan stage. The director must approach the designer with a fairly complete knowledge of the play's staging requirements and a fairly sure sense of how he wishes the play to move. Platforms, doorways, windows, walls, and furniture arrangement must always be examined from the standpoint of how they will be used, not simply how they will look. The director must have a firm sense of where entrances and exits will be made, how many people will be entering the stage at any time, and how many specific staging requirements, such as duels, battles, dances, hiding-in-closets, and so on are to be accommodated by the sets he is asking to have designed and built. He must have an overall vision of the movement in the play, both in terms of spatial direction and vigor, which he must convey specifically to the designer.

The sensitive collaboration between director and designer at this point will probably involve several meetings, some mutual rethinking, and some compromise. The nature of the collaboration depends, obviously, on the talents and mutual regard of each party; the most profitable collaborations involve a general sharing of ideas and aesthetics. Like all collaborations to which the director is a party, it is ordinarily most fruitful when unihibited by artistic arrogance.

Choosing a Ground Plan

The director will consider the following aspects when examining or drawing up a ground plan:

1. Does it allow for the action of the script?
2. Will it allow the action to be forcefully projected?
3. Does it encourage desirable movement? Tableaux? Improvisation?
4. Does it provide mechanisms for establishing focus?
5. Does it communicate the atmosphere of the play? The inner world of the play?
6. Is it dynamic?

The first criterion establishes the basic qualifications of the competent ground plan; the remaining criteria, those for the better-than-competent one.

THE GROUND PLAN ACCOMMODATES THE ACTION OF THE PLAY

Accommodating the action is, of course, a prime function of the ground plan. If, for example, we are dealing with a realistic play, performed "by the book" on a single realistic interior set, then we must have doors for people to enter through, chairs to sit on, beds to lie on, and enough furniture to make the setting plausible and the actors comfortable. The ground plan must also provide the necessary crossover (backstage) space. If a character enters from outside, goes into a bedroom and then into another bedroom, and then comes out of the bathroom, there will have to be four doors in some kind of architecturally proper pattern if we are to understand what is going on. Designing a ground plan of this sort, the director must read through his play with nothing else on his mind but what is needed in the way of functioning scenery. Sets have been completely built without the window through which Uncle Harry is supposed to be seen coming up the walk.

THE GROUND PLAN FORCEFULLY PROJECTS THE ACTION OF THE PLAY

This second task of the ground plan is much more than a technical operation. There is obviously more to designing the plan than arranging the doors, windows, and furniture in an obliging pattern. The placement of all the objects on the set determines in advance the positioning of the actors at many crucial scenes, particularly entrances, exits, and scenes involving furniture. These placements must be figured out with great care, ordinarily before rehearsals have even begun; they certainly cannot be changed at the whim of a director after the design has been built.

Let us first examine the problems involved in a single realistic interior which is to be used in a standard proscenium theatre, the set appearing upon the raising of the curtain, and the scene ending when the curtain falls. The ground plan will ordinarily be located in the trapezoidal space bounded by the curtain, the rear wall of the theatre, and the two lines, nearly vertical in the figure, which are extensions of a line drawn from the last seat on either side of the first row of the audience to and past the nearest proscenium edge. Notice that these lines are not truly perpendicular to the curtain line, but are "raked" inward about ten degrees. This is because in most theatres some audience seats are positioned beyond the

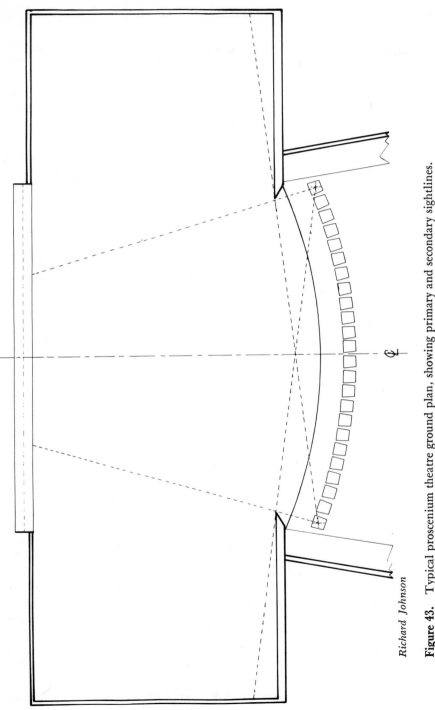

C_L

Richard Johnson

Figure 43. Typical proscenium theatre ground plan, showing primary and secondary sightlines.

97

width of the proscenium. As the plan makes clear, scenery or action located outside these raked lines will be invisible to a portion of the
audience.

Obviously the ground plan need not be absolutely bound to these
perimeters. The left and right boundaries may be broken at will as long
as total visibility from every seat in the house is not of major concern. The
curtain line is not an absolute limit; scenery or furniture can be placed on
whatever apron lies in front of it. Even the rear wall is not particularly
sacred if an alternative can be fashioned. Alexander Dean, in a production
of Pirandello's *Six Characters in Search of an Author* in the early years of
the Yale Drama School, made use of the fact that the scene shop was
located immediately behind the stage. He raised the huge loading door
and then opened the tiny door at the rear of the shop, more than a hundred feet behind the curtain line. Through this tiny door came the six
characters, who walked mysteriously into and through the shop, through
the loading door, onto the stage, and down to the curtain in a staging that
has been remembered ever since.

The director must first define his usable perimeters, whether or not
they are entirely within the trapezoid, and then form his ground plan
within them. If his job were merely functional, this would be easy. He
would simply make the back wall of the set parallel to the back wall of
the theatre (allowing sufficient crossover space behind), make the side
walls follow the raked sight lines, and puncture his set with as many doors
and windows as the script requires. He would then place furniture in the
classic position (two chairs and a table stage left, a sofa stage right, both
canted slightly inward, and perhaps occasional chairs at one or both far
downstage corners) and let his designer "dress" the set with pictures, bookcases, fireplaces, and a raised landing or two. Perhaps half of the amateur
productions of modern drama in the United States are designed in such
a way.

However, this form of ground plan design does nothing to project
the specific action of the play. Implicit in its statement is that all plays
and all interior sets are the same; that whether the play is a farce or a
melodrama, a classical domestic tragedy or a Neil Simon comedy, the same
set can work. Nothing could be less creative, or farther from artistic truth.

A ground plan must be designed, first and foremost, for the play being produced. What does the play say? What does it mean, or existentially,
what does it *do?* These questions of interpretation are vital. Whether the
interpretation actually precedes the design in the director's mind is a moot
point, for different directors work in different ways, and it is certainly possible for the director to conceive of a ground plan before he has consciously articulated his interpretation. Still, at the unconscious level at least, the
director's ground plan is based on his concept of what the play is about,

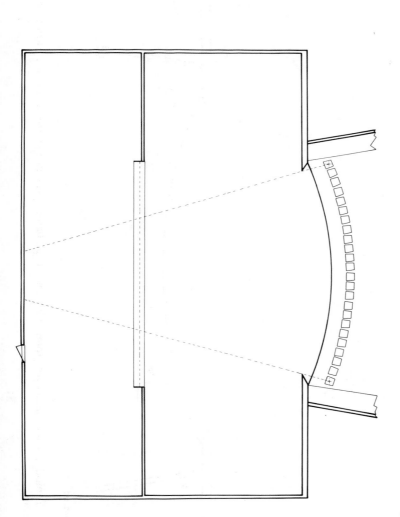

Richard Johnson

Figure 44. Reconstructed ground plan of the Alexander Dean staging of *Six Characters in Search of an Author*. The staging area extends into the workshop behind the "stage."

99

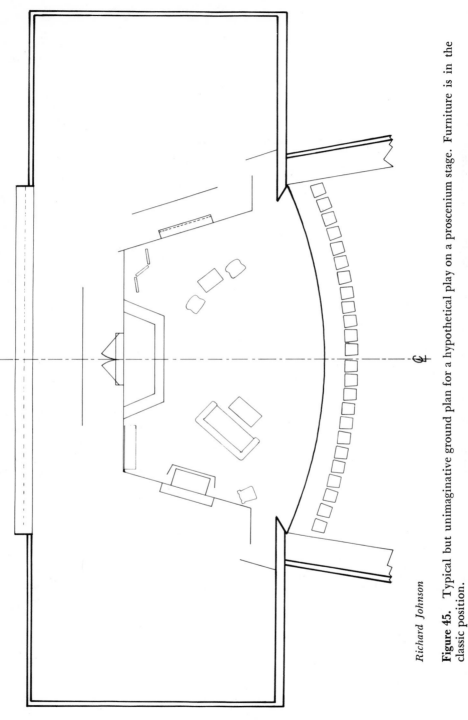

Richard Johnson

Figure 45. Typical but unimaginative ground plan for a hypothetical play on a proscenium stage. Furniture is in the classic position.

and how it is to be presented to the audience. The movement from interpretation to ground plan design can be either inductive or deductive.

Inductive ground plan design. Sometimes the director works inductively; that is, in his mind he "sees" the entire play. He "sees" the kind of room (assuming the scene involved is a room, of course), its shape and configuration vis-à-vis the audience, its style, its levels, its overall atmosphere. Inductively, the whole play dictates the whole set, at least in its broadest details, and then the design is more precisely articulated as the director goes through the play's action and shapes the setting around it. One can imagine the Kazan-Mielziner set for *Death of a Salesman* being created in this manner, Kazan deciding that it would be theatrically expedient (and artistic) to show the entire house simultaneously, rather than in sequential scenes, and building a ground plan which would show the bedroom over the living room for that purpose.

Deductive ground plan design. Occasionally a director chooses to work deductively. He has no general idea of what he wants for the whole play or scene, but he isolates in his mind from one to a dozen vital moments in the play and "sees" them as occurring in specific places with regard to the audience. These moments could be simple ones, such as vital entrances or exits, or moments of great dramatic action, such as Hamlet's killing of Claudius, or Orgon's hiding under the table (in Molière's *Tartuffe*). They could also be repeated moments, like the comic entrances in Neil Simon's *Barefoot in the Park*. Or they could be entire subscenes revolving around a piece of furniture, for example, the scene by Leslie's bed in Brendan Behan's *The Hostage,* or the scene between Joan and the dauphin on the throne in Shaw's *St. Joan.* The placement of these scenes, and the furniture necessary for them, can be determined first, and the ground plan designed around that placement.

Why is one placement better than another? Why would a director visualize a scene in one place instead of another? Why would one placement project a scene to the audience better than another? Successful staging in principle means that the audience sees what it is supposed to see, hears what it is supposed to hear, and most importantly, feels what it is supposed to feel. The goal of the ground plan in these respects is to create movement and positioning which will make the characters face the audience, naturally, as much as possible. For this reason the classic position of furniture is, as described, a sofa downstage center left and a chair-table arrangement downstage center right (or the reverse), both canted slightly inward toward center for maximum visibility. Characters seated on the sofa and chairs face not only each other, but the audience as well, at least in a proscenium stage setting. It is the director's business in blocking the play to have the actors' faces as visible to the audience as possible, not only for visibility and audibility, but so that the audience can "read" the emotions on the actors' faces. His ground plan lies at the heart of his blocking. Obviously if the sofa and chairs faced upstage, actors sitting on them and talking would be closed off from the audience.

The actual implementation of this principle, however, allows great leeway for experimentation, and the classic furniture position is so far from sacrosanct that it is often considered a last resort. Novelty and visual excitement, which are highly desirable theatrical attributes, suggest more vital ground plan arrangements than the symmetrical and undynamic "classic" one. Act II of *St. Joan,* for example, takes place in the throne room of the dauphin, Charles. At the end of the act Joan thrusts Charles onto his throne and convinces him to let her make him once more the rightful ruler of France. The "classic" way of staging this scene is with the throne upstage center, facing the (proscenium) audience. But a more vital, dynamic staging places the throne downstage left, facing upstage right, raised on a small platform (see pages 104–5).

So far we have considered relatively arbitrary interiors. However, realistic plays frequently call for specialized ground plans, such as a courtroom or the interior of a railroad car, requiring great care and ingenuity from director and designer. Courtroom scenes are common in contemporary plays. Such scenes usually involve a jury box, a judge's bench, and a witness stand. In a proscenium theatre this arrangement presents no problem. But sometimes an "audience" is also required (in addition to the theatre audience), as are tables for counsel, a stenographer, and the press. To crowd all these on stage and still open up the action requires great skill on the part of the director. In such matters his advice to, and authority over, the designer become especially vital, because the ground plan will virtually dictate the staging.

Realistic plays must conform to realistic conventions—unless a deliberate choice to use more abstract forms is made—and that means a basic adherence to normal architecture for ground plans. In designing ground plans for nonrealistic plays the director can be more flexible in projecting his action, since scenery does not have to conform to normal architectural relationships. The custom in Japanese Kabuki theatre of thrusting one or two gangways (*hanamichi*) from the stage into the audience can be adapted to many Western plays that involve direct audience-actor rapport (*The Hostage,* for example). Many ground plans for nonrealistic plays use similar devices to bring the play directly forward to the audience and project it without the guise of natural placement.

THE GROUND PLAN ENCOURAGES THE MOVEMENT PATTERN

The third task of the ground plan is to encourage movement. In most plays movement is desirable, and in plays in which it is not, the ground plan should encourage the desired stasis. But ordinarily we enjoy in the theatre a fluid, mobile play whose actors meaningfully create outward action that helps transmit the play's inward action. Actors like to move and audiences like to watch them move.

In a realistic play the ground plan is an essential element in starting up the movement pattern. In real-life situations people tend to move very little for long stretches of time. They eat leisurely dinners around a table, each in his own chair; they converse while sitting around a fireplace for hours on end, without anyone going anywhere but to the bathroom; they quietly plot assassinations, love affairs, and coups d'état across a counter with barely a toss of the head. On stage, however, a lack of physical action can produce boredom, and playwrights and directors are usually well advised to get their plays moving. The director uses first whatever the playwright gives him. Phones ring and are answered. Drinks are mixed, served, and consumed. Books are taken from bookcases, cigarettes from cigarette cases, and clothes from suitcases. Even in Samuel Beckett's *Waiting for Godot,* the classic play of inaction, people come in and go out, eat carrots, fall to the ground, run off stage to relieve themselves, do exercises —hundreds of physical acts. All the stage actions specified in the script (we shall call them *obligatory stage actions* since the playwright has required them) can be performed quietly or theatrically, according to the sense and imagination of the director. When the director is given obligatory business by the playwright, he has an initial ready-made pattern of movement which he can either elaborate or leave alone.

Even in a realistic play there may be little obligatory movement, however, so most of a director's blocking is self-initiated. In these cases as well, an effective ground plan can stimulate realistic business. A bar, a box of cigars, a telephone, a mirror, a photograph on the wall—such items of scenery or properties can be situated and used with great finesse to create a fluid, motivated movement pattern in a naturalistic play, even though they are not directly mentioned in the text. A good ground plan liberates business and behavior on stage; it does not box it in between furniture pieces or set it upstage.

No ground plan is "best" for getting a play to move; like everything else in the design, the ground plan must be shaped to the specific play, theatre, interpretation, and occasionally even to the intended cast. Still, to provide a fluid movement pattern a ground plan should be laid out in terms of its dynamic use rather than its static appearance. Important set and prop pieces should be spread about the stage, not cluttered in one corner. Similarly, entrances and exits should create movement. Many real-life rooms have two doors next to each other; however, this is rarely useful on stage. The setting arrangement should provide movement in three dimensions as well as two; it is not impossible to conceive of entrances up through trapdoors or down stairways, ladders, ropes, or firepoles.

Furniture can be butted against a wall or located so that it can be

Don Hamilton

Figures 46–49. Staging possibilities for the scene between St. Joan and the dauphin in Bernard Shaw's *St. Joan*, with the dauphin's throne in the classic upstage center position. Despite the actors' intensity, the ground plan has limited the stage picture to a series of weak, awkward confrontations.

Don Hamilton

Figures 50–53. The same scene from *St. Joan,* but the throne is placed downstage right and canted toward upstage center. The improvising actors naturally find themselves in more theatrically vivid positions.

walked around as well as toward, creating greater movement possibilities. Telephones can have long cords so that actors can walk while talking on them; chairs can swivel, bars can roll, railings can be sat on, windows can be entered through. It is vital that the director anticipate at the design stage the movement patterns he will use, and not wait for the blocking rehearsals, so that the ground plan can include enough movement possibilities and so that shop technicians can build the scenery sturdy enough to support or accommodate the anticipated movement. A railing cannot be sat on if the stage carpenter builds it of cardboard, assuming that it will be a "nonpractical" piece of decor.

The Ground Plan Encourages Effective Tableaux

A *tableau* is a frozen stage picture in which the arrangement of actors and scenery conveys a striking impression or effect. The golden age of tableaux was the nineteenth century, when almost every scene ended with one; imagine, for example, Hamlet staring off after the departed ghost, wringing his hands, while Horatio and Marcellus kneel beside him, swearing on the hilt of the sword which has been plunged, crucifix-like, into the stage floor. As the characters freeze with appropriate devotion on their faces, the curtain falls and the audience applauds madly. Today's tableaux may seem more subtle to us, but in fifty years they will presumably appear as contrived as earlier ones do now. The tableau is used today for much the same reason for which it was originally invented: to put into visual terms a vivid moment, thought, or feeling.

Technically, a tableau is a frozen moment, a framed picture. The film medium has turned to the tableau with great relish in the past decade, with the freeze-frame becoming a common method of terminating a scene or a film. But the freezing need not be unnatural (as in the freeze-frame, or with actors suddenly becoming, to all appearances, lifeless); it can be realistically performed, as in the conclusions of the films *Midnight Cowboy* and *The Graduate*—both tableaux occur in the back seat of buses—or of the famous nude scene that terminates the first act of *Hair*.

Tableaux may occur throughout a play to mark significant dramatic points such as an entrance, a departure, a revelation, an introspection, a kiss, a touch, or any other emotional transfer. For a moment, a single beat, the characters stop and think; the audience thinks too, and the picture of the setting and the characters is etched (we hope indelibly) on their minds. Then the action continues.

A good ground plan encourages tableaux to be memorable and effective. In a proscenium theatre the goals are similar to those of pictorial composition: the stage picture should have balance, focus, dynamism, and inner life. The last of these is most important, the inner life in a frozen situation. It is not accidental that paintings of immobile objects are called still lifes, for the interaction of the objects, which may not themselves be alive, creates an artistic vitality akin to life itself.

If the ground plan is deductively designed, it will probably derive from the director's envisioning several tableaux throughout the play, or possibly just one or two vital ones. But the staging must of course be effective in the quieter moments of the play as well. Stage composition is a fluid enterprise that, when properly handled, creates exciting stage pictures throughout a production, not just at its crucial moments. Thus the ground plan must be examined in relation to every moment in the play, to determine where a character can enter, stand, sit, talk, listen, and exit so that his words and feelings are strikingly conveyed to the audience.

The compositional goals of balance and focus are so vital that several books have been written to explain them in precise mathematical detail,[1] and many studies on compositional instruction have been published over the past 150 years. Yet this is a subject that is probably better intuited than learned; the factors in creating vivid stage tableaux have never been successfully reduced to mathematics or rigid academic strictures, and no working professional director today operates within formalistic limitations of this sort. To create successful tableaux, the director tends to rely on his native aesthetic taste and judgment, abetted by his familiarity with a wide variety of options and models from all media.

THE GROUND PLAN STIMULATES EFFECTIVE IMPROVISATION

Improvisation means that some movements, business, and stage behavior are left up to the actors to work out, usually in rehearsals in which they are encouraged to initiate movements instead of being told what to do. All productions are to some degree improvisational, and some are overwhelmingly so; in recent years improvisation has become much more common in professional theatre, and occasionally entire "plays" are improvised, dialogue and all, night after night.

The ground plan can stimulate improvisation, particularly in realistic plays, by being as real as possible. If the setting is a room, the ground plan represents a real room with real furniture scattered about in relationships different from the "classic" stage positioning. Set pieces are chosen or built strong enough to do what their real-life counterparts would: windows can be opened, hanging chairs can be swung on, doors can be slammed. This is not always practical or economical, but the improvisational dividends are high. In improvisational rehearsals the director wants

---

[1] For example, see Alexander Dean and L. Carra, *Fundamentals of Play Directing*, rev. ed. (New York: Holt, Rinehart and Winston, Inc., 1965).

the actors to be as free as they would be in an equivalent real-life situation; they cannot be so if they must worry continually about which walls they can lean against. Similarly, fine improvisational results can be obtained by placing furniture in nonclassic positions, for example, a sofa that forces a traffic detour, a chandelier that people run into, a chairless room that forces people to sit on kitchen counters, the floor, or bedrails. Actors improvise not merely with the text, but with the setting, and if the setting contains elements that lack fixed functional purposes (such as the nineteenth century use of andirons downstage center, so that the principal actors could come down front to warm their hands over a make-believe fire) the actors will be able to create novel and exciting movements and tableaux.

It is often said that a ground plan should provide for free, unhindered movement, and that the primary goal of ground plan design is to create a large, unobstructed acting area. This is rarely if ever helpful advice for a creative production. Some of the best ground plans, on the contrary, intentionally create obstacles. Actors, particularly good ones, tend to follow their intentions in a straight line, with regard to both movement and inner action. One of the goals of directing, however, is to put obstacles in their way, to force those dull straight lines into more theatrically exciting curved or broken ones. In a film chase scene, the characters never chase each other down a straightaway track; their path follows as varied a path as the director can contrive. Similarly, in the tiny confines of a stage, the ground plan should allow nothing to be too simple, lest the directness of the movement imply a dullness and simplicity in the inner action. The audience wishes to see not only the intention of the character, but also the contour of his path in pursuit of that intention; the director frequently has to create that contour, or at least elaborate it, by placing hindrances, generally physical ones, in the actor's path.

THE GROUND PLAN CREATES FOCUS

A ground plan creates focus even if no actors are on stage. Some elements of the stage are more important than others. There may be an empty throne, as in *St. Joan;* a doorway behind which lives a character who never comes on stage, as in O'Neill's *Touch of the Poet;* or a doorway through which someone is expected to enter *(The Inspector General)* or through which someone does enter.

The director often determines at some point in the design process what is the most important element in his setting. In most cases he wants to assure that it has spatial prominence and is not lost in the background. Elements in the stage set that have a sense of mystery should be presented with that mystery intact, so that it tantalizes the audience until they almost beg to have the mystery revealed.

The Ground Plan Creates Atmosphere

The ground plan helps to create the atmosphere not only of the setting, but of the play. If the setting is a cramped attic apartment, for example (as in Henrik Ibsen's *The Wild Duck*), the ground plan must be contained in size and probably jumbled with architecturally superfluous levels, steps, and obstructions. If the atmosphere of the play, moreover, is of cramped minds and limited vision, the ground plan must go even farther. Ground plan atmosphere is left largely to the designer, but it is a good idea for the director to use many adjectives in describing what he wants. A room can be stifling or airy, comfortable or restricted, expensive or cheap, lofty or dreary, light or dark, peaceful or frenetic, cluttered or spare. These qualities will be built into the architecture of the set, not just into its decoration, and they are a matter for agreement and creativity at the level of ground plan design. They create the inner world of the play at an exterior level.

The Ground Plan Is Dynamic

Dynamism is the synthesis of all the other ground plan design elements. The plan must be fluid and encourage fluidity; it must be meaningful in itself and encourage meaningful activity; it must convey a sense of the inner world of the play while the play moves within it. It must place the actors in dynamic relationships with each other, perhaps along diagonals, up and down different levels, confronting each other while running up steps or ramps, leaping down from railings, or swinging on ropes. In a different kind of play, it may do this by setting the actors adrift on a bare platform in the midst of an audience.

In addition, the ground plan must place the actors in a dynamic relationship with the audience. That makes of the audience either participants (for example, in some forms of communal, environmental, or improvisational theatre), or voyeurs. In either case, the play must be dynamically projected to the audience; it must open out to them, reach across to them, seize their emotions and their minds, and give them an experience they have never had or felt before. This is the function of theatre, and the final goal of the ground plan which helps to achieve it.

6

Blocking

Once he has a cast, a ground plan, and a rehearsal space, the director can proceed to block his show. In this one task he has complete freedom. Blocking is the one duty of the director that has not traditionally been collaborative, and many directors still define the sum of their responsibilities as blocking and taking occasional notes.

Terms

Blocking is not synonymous with movement, although they are occasionally used interchangeably (with confusing results). Characters may be blocked to sit about a table and not change their positions for an entire act—this is still blocking. *Movement,* as used here, refers to the major spatial changes as a character moves from one place on the stage to another—entering, crossing, standing, sitting, lying, exiting—and not to the character's individual movements—breathing, head scratching, moustache twirling—which are called *business*. *Blocking* refers to the placement and movement of all characters on stage at any time. *Business* is dealt with separately.

Called For Stage Actions

"Called for" stage actions are the external actions that define plot events of the play, such as Hamlet killing Claudius in the last act. They are the actions which, if you were attending a play in the company of a blind person, you would have to explain to him so that he would understand the story line. Story-telling actions such as these ordinarily involve a small fraction of playing time; still, since they are generally the key moments in every play, they must be accomplished with utmost clarity and with powerful theatrical effect.

Let us make this clear by example. Consider the scene in *Hamlet* (III. ii) where the "Murder of Gonzago" is being performed by itinerant players to "catch the conscience" of Claudius. Hamlet has inserted dialogue into this play-within-the-play to see whether Claudius reacts guiltily to the performance of an assassination similar to the one he instigated earlier. Hamlet has also asked Horatio to note Claudius's reaction. At the moment of the reenacted killing of Gonzago, the Shakespearean text reads as follows:

> HAMLET. He poisons him i' the garden for his estate. His name's Gonzago: the story is extant, and written in very choice Italian; you shall see anon how the murderer gets the love of Gonzago's wife.
> OPHELIA. The King rises.
> HAMLET. What, frighted with false fire!
> QUEEN. How fares my lord?
> POLONIUS. Give o'er the play.
> KING. Give me some light. Away!
> POLONIUS. Lights, lights, lights.

Then, presumably, everyone leaves the stage except Hamlet and Horatio.

Notice the number of discrete events we (the audience) must see clearly at this moment. Above all, we must see that Claudius's action stops the show. This is not as easy as it might seem. First, recall that the stage is filled with people, the entire court as well as the king and queen, Polonius, Ophelia, Hamlet, Horatio, and the players—perhaps thirty people or more. Then realize that (in a modern production, at least) the lights are dim and focused on the players; otherwise the king's cry for light makes little sense. Then realize that the audience is supposed to be watching the performance of the players, not of Claudius. Claudius has no words to speak during the moment of his deepest revelation, which is that Hamlet has somehow discovered his regicide. Amid all this confusion and split focus, the audience must clearly see the dramatic inner torment of the king, and that it is his silent perturbation which forces Polonius to abort the performance of "Gonzago." Then the king, whose sole line is "Give me some light. Away!," must hurriedly leave the stage, confirming our knowledge that he now understands the reason behind Hamlet's feigned madness.

But that is not all we must see. We must also see the reactions of Gertrude, Hamlet, Horatio, and Polonius, whose later actions make sense only in terms of what they observe here. Even the courtiers and players must have an observable reaction to this series of events, for their behavior and lives are also to change because of the happening. Not a few professional productions have bungled this scene entirely, and audiences have questioned each other during intermission (or worse, during the playing of the following scene), asking "What happened?" In such scenes, successful blocking is utterly vital to tell the playwright's story. If the blocking fails, even the most brilliant interpretation of the events will be wasted.

The Chosen Actions

Most blocking is chosen by the director in the absence of ruling stage directions; it is not called for by the playwright, but simply arbitrary from the point of view of story telling. This is a different kind of blocking; it is one thing to block Claudius stopping the show, and another to show Laura (in *The Glass Menagerie*) having her feelings hurt. About 95 percent of a director's blocking serves purposes other than gross story telling, instead heightening the inner actions and character relationships which form the greater part of the fabric of a play.

Blocking Creates Clarity

Blocking is the director's prime device for making the action (inner or outer) clear to the audience, which is, after all, the sine qua non of successful directing. We have already discussed clarity in terms of the principal actions of a play, the called for actions. But clarity is vitally important for the inner action as well. At any moment in the course of a play the audience will want to know, "Did he hear her line?," "Does he realize what she means by that?," "Does she know that a man is behind her?," "Where is he going?," and so on. One of the worst pitfalls in directing is to develop too great a familiarity with the play being produced.

By the final dress rehearsals an inexperienced director may "read in" answers to these questions that a first-time audience cannot begin to answer.

Suggestions for Clarity in Blocking

• Make the actors visible. For example, when Claudius stops the play, he should be visible from every seat in the house. He should be higher than anyone else, or downstage (in a proscenium theatre) of everyone else, and he should be illuminated enough to be seen. Ideally, all the actors should always be visible to the entire audience. While this may be impossible with a large cast or in a large, pillared theatre, it is ordinarily a good rule of thumb.

• Make the focal actor's face visible. If Claudius is stopping the play, and his reaction is important, then his face should be seen. This is difficult to arrange in arena staging, but at a key moment like this it would not be out of place for Claudius to say his line while turning 360 degrees and speaking it to everyone on stage, thereby showing his face to everyone in the audience. It is always preferable to let the audience see the actor's communicative tool, whether it be his face, body, or voice. His dialogue is more understandable if we can see his lips as he speaks.

• Isolate the beats in the scene. Beats are moment-to-moment actions, miniscule events. For example, after Polonius says "Give 'oer the play," the following beats could occur:

1. Hamlet and Horatio exchange a glance.
2. Claudius observes Horatio.
3. Claudius follows Horatio's gaze and sees Hamlet.
4. Horatio raises his eyebrow as a sign to Hamlet that the king is looking at him.
5. Hamlet turns his head and smiles at Claudius.
6. Claudius gives Hamlet a look that says, "I know what you've done and I'm going to kill you for it."
7. Hamlet laughs, mocking Claudius. His gaze lands on Gertrude.
8. Gertrude looks at Claudius, inquiring, "What's going on between you two?"
9. Claudius grabs Gertrude's arm to lead her away from her son's influence, crying, "Give me some light, away!"
10. Gertrude glances over her shoulder at Hamlet in despair.
11. Hamlet points his finger at Claudius as if to tell Gertrude, "He's the man who killed your husband."
12. Polonius, realizing what has just transpired, shouts for lights to distract the others.

Friedman-Abeles

Figure 54. *Blocking toward the audience.* Whenever possible, the director maneuvers his characters into positions where they can speak to each other while still having their faces visible to the audience. This scene, from David Rabe's *The Basic Training of Pavlo Hummel,* directed by Jeff Bleckner at the New York Shakespeare Festival Theatre (1971), shows a classic "two shot," with both actors facing front while communicating with each other.

Friedman-Abeles

Figure 55. The two shot expanded by an additional character into a three shot. Bleckner's production of Rabe's *The Basic Training of Pavlo Hummel.*

This series of beats is hypothetical. None is specified in the script, so they must be considered discrete subtextual events. All the same, it is entirely possible for experienced actors under expert direction to convey these twelve events or beats accurately in the two-second pause between Polonius's cry and the king's exit. (In film, of course, it would be comparatively easy to do this.) The beats convey clearly what the text does not: that Gertrude is only now made to suspect that Claudius killed her husband, that Claudius is now conscious that Hamlet knows of his crime and is plotting against him, that Hamlet will try to enlist his mother's help, and that Claudius knows that Hamlet and Horatio are together against him. To make these points (which are, of course, a matter of interpretation), the director must say to the actors, "I want to see all twelve of these beats." And the actors, probably at "walk through" pace at first, will play them.

• Discuss the action of the play fully with the cast. It is useless to ask the actors to play the twelve beats enumerated above if they do not fully understand them. Clarity cannot be achieved through blocking if the actors do not understand the action as the director has interpreted it. The director should ask the actors to explain the beats to him; they may see things that he does not.

• Isolate the principal actors. In the scene from *Hamlet* we have only a fraction of a second to follow Claudius's gaze to Horatio, Horatio's to Hamlet, Hamlet's back to Claudius, Claudius's back to Hamlet, Hamlet's to his mother, Gertrude's to Claudius, Gertrude's to Hamlet, and Hamlet's back to Gertrude. The human eye works with lightning speed, but all will be lost if the characters involved are hidden in a crowd of lookalikes.

• Make the actors take definite movements and positions. Each action should be able to be defined in terms of its intention. Avoid aimless movement (movement without communicative function), as it will only blur the focused movements and confuse the audience. Make the blocking points register by setting them against a fixed background.

• Check the clarity of the blocking. Invite friends unfamiliar with the play to rehearsals to see if the points are coming across. Do not rely on generalities, but ask them direct questions that they can answer only if they have really understood ("What do you think Gertrude feels after the king stops the play?"). If they cannot tell what the director thinks he has put into the scene, he has not yet succeeded.

Blocking Creates Focus

Focus is the means by which the director "orders" the audience's attention to the line, face, or gesture which is most important at a given moment. Consider for a moment the difficulties a stage director faces in contrast to his film counterpart. The film director (together with his editor) can aim his camera at as large or as small a subject as he wishes. When a character speaks a line, the camera can follow with a close-up of another character's reaction. The camera can zero in on a prop, a clenched fist, a pained expression, a "two shot" isolating a glance between two characters, or it can draw back to show the whole scene at once. The cameraman can also convert to slow motion (within most contemporary film styles) or freeze frames without breaking the stylistic realism of his scene, thereby fixing the audience's attention on an action of supreme importance or emotional content. Imagine the possibilities open to the film director in the "mousetrap" scene in *Hamlet,* discussed above: close-ups of the king's face, of his hand clenching the arm of his throne; two-shots between Hamlet and Claudius exchanging potent looks, between Claudius and Gertrude, between Horatio and Claudius, between Hamlet and Horatio. By contrast, the stage director is faced with a full setting all the time, and if he wants the audience to look at Hamlet instead of Polonius, he has to contrive that they do so.

Focus is just as important, however, in relatively simple and outwardly nonactive scenes. A scene with only two characters on stage, for example, is ordinarily watched as one watches a tennis match; the audience has eyes only for the speaker, and shifts back and forth as the characters exchange lines. But a scene is not a tennis match; sometimes its central points are made "between shots." Sometimes a character's line is the most important focal point of the moment, but sometimes a director would rather have the audience see the other character's reaction. The director must then find ways to interrupt the audience's natural desire to follow the dialogue, and focus their attention instead on the more important event taking place. Antigone is arguing with Ismene; does the director want the audience to watch Ismene develop her line of reasoning, or watch Antigone quietly considering it? Lear is jesting with the fool; should we watch the fool's antics or the reactions they are drawing from the tormented king? These are questions the director must answer and then implement, or the play's internal workings will be muddled and arbitrarily presented. In scenes with three, four, or a dozen characters, the problems of achieving valid focus grow exponentially. Fortunately, the director has many ways of handling them.

PRINCIPLES OF FOCUS

More than any other staging accomplishment, focus requires the complete compliance of the audience. Ultimately the audience will decide for itself what it wants to see, and if the production is dull, the audience may choose to focus on the patrons instead of on the actors—in most cases a disastrous occurrence. In Elizabethan times, we are led to believe, it was a major accomplishment if the play drew the patrons' attention to the stage, away from the galleries!

The director collaborates with the playwright as well as with his actors and designers to induce the audience to see and hear precisely what he wants them to. Theatre conventions will assist him, of course; the houselights will ordinarily be darkened, the ushers dressed in muted tones and speaking discreetly; the patrons, by common consent, will keep their thoughts and words to themselves except for periods of applause and laughter, and stay in their seats. Of course this varies with cultures and climes (in gold rush days, mining camp theatres pleaded with patrons not to stamp on the floor or stand on the chairs), but certainly in today's American and English theatre the director can expect compliance with his task. The rest is up to him and his production.

The principles that govern focus are complex, because manifold factors come into play. We shall list a number of these factors, roughly in descending order of importance. Those listed first, therefore, can in most cases override those below, all else being equal.

FOCUS INTRINSIC TO THE SCRIPT

The first principles of focus are intrinsic to the script itself, and to the story. Ordinarily the audience is more interested in the story of the play than in what the director does with or to it, and for this reason focus intrinsic to the script overrides all other forms.

A character has focus when he is *vulnerable*. This depends on the situation of the play more than on the blocking. Just as in the tennis match effect, where the spectators all watch the man to whom the ball has just been hit, instead of the one who has hit it—so in the theatre we always focus on the character who has been asked an important question, or required to perform a risky task. This is largely intrinsic to the inner action of the play, but the director can, by enhancing the inner action, create a stronger focus.

A character has focus when he has a *stronger intention* than the others. In the scene before the arrival of Othello's ship at Cyprus, for example, Iago, Desdemona, Emilia, Cassio, and various others are engaging in what appears to be small talk. Because Iago's known (to us) inner intentions are so fierce, he will have focus no matter what staging is used.

A *title* character will have focus, as will a principal character, or a star performer. This is partly justifiable; if the play is called *Othello*, Othello has focus by dint of his name, since we assume the play is going to be about him and we will have to watch him closely. And when Katharine Hepburn steps on stage, we watch her because we know she is being paid a fortune for her efforts and we want to get our money's worth. Little can be done about this, so the director had better accept the situation.

FOCUS INTRINISIC TO THE STAGING

Purely compositional methods of achieving focus can overrule the above, but they are most often used to supplement and enhance them, as well as to determine focus when the already mentioned factors are not in play, or are self-cancelling, as is frequently the case. These compositional methods follow in rough order of their potency.

A character "pointed at," all else being equal, has focus. The pointing need not be literal; in fact, it usually involves simply having the other characters look at the focal character. This is one way of throwing the ball to him.

A character speaking, all else being equal, has focus. If he clears his throat or stammers first, he will have focus before his first word. This is ordinarily a cheap trick—and if initiated by the actor, an offensive bit of upstaging—but it is frequently the only way of drawing sudden focus to a character who is in no other way the point of attention. Some actors have made this a stock in trade.

A character facing the audience, all else being equal, has focus over those not facing the audience. Again, if initiated by the actor, this can be considered upstaging. (The term means that the upstager moves with respect to the upstaged so that in a face to face confrontation the upstager is facing the audience and his smouldering colleague has his back to them.) Upstaging arranged by the director is perfectly correct, though it occasionally causes bruised nerves. A character delivering a long speech to another is frequently blocked upstage center with the other downstage left, for example, since it is desirable at that point to see only the speaker's face. When the listener's reaction becomes important, he can turn to face the audience; the scene is what is called in films a "two shot," with both faces pointing to the audience. (See the photograph on page 114.)

A character moving, all else being equal, has focus over those who are still. Movement attracts attention, and even the most free, improvisational directors sometimes stop actors from moving about while others are supposed to have focus. In most productions calling for large numbers of actors on stage, the less important characters are told to freeze during their still moments; even a fidgeting finger can steal the focus from Hamlet if it is within the peripheral vision of the audience. Major movements, such as entrances, exits, full stage crosses, or anything done rapidly, are certain attention getters on stage, proving it desirable for directors to externalize inner actions as much as possible. Finally, a brief movement be-

Photos by Hank Kranzler. Courtesy American Conservatory Theatre.

Figures 56 and 57. *Blocking for focus.* Principles of focus, illustrated in production shots from the American Conservatory Theatre, San Francisco. Above, *The Merchant of Venice,* directed by Ellis Rabb (1970). Subtle focus on Shylock (center) and Antonio (right) because of the contrast between their stillness and downstage gazes and the frenzied movement and upstage faces around them. Below, *Hamlet,* directed by William Ball (1967). Strong focus on Ophelia, center, because of her whirling movement and white dress, which contrast with the darkness and immobility of the others; the focus is reinforced by the others gazing toward her.

fore a line, like a stammer, will draw focus before the actor's first word, and is a common technique.

A character who is isolated, all else being equal, has focus. If ten actors are on stage right and one on stage left, the one on the left has a high degree of compositional focus. The same principle applies if ten are on the stage floor and one on a raised platform or vice versa, or ten upstage and one downstage.

A character who is moving in a different pattern from the others, all else being equal, has focus. If he limps and the others stride, if he runs and the others walk, he will be looked at.

A character who is more brightly lit, or is placed in a more interesting part of the stage, or has a more exciting costume, has focus. Actors have been known to make friends with lighting technicians and costume designers for this purpose. If a large canopied chair downstage left remains unsat in for a while, the first actor to sit in it will tend to draw focus to himself.

An actor who is downstage, all else being equal, has focus. Early textbooks on directing laid great stress on areas of the stage that had high innate compositional focus, and decided that downstage center had the highest, followed by upstage center, downstage right, and downstage left. We find this fairly arbitrary. Of course, if six actors stood motionless and impassive, all facing the audience, one in each of the six main areas of the stage, we would tend to look at those in the first row more than those in the second because the former were closer. We might look first at the one downstage center, because we are trained to look there, but our eyes would finally come to rest on the one closest to us: the actor downstage right for those on house left, and the actor downstage left for those on house right. If one of the actors were somewhat more attractive than the others, we would probably stare at him wherever he were located. The point is that focus by stage area has such minor effect that any other focal principle overrides it.

We have cautioned throughout, "all else being equal," knowing of course that all else is not equal. Obviously, if Marlon Brando, playing Molière's Tartuffe, enters (after a big two-act buildup from the other characters) in his all-black costume, strides gallantly to an otherwise unused, raised downstage chair as the other actors stare at him, cries, "Where is my hair shirt and flagellator?", and is illuminated by a 5000 watt followspot as he sits down, he will have focus! But invariably focal matters are more complex. One character is speaking, one moving, one looking at someone else, one isolated in a corner, one downstage center, yet focus must still be achieved. The director works this out by his understanding of the principles of focus, and of which ones are strongest in various situations. His synthesis of these principles is not scientific; it comes from his

Photos by Hank Kranzler. Courtesy American Conservatory Theatre.

Figures 58 and 59. Above, 1967 ACT production of *Hamlet*. Focus on Hamlet (right) because of the contrast of his dark costume and leftward-downward gaze and the light costumes and rightward-upward gazes of the others. Below, Edmond Rostand's *Cyrano de Bergerac,* directed by William Ball (1973). Focus on Cyrano and Montfleury because of their downstage positions, elevation, and brighter illumination than the muted, seated, upstage characters around them. A secondary focus on Roxanne, who is brightly illuminated, tiaraed, raised, and facing front in the left rear of the stage.

understanding of the theatre itself—even of life itself—and from his intuitive and experiential knowledge of which principle will override in each case. In this area, too, the director should check his choices against the findings of visitors at rehearsals if he is at all diffident about the validity of his intuition.

Upstaging

Actors are intuitively aware of devices to attain focus, and many try to use them, either consciously or unconsciously. Actors should not be condemned, of course, for what is a vital ingredient of an actor's talent. A highly mobile and exciting actor may be a dream as Hamlet, however, and a curse playing Horatio opposite a phlegmatic prince. The old actor who cagily lights a cigarette while another is speaking, the five-year-old girl who rolls her eyes at the audience while the leading lady is pontificating, even the novice actor who drifts upstage in a face-to-face scene to "see" the audience better, are all upstaging and should be checked; if they are doing so involuntarily and cannot stop, they should be removed or the play is doomed. Incidentally, some actors continually upstage themselves, for various psychological reasons; for the production this can be just as disastrous as an actor who upstages others (though it causes fewer hurt feelings among the cast).

Blocking Establishes Credibility

The problem of achieving character credibility is to a certain extent an acting problem, a problem for the director insofar as he is working with the actor. But blocking is also an integral part of credibility; the greatest naturalistic actor in the world would be hamstrung if directed to stand, sit, and cross like no real person. Actors represent people, and in most dramatic situations people move and position themselves in response to the situation. In any play which is directed within a framework of realism, characters should move as we expect people to move; they should sit when they are tired, stand when they are excited, run when they are in a hurry, cross to someone when they want to make love. The *arbitrary* (and we emphasize arbitrary) disregarding of these and similarly obvious principles leads to noncredible action and is never tolerated by audiences or, for that matter, by actors. Again, in plays directed more or less realistically, the most theatrically effective bit of staging will collapse if it makes no sense that the characters execute it at that moment.

While we have considered only realistic plays to this point, the principle of credibility applies to all styles and forms of theatre. No one

would call *Hamlet* a realistic play—it is written in verse, for example—
yet in all but the most abstractly styled production we expect Hamlet and
the other actors to be credible. We want to see them walk, sit, and stand
like human beings, and we expect that when Hamlet crosses to the audience to deliver a soliloquy, he crosses to us because he has something important to say to us. Even in the wildest theatre of the absurd, we expect
the actors to be credible within the context of the style of the play. The
director must block his play to ensure that ultimate consistency of credibility.

Considerations of credibility in blocking must be carefully weighed
against considerations of focus and clarity, for while credibility requires
an attempt to simulate real-life behavior, clarity tries to make inner actions clear to an outside observer, which is not a consideration in real life.
An outsider could observe a heated family argument without ever getting
the gist of the disagreement or the internal shifts, but this must not happen in the theatre. Clarity must always prevail, even at the possible risk of
loss of credibility. But a loss of either is urgently to be avoided, and can
be avoided by careful staging. Just as in a naturalistic play the playwright
tries to shape and compress his dialogue into a telling two-hour product,
so the director must eliminate extraneous movement and try to make his
directorial points through credible human physical actions. For ultimately, if the blocking and acting are not credible, the failure of the play will
be as great as if it is not clear.[1]

METHODS OF BLOCKING FOR CREDIBILITY

• Familiarize the actors with the set and the situation. This is ordinarily the first task of a director trying to achieve any kind of naturalistic
performance. If the setting is an interior room, for example, make it as
easy as possible for the actors to feel at home in the room (particularly if
it is supposed to be their home). While rehearsals rarely take place on a
prebuilt set (and the results are extraordinary when they do), arrange the
rehearsal space to resemble the set as closely as possible. Use furniture
that resembles the stage furniture (or use stage furniture) so that the actors can use it as they will in performance. Let them practice living in the
set, using its doors, furniture, fireplace, bookshelves, and so on. Improvise

---

[1] We admit exception to this. Countless Broadway plays, especially when well into
their runs, are performed with only the vaguest simulation of credibility. Regardless of
theoretical considerations, the audience seems not to mind. What they do find intoler-
able, however, is not knowing what is happening, or not being able to hear. This state of
affairs is painful to anyone concerned with the art of the theatre, but it exists and bears
reporting. Still, we are concerned with the art of directing, not the practices of a commercial industry, and we stick by our point.

scenes not in the play that could take place on the set. Give directions in terms of the set as a room, rather than as a stage ("Go to the bathroom" instead of "Exit up stage left door"). Give the actors the props they will use. Let them bring in set dressing and furniture if possible, and use it in the performance, too.

• Work with the actors on establishing their characterization down to the details of ordinary living: how would they sit in a chair, set the table for dinner, brush their teeth, and so on. Have the actors do these routine things on the set, or the set simulation.

• Use set pieces with the structural counterparts of the real objects they represent. If you are doing *Zoo Story*, which takes place on a park bench, obtain a bench on the back of which Jerry can sit, as he could on a Central Park bench. If the set has wide window sills, and there are teen-age boys in the play, have the carpenter build the set so that the boys can sit on the sills as they could or would do at home. Use furniture that is not too fragile to experiment with—couches that the actors can climb on, trip over, sit on the arms of, and so on.

• Let the actors improvise much of their blocking. Credibility is the one directorial objective which the actors, if they are good, can probably establish better through their movement than you can.

Blocking Establishes and Heightens the Inner Action

Blocking intensifies the inner action of a play (see Chapter 3). Inner action is the emotional or intellectual (mental) shifts within characters: realizations, resolutions, alterations of plans, alterations of attitudes, and so on. Falling in love, for example, is an inner action which does not necessarily correspond to any outward physical activity, yet it must in some way be made apparent to an audience if the story of the play depends on it. The following scene from *Othello* contains intense inner action unaccompanied by any specified outer action.

> IAGO. My noble lord—
> OTHELLO. What dost thou say, Iago?
> IAGO. Did Michael Cassio, when you wooed my lady
>   Know of your love?
> OTHELLO. He did, from first to last. Why dost thou ask?
> IAGO. But for a satisfaction of my thought;
>   no further harm.
> OTHELLO. Why of thy thought, Iago?
> IAGO. I did not think he had been acquainted with her.
> OTHELLO. O, yes, and went between us very oft.

IAGO. Indeed?
OTHELLO. Indeed? Ay, indeed! Discernst thou
      aught in that? Is he not honest?
IAGO. Honest, my lord?
OTHELLO. Honest? Ay, honest.
IAGO. My lord, for aught I know.
OTHELLO. What does thou think?
IAGO. Think, my lord?
OTHELLO. Think my lord?
      By heaven he echoes me,
      As if there were some monster in his thought
      Too hideous to be shown. Thou dost mean something . . .

On one level, nothing is happening except talking. On an intellectual/emotional level, however, Othello's entire psychic foundation is being attacked, and his life will never hereafter be the same. Similarly, Iago is for the first time taking criminal risks with his security to plant the seed of jealousy in the Moor's ear. The nature of the action is in fact as urgent and compelling as Hamlet's killing of Claudius, but it is entirely mind-to-mind, not body-to-body.

The inner action of a scene is occasionally called its subtext. While it might be valuable to distinguish these terms (an inner action may be fully textual, for example, as in a soliloquy), for most purposes they are the same. Subtext involves all the inner action of a scene or play which is not specifically noted in the text; it is under (*sub*) the text, there to be found by the diligent interpretive study or intuition of the director and actors. It is also there for the study and intuition of critics and audiences, so the director must work carefully if he is to avoid universal censure.

The subtext of a given moment is the composite of three components which, in the lazy parlance of the theatre, are frequently mistaken for the whole thing. They are not, and they should be precisely understood:

1. The character's intention (what he wants to do)
2. The character's motivation (why he wants to do it)
3. The character's inner monologue (what he is thinking when he does it)

The subtext of a play, therefore, is a highly complex network of conscious and unconscious impulses that are as real and theatrical as the external actions. The text is the mere external tip of a giant iceberg of inner action.

As an example of the complexity of this problem, let us look at Othello's single line, "Indeed? Ay, indeed!" A possible interpretation of the subtext of that moment follows.

Othello's intention: to make light of Iago's hint by mocking Iago's unusual inflection, thereby diverting Iago from continuing.

Othello's motivation: to prevent himself from hearing what he dreads to hear.

Othello's inner monologue: "What the hell is he driving at?"

Iago's intention (while listening to Othello's line): to note how much the hint rattles Othello.

Iago's motivation: to see how fast and hard he should pursue this line of hinting without overstepping his bounds.

Iago's inner monologue: "Yes, he's upset, he's going to pursue this."

The subtext of the moment: Othello, frightened by the possibilities that Iago's hint has opened to examination, tries to avoid further discussion of the subject by the psychological defense mechanism of mocking his subordinate. Iago, a superior psychological analyst, sees through Othello's mechanism, recognizes it for what it is, and discovers that the Moor is open to further suggestion.

Multiply this subtext by every definable moment in the play, and every character on stage at every moment, and the magnitude of the subtextual play becomes apparent.

The director "finds" or "chooses" the interpretation of the play and its moments (see Chapter 3) and communicates it to his actors so that they can think about it, feel it, and play it (see Chapter 9). No matter how great the contribution of his actors in this regard, he is still responsible for the understanding and projection of every action, inner and outer, in the course of the play. Blocking is one of his major vehicles in this task.

Blocking intensifies inner action by making it outer action. Blocking is the principal mechanism by which a play moves off the page into the theatre. It gives life and fullness to dialogue, demonstrating that something important is happening. It is entirely possible for guests at an intimate cocktail party to sit in the same positions without moving for an hour at a time, even if their discussion leads to shattering revelations and emotional shifts. But stasis is rarely successful in the theatre, because plays usually involve dramatic confrontations causing characters to become highly disturbed and active. The audience expects the characters to become deeply involved in the situation; if the characters are not involved, why should the audience be? Character involvement is usually communicated across the footlights by movement, by doing things and by physically reacting to stimuli. Even when the entire point of a play is stasis (as in Chekhov's *The Three Sisters*) directors ordinarily find that movement which can be shown to be self-defeating is the most effective way to project the stasis. Only rarely (we are reminded of Ralph Richardson and John Gielgud in *Home*) can even superior actors remain still on stage for long periods of time and hope to engage the audience with philosophical reflections and internal reactions. The plays of Bernard Shaw, filled as they are with rhetorical dialectic and devoid of external action, are usually most successful when staged with movement to emphasize the "points" of the playwright.

Thus a play's blocking creates a sense that things are happening. A familiar adage in the early days of cinema was that "moving pictures move." The same is true, perhaps to a lesser extent, in the theatre. Placement and movement tell not only the external story of the play, but the characters' thoughts and feelings. A well blocked production can be attentively (if not perfectly) followed even if the dialogue is in an unknown foreign language; for proof of that one need only attend productions of the late Bertolt Brecht, still playing at his Berliner Ensemble in East Berlin.

METHODS OF BLOCKING TO HEIGHTEN INNER ACTION

• Establish the inner action precisely in terms of beats. Discuss the beats with the actors to make sure that you and they see them the same way.

• Externalize inner action. If an actress is saying, "I want to get out of here, Charlie," it might be effective to have her back toward the door, facing Charlie, while she speaks. If, on the other hand, she is saying, "I'm going to kill you, Charlie," she can emphasize her inner action by reaching for a weapon.

• Dramatize inner shifts of emotion. It is possible, sometimes even likely, that real-life people would remain outwardly impassive while their world is crumbling. It is also possible that they would externalize the inner shift through movement. A director is free within the bounds of credibility to choose either course; the latter is ordinarily more theatrical. When Juliet first hears that Romeo is a Montague, for example, she could make no visible response. But she could also run downstage, throw herself on her bed, pound on the bedstead, whirl back at the nurse who has informed her, and finally bury her face in the pillow. The first reaction may be considered more naturalistic and the second more melodramatic, but each is reasonable for a fourteen-year-old girl, and each has a valid place on the stage.

All mechanisms for intensifying stage action can tend to lead to melodramatic spectaculars, mugging on the part of the actors, and empty theatrics. They must be used with caution or they will be laughable. Once clarity is achieved, the level of intensification is a variable that the director should handle with care, but he should not be afraid to use it. Actors, particularly those trained in naturalistic styles, often wish to play their scenes with an outward display of cool dispassion. When this tendency is uncorrected, the inner action the director wants to project may remain in the actors' minds, and not reach the audience's emotion.

Blocking Creates Behavior

This is one of the least understood yet most important aspects of blocking; it is fair to state that few directors until the last two or three decades have even been aware that blocking creates behavior. Yet it is a major part of most contemporary professional directing. As Elia Kazan noted, "Directing finally consists of turning Psychology into Behavior."[2]

Behavior is movement on stage which is not called for in the script and which seems to have no direct correlation with the play. It is movement for the actor to "play against," rather than with which to express himself and his feelings directly. It allows him to set up a pattern of audience expectations through which, by making deviations, he can allow his deepest feelings to be inferred.

For example, consider a meaningful but not climactic speech in the middle of a modern play, a speech that could (and with an unimaginative director certainly would) be delivered straightforwardly from the middle of the stage. Now imagine the same speech delivered while the actor crosses to the bar, mixes himself a Manhattan, drops a cherry into it, crosses back downstage, and concludes his line by taking a drink. Consider the possibilities of subtextual communication this bit of blocking provides. The actor's inner action, which could otherwise be conveyed only by his inflections and facial expressions, which can easily become mugging, can now be revealed by his manner of walking to the bar (compulsively? casually? is he comfortable in this room? is he uptight?); by how he pours the drink (do his hands tremble a bit? is he composed enough to measure the vermouth carefully?); by how he drops the cherry (is he trying to show how composed he is by adding that little extra, perhaps victorious, touch? or is he trying to disguise his worry about his drinking by elegantly plopping in the cherry to show that he retains his control?); or by how he crosses back downstage (triumphantly? nervously? proving something?) and takes the first swallow (desperately? savagely? savoring the taste?). What a wealth of inner action such a minor piece of blocking can convey!

[2] Elia Kazan, "Notebook for *A Streetcar Named Desire*," in Toby Cole and Helen K. Chinoy, *Directors on Directing*, rev. ed. (Indianapolis: The Bobbs-Merrill Co., Inc., 1963), p. 346.

Consider the possibilities of staging the scene from *Othello*. Suppose that in an experimental modern dress production, or a rehearsal for a more traditional production, Othello is lifting weights while Iago sits at his feet. Imagine Othello pausing, the weight in mid-air, as he ponders Iago's point, then renewing his workout with greater energy as he tries to shake off Iago's comments. Imagine Othello playfully tossing Iago one of the weights, and Iago redoubling his efforts because of the discomfort the Moor's action causes him. Imagine the lines spoken as the two men jog around the stage, drink at a bar, or fire at a rifle range. The creation of behavior can unlock all sorts of internal feelings that mere face-to-face confrontation, and even the abstract "cross left, cross right" directing, cannot.

The creation of behavior is inextricable from the creation of style, and it is not normally considered under the general heading of stage composition. But ultimately the director's blocking creates it. In this area, within the bounds of what will be effective, the director can make an enormous contribution to the play. Behavior is a director's creative option because he is invariably the one who invents it; actors are trained to follow their intentions without deviation; and behavior will tend to be an obstacle to, rather than an intensifier of, their intentions.

Methods of Blocking to Create Behavior

• Consider creating obstacles. Suppose a character receives an on stage telephone call in the midst of a conversation. If he is next to the phone when it rings, it must be made to ring just as he completes his last sentence. He picks up the receiver and answers. Consider this alternative: the character, standing behind a sofa at upstage right, is talking to a friend who is sitting on the sofa. The phone rings in mid-sentence, and, still talking, he crosses down left to the telephone, picks up the receiver, and begins to speak. The action is more fluid, more interesting (more credible, for that matter), and more open to subtextual acting. Now suppose that during the phone conversation he reaches into his pocket and pulls out a cigarette. He fumbles for a match but has none (the obstacle). His friend, seeing his distress, picks up a lighter from the coffee table. The actor on the phone picks up the body of the telephone and, still talking, crosses back to the sofa, where his friend lights the cigarette. At that point the person on the other end of the line says something of great importance. "What?" exclaims our actor, wheeling back to a full-face position. Talking furiously on the phone, he crosses urgently back to the telephone table, where the ash tray is located. Finally he sits by the phone while his friend lights a cigarette of his own. This staging sequence is arbitrary, to be sure, but it can greatly heighten the excitement of the scene. The obstacle has forced the actor to move, to turn, to be frustrated (at not having a match), to be satisfied (with his first pull on the cigarette), and to further identify his relationship with the other actor on stage, who has demonstrated some empathy by realizing that his friend needed a match, but not enough empathy to cross to him and light his cigarette. Only in action can we discover the full measure of a character.

• Think of the possibilities for behavior suggested by the setting. Are there dishes to be cleaned, ash trays to be emptied, pillows to be fluffed, a floor to be swept? Tennessee Williams's plays are filled with marvelous behavior that renders the subtext vividly. Recall the scene in *The Night of the Iguana* in which Maxine and Hannah are having a life-and-death struggle, in utterly quiet tones, while setting the tables for dinner. The handling of knives and forks and the rattling of dishes becomes the prime vehicle whereby the actors reveal what is on their minds. Recall also the scene in Arthur Miller's *The Death of a Salesman* in which Willy accidentally turns on the wire recorder, and struggles insanely to turn it off.

• Consider the possibilities for behavior suggested by the characters. What is Othello doing when Iago accosts him? Standing around waiting to be accosted? Think creatively: what *could* he be doing? "Enter Hamlet reading on a book," says Shakespeare in one of his few behavioral stage directions. How is Hamlet reading it—avidly, absent-mindedly, at a desk, in a chair, walking? What are Benvolio and Mercutio doing as they jest with Romeo? Playing catch? Practicing their dueling skills? Carrying each other on their backs?

• Stretch the actors' capacity. In the tea scene of Giraudoux's *The Madwoman of Chaillot*, for example, there may be pressure to use imaginary tea and no cream, sugar, or lemon. This pressure may come from the prop department (it would mean less work and expense), but it might also come from the actors, who may consider that the real props "get in the way." "In the way of what?" the director should ask. No play is simply the sum of its verbal content. Imagine the possibilities for hilarity, as well as for character revelation, when the three old madwomen struggle with tea, an antique teakettle and teakettle warmer, china teacups, cream, sugar, spoon, lemon, napkins, spills, mop-ups, burned tongues (too hot), wry faces (too much lemon), and satisfied, semisenile sighs (just right).

• Think imaginatively about where a scene is set. Elizabethan and multiscene plays in particular provide a great deal of choice in this matter. The so-called "First Court Scene" in *Hamlet,* for example, Shakespeare calls simply "scene two." No lines specifically define the setting as a court, so why could it not be in set a meadhall? Claudius, a heavy drinker, could receive Cornelius and Voltimand wherever he chooses; the play is full of lines and imagery about drinking (Hamlet: "They klepe us drunkards"), so why not play the scene among courtiers carousing over pints of ale? Imagine Claudius's effect when, redfaced and befuddled, he turns half-drunkenly to Hamlet (a nondrinker?) and says, "But now, my cousin Hamlet, and (burp) my son."

• Set up behavior opposite to the inner action of the scene. Interrupting or shifting the behavior will make the drama of the scene more chilling or poignant. In *Romeo and Juliet,* Paris finds Juliet apparently dead on their wedding day. In Mel Shapiro's production of the play at the Old Globe Theatre in San Diego, Paris came in with a hired group of strolling musicians, who played their joyous serenade right down to the discovery of the presumed corpse. This practice parallels what the actor calls "playing against the obvious," whereby a character who is supposed to cry tries instead to laugh, yet his tears show through the laughter for greater poignancy. Blocking against the obvious means blocking against the normal system of intensifying the inner action; the actress who says, "I'm going to kill you, Charlie" does not in this case cross to the rifle rack, but backs timidly toward the door. The effect is one of surprise, intrigue, and a feeling that something unknown is going to happen. (Of course, something should then happen, or the movement will look absurd.)

The danger in blocking to create behavior is that it might appear gimmicky. In classical productions (as of Shakespearean plays) some critics will attack anything other than the actors standing and delivering their lines straightforwardly ("It might be theatrical, but it certainly isn't Shakespeare," or "Imagine old Will rolling over in his grave"). Of course behavior can be gimmicky, as can anything in the theatre, which after all is only humanly created illusion. Transparency in a director's achievement is rarely commendable; if the audience dismisses a bit of created behavior as a cute directorial device, the bit will fail because it has not satisfied its primary objective: to project character and action more deeply than would a line reading. Still, the creation of behavior may ultimately be that which gives a produced play its greatest sense of vitality, and it should be creatively, and intently, pursued.

Blocking Creates Special Effects

So far we have been speaking mainly in terms of the goals of blocking in serious, realistic plays, since those general principles apply to almost all theatrical modes. But much blocking is executed for what we might call special effects, especially for farcical effects. Pratfalls, for example, are blocked actions which cannot really be justified on the basis of clarity or credibility, and can only by stretching the point be considered to derive from the director's wish to heighten inner action. A pratfall is staged for one reason, to make the audience laugh, although it is selectively employed to make a statement about the character who falls. In plays that permit or require them, extensive chase scenes, slapstick beatings, characters backing into each other, speeded-up motion or slow motion, and wildly exaggerated tantrums can produce the same effect. While these farcical staging bits are as old as Aristophanes, they are frequently employed today with great effect, in the appropriate stylistic circumstances.

Blocking can also create nonfarcical theatrical effects. Slow motion and nonnaturalistic freezes can delineate dramatic confrontations superbly. Actors advancing en masse on the audience can be chilling, as in Peter Brook's *Marat/Sade*. Actors accomplishing seemingly superhuman feats, as in the Polish productions of Jerzy Grotowski, can be awesome and thrilling. Blocking which fills the stage with hundreds of extras, horses, and elephants, such as the summertime Roman production of *Aïda,* can be breathtaking. Blocking for these purposes, needless to say, involves a high level of advance planning and consideration of the style of the production.

This sort of blocking also involves the most delicate originality. While books of comic *lazzi* (time-honored comic bits) and spectacular staging effects could be compiled, the success of these special feats is in their newness, their appropriateness to the play and the character involved, and in the unique imagination of the director, his playwright, and his cast.

Blocking Creates Aesthetic Effects

The goal of creating aesthetic effects is given such priority elsewhere that it may seem strange to put it near the bottom of a list of directorial blocking effects. However, textbooks on directing have often been little more than manuals of composition, which itself has been primarily thought of as an aesthetic "picturization" of the stage which is supposed to accompany the speaking of the dialogue. It is not our purpose to ignore the director's pictorial goals, but simply to put them in what we consider to be their proper place.

Historically, one of the first goals of a director was to arrange his actors in an aesthetically pleasing composition. In the nineteenth century the models of this sort of composition were art masterpieces such as Raphael's *The School of Athens,* which displays dozens of men and women grouped so that the canvas is balanced and the focus is on the central group. The danger of seeing stage composition in similar terms is manifold. In the first place, it speaks only to proscenium staging and is generally inapplicable to thrust, arena, or environmental staging. Second, it assumes a single vantage point (the center of the auditorium) from which the stage picture is perfect. But even proscenium theatres have two fea-

Virginia Museum Theatre photo by Ron Jennings

Figure 60. A ground plan and blocking which direct the actors into a mass confrontation with the audience, creating a chilling effect. *Marat/Sade,* directed by Keith Fowler at the Virginia Museum Theatre, Richmond (1969).

tures that Raphael did not have to contend with: a multiplicity of vantage points and a real (not simulated by perspective) depth of stage (versus canvas). To stage *The School of Athens,* for example, on a proscenium stage would cause enormous difficulties.

In fact, the aesthetic compositional goals of the stage director are very different from those of the canvas painter or even the sculptor, though occasionally paintings (David's *The Assassination of Marat*) and sculptures (Rodin's *The Burghers of Calais*) have been used as stage models. The stage director's goals are partly shared by other visual artists, but are also partly different and their implementation is considerably so.

The compositional subgoals of a director might be to create

1. Balance (or imbalance)
2. Visual focus (or mass confusion)
3. Sweeping movement (or formal stasis)
4. Use of all stage areas (or of one stage area)
5. Prettiness (or ugliness)
6. Dignity (or grotesquery)

These subgoals (and there are probably a thousand others) may be desirable for their independent aesthetic effect (that is, independent of the goings-on of the play's story); if they are in keeping with the nature of the overall play and production, they may certainly enhance the success of the venture. They can hardly, however, ensure it.

"Composition" is no longer a required course at most collegiate art schools (it is not even offered at many), and the days of the "rules of composition" are even deader in the theatre than in the painting studio. This was inevitable in an age where Picasso, Mondrian, Larry Rivers, Frank Stella, Claes Oldenburg and Andy Warhol decided to take the "rules" into their own hands. No one, of course, would say that composition does not exist—merely that codified principles are no longer prescriptive. The old goals of balance and visual rhythm were fine in Renaissance painting and nineteenth century staging, but as ends in themselves they are archaic today. The compositional goals of a contemporary director are more than likely guided by his intuitive aesthetic sensibilities.

Blocking Creates Variety

There is no question that blocking creates variety, but whether movement should be inserted into a play for that reason alone is debatable. Many directors insert a series of sits, stands, and crosses simply to keep the audience alert; perhaps nothing is more indicative of poor directing, in fact, than to see the characters moving aimlessly around the stage because the director told them to do so. It is not enough merely to remind the director that every move must have a character motivation; every move on stage should have a directorial purpose, more than for variety. Indeed, if a play is creatively blocked to clarify the external action, to intensify the inner action, and to develop credibility, behavior, and the desired special effects—and if the play is a good one to begin with—it is difficult to conceive that the necessary variety will not be present.

The theatre has no innate need for movement. Samuel Beckett's short play, *Play,* requires three characters to be immersed to their necks in urns for the play's duration, and to remain impassive and expressionless to boot. In *Home,* John Gielgud's most vigorous movement during the entire play was to stretch his legs. One should not underestimate the audience's ability to stay involved, *as long as valid action is taking place on stage.*

Still, not all plays are devoid of dull passages, and the director may be said to have a responsibility to enliven these with effective movement. No one really questions this, in practice; still it seems far more effective for the director to find something in the inner action, or to create some behavior, than simply to say to himself "They've been sitting there long enough. I'll move them over to stage right." Such arbitrariness can often bewilder the audience as well as the actors, leaving the audience more bored than before.

Blocking Creates Abstract Effects and Symbolic Patterns

We have mentioned a few cases where directing creates special effects, such as actors moving en masse toward the audience. Particularly in non-naturalistic plays directors often create what we must consider nonnatural character movement or placement for abstract purposes. For example, in the last scene of Dürrenmatt's *The Visit,* as staged by Peter Brook, the actors formed a perfect semicircle around Anton Schill, then slowly converged on him as he was killed. This not only created an abstract feeling of horror, it also conveyed the symbolic meaning that people can be turned into machines, given proper stimulus (in this case, money). Otherwise, the action of this play was realistically directed.

When abstract or symbolic movements repeat or reverse themselves, the director is using a blocking pattern. In comedy or farce, this practice is familiar as the running visual gag: an actor always trips on the last step of the stairway, always knocks over the same chair. In highly stylized plays the pattern may be consciously symmetrical, for example, actors on opposite sides of the stage rise simultaneously and cross to meet each other at exact center stage. Other patterns are much more subtle; for example, one character may always move in a circular fashion while others are blocked back and forth in straight lines. In styles that permit it, actors can move simultaneously, as in *The Visit,* or with identical strange mannerisms, such as goose stepping, to indicate a greater than normal sense of menace. Or an actor can be positioned in a realistically abnormal manner, such as at the proscenium edge or in the audience, to establish a relationship with the audience that exceeds the limits of the regular play. An actor can establish one area of the stage as "his," thereby making his presence felt even when he is not on stage.

Abstract and symbolic blocking can be received with enormous approval or disapproval. On the positive side, they may be considered the director's great contribution to the play, as memorable as Alexander Dean's entrance of the six characters, mentioned earlier. Or they may be quickly dismissed as meretricious, the director's "showing off." They may also sound exciting in theory yet be lost on the audience. More than one director has proudly said, "What a great idea! See, she comes in that door in the first act and goes out the same door in the last act!"—and the point is completely wasted because no one but himself noticed it, even subliminally.

The most that can be said about abstract movement patterns, in terms of a director's goals, is that the best of them are sensational, many are a waste of time, and the worst are utterly disastrous. They are risky (particularly because they are so easy) and should be considered and even reconsidered carefully.

The Director's Blocking Tools

To accomplish all his blocking goals the director has only two tools: actor placement and actor movement (including direction, velocity, and manner). However, if we consider that in a three hour Shakespearean play with an average of six people on stage at a time, the director stages over 1000 man-minutes of stage time, we realize that a lot of blocking goes on in the theatre. Even a much smaller play involves thousands of moment-to-moment blocking decisions on who is where, who moves where, how fast, and in what way.

Blocking Terms

The director communicates blocking to the actor by using a set of accepted terms. An actor stands, sits, lies down, falls to the floor, enters a room, or exits just as he would if asked to do so in real life. If he is told to move left or right, he does so from his vantage point, not the director's, which of course means that a director in a proscenium theatre who wants an actor to move left must ask him to move stage right. If that seems confusing, there is no need to worry; directors who have been in the business forty years get confused, too. If the director wishes the actor to move away from him, he asks the actor to move upstage; if he wishes the actor to come forward, he requests downstage. This terminology originated in the seventeenth century when stages were raked (angled) toward the audience, so that the back part was actually higher than the front; today the term is firmly fixed in theatrical jargon. Occasionally it is unclear, as when an actor who is asked to "come down" from a platform instead comes forward and remains on it. The terminology is still in common use, however—though a few directors simply say "come forward" or "go back." *Above* and *below* are terms used to mean on the upstage or downstage side, as in "cross above her." The terms are used together in most stage directions, for example, "cross down left and sit in the upstage of the two chairs there." This theatrical shorthand is useful in making immediate communication with new actors, but a director can use any terminology as long as he is clearly and quickly understood.

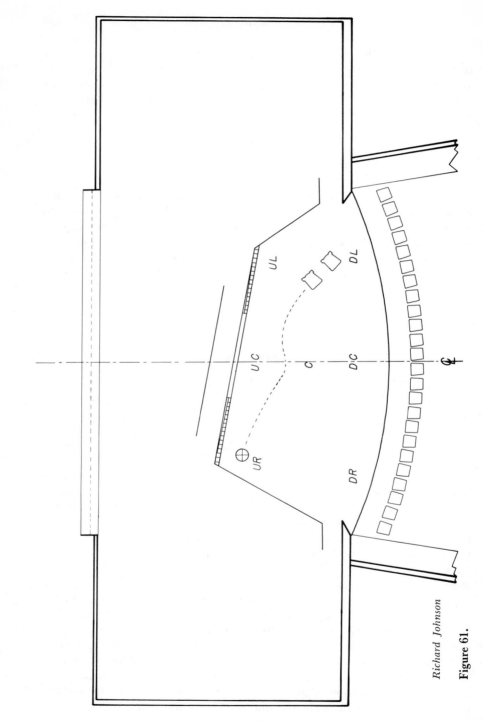

Richard Johnson

Figure 61.

In the illustration on page 138 Harry crosses down left and sits in the upstage of two chairs. The other stage positions are listed appropriately. Theoretically stage center is flanked by center right and center left, but those terms are never used. Actually, most stage directions are given in terms of course rather than destination; a character who is up left is asked to cross down right, but he may end up at center. The direction means down right *from where the actor is now,* unless he is told to go *to* down right.

Working Out the Blocking

There are an infinite number of ways of working out the blocking of a play, but they fall within two fairly well defined extremes. The authoritarian director (and this term is not meant to be pejorative, but simply to indicate strictness of directorial control) preblocks his show, and the improvisational director allows the actors to block themselves. Most directing, of course, falls between these two poles.

In preblocking a play the authoritarian director prepares a promptbook well before the first rehearsal; he also works out every detail of the setting, lights, and costumes with his designers and notes them in his book. Many directors prepare their production book with a mimeographed copy of the ground plan facing every page of text—or every half or quarter page. The ground plan is complete, with every piece of furniture drawn carefully to scale. Then the director plots on paper every movement and position that the audience will see three months hence. The more he puts into his book, the more he is preblocking; and the more he puts down in ink rather than in pencil, the more he is rigidly preblocking.

The improvisational director, in the extreme case, assembles his cast even before the set has been designed. Together they read the play and then improvise staging for it. If a chair is desired, a chair is added to the prop list. If a wall is desired, or a door, the designer is informed. Gradually, and simultaneously, a set and a production are created.

The advantage of preblocking, in theory at least, is that the production is plotted out with the extreme intellectual care that can be attained only in the director's study. The performance will come off with precision and polish. The design staff is delighted, for they have months to build their scenery and hang their lights without fear that design changes will send them into overtime. The advantage of improvisational blocking, again in theory, is that the production achieves greater spontaneity, charm, delight, and above all, honesty. It is not compromised by earlier design decisions, and the actors' and director's on-the-spot creativity is

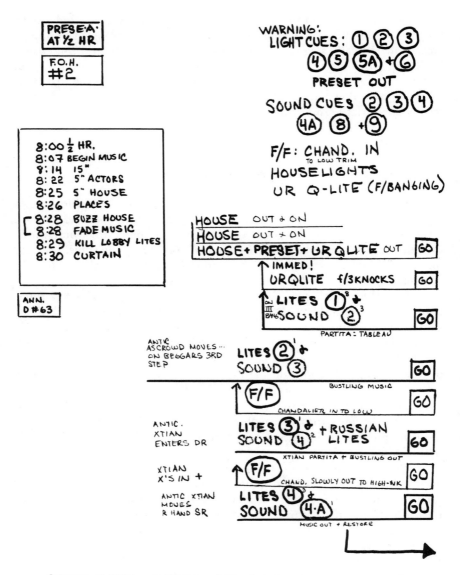

Figure 62. Promptbook pages from ACT's 1973 productions; William Ball
was the director, James Haire the stage manager. Above, cue sheet for the
beginning of *Cyrano de Bergerac*. Light, sound, house, and timing cues are
recorded in different colors.

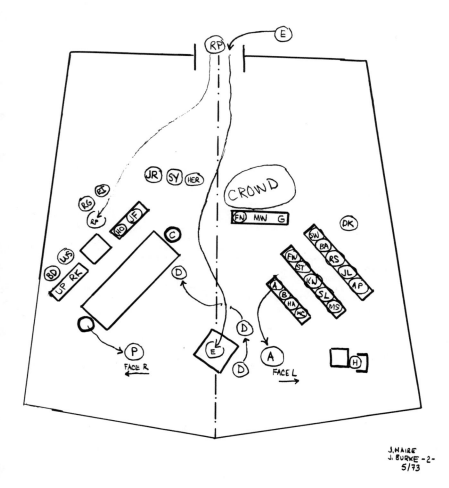

III 107-108
ENTRANCE
OF ELIZABETH

A.C.T. 5/73
THE CRUCIBLE
ACT III

J.HAIRE
J. BURKE - 2 -
5/73

Courtesy of William Ball, General Director, American Conservatory Theatre

Figure 63. Blocking for Elizabeth Proctor's entrance in Act III, *The Crucible*. All actors are placed exactly (A is Abigail, D is Danforth, E is Elizabeth, P is Proctor), their moves indicated by arrows.

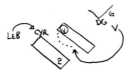

VALVERT
    Observe: I myself will proceed to put him in
    his place.
    (TAPS CYR ON SHOULDER:)   (Walks up haughtily to CYRANO)
    Ah, sir, ~~your nose...ah..~~your nose is...rather large.

                    CYRANO
    TURNS (coolly)
    Is that all?

                    VALVERT
        (Turning away with a shrug)
    Well, of course...

    oh no young sir, why waste *PUSHES V--WHOSITS DS 2 BENCH*
                                        CYRANO
    ~~What? Nothing more? With~~ such an opportunity for
    eloquence? Consider all the things you might have
    said! For example, ~~the~~ *THUS* AGGRESSIVE ~~approach~~: Sir,
    if that nose were mine, I'd have it amputated on
    the spot! DESCRIPTIVE: 'Tis a rock, a crag, a
    cape! A cape? Nay, say rather a peninsula!
    KINDLY: Ah, do you love the little birds so much
    that when they come to sing ~~to you~~, you give them
    this to perch on! *HE HE HE HE*   *HO HO HO HO*
    HUMEROUS: ~~INSOLENT~~: Sir, when you smoke, the neighbors must
    suppose your chimney is on fire! *CAREFUL WHEN YOU TURN YOUR HEAD*
    CAUTIOUS: ~~Take care when you walk. With all that~~ *YOU MAY CLUB*
    ~~weight in front, you could easily fall head first~~ *ME WITH IT,*
    ~~into the street!~~
    PEDANTIC: Does not Aristophanes mention a
    mythological monster called the Hippodragonocamelephantos?
    Surely we have here the original! *DO YOU MIND IF I*
    FAMILIAR: Hey, ~~that thing must be convenient to~~
    hang ~~your~~ hat on. *IT?*   *(STANDS ON 4 STAGE -- T 5 STEPS)*
    ELOQUENT: When it blows, the typhoon howls! When
    KNEELS L it bleeds, the Red Sea!
    OF VALVERT ENTERPRISING: Stripe it -- you've got a barber's pole!
    ┌INQUISITIVE: What do they call the monument? *MAN OF PROMINANCE*
    RESPECTFUL: Sir, I recognize in you a ~~forward-looking man!~~
    RUSTIC: What? You call that a nose? What kind of
    a fool do you think I be? That ain't no nose--it's *A NEW KIND OF*
    ~~a~~ bulbous cucumber!
    MILITARY: The enemy is charging! Fire your cannon!
    PRACTICAL: At least it keeps your feet dry in the
    STEP S ON rain! Or, parodying Faustus in the play, "Was this
    DS EDGE the nose that launched a thousand ships and matched
    #2 BENCH the topless towers of Illium?" These, my dear sir,
    are things you might have said, had you some tinge
    of letters or of wit to color your discourse. But
    wit? Not so -- you never had an atom! And of letters
    you need but three to write you down -- an ASS! *LE BELL*
    SITS DS   *X'S DSR*
    EDGE #2 BENCH

*Courtesy of William Ball, General Director, American
Conservatory Theatre*

Figure 64.   Annotated and cut text from Scene 1 of *Cyrano*. Stage furniture is numbered; actors' moves are recorded by abbreviations (DSR is downstage right, and so on).

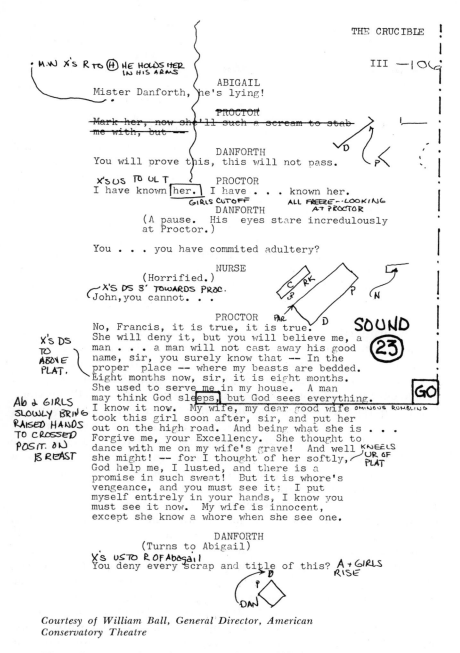

THE CRUCIBLE

III —10⑤

• H.W X's R to Ⓗ HE HOLDS HER IN HIS ARMS

ABIGAIL

Mister Danforth, he's lying!

PROCTOR

~~Mark her, now she'll such a scream to stab me with, but --~~

DANFORTH

You will prove this, this will not pass.

X's US TO UL T

PROCTOR

I have known ⌐her.⌐ I have . . . known her.

GIRLS CUTOFF   ALL FREEZE--LOOKING AT PROCTOR

DANFORTH

(A pause. His eyes stare incredulously at Proctor.)

You . . . you have commited adultery?

NURSE

(Horrified.)

X'S DS 3' TOWARDS PROC.

John, you cannot. . .

PROCTOR   PAR

X'S DS TO ABOVE PLAT.

No, Francis, it is true, it is true.

She will deny it, but you will believe me, a

man . . . a man will not cast away his good

name, sir, you surely know that -- In the

proper place -- where my beasts are bedded.

Eight months now, sir, it is eight months.

She used to serve me in my house. A man

may think God sleeps, but God sees everything. OMINOUS RUMBLING

Ab & GIRLS SLOWLY BRING RAISED HANDS TO CROSSED POSIT. ON BREAST

I know it now. My wife, my dear good wife

took this girl soon after, sir, and put her

out on the high road. And being what she is . . .

Forgive me, your Excellency. She thought to

dance with me on my wife's grave! And well KNEELS UR OF PLAT

she might! -- for I thought of her softly,

God help me, I lusted, and there is a

promise in such sweat! But it is whore's

vengeance, and you must see it; I put

myself entirely in your hands, I know you

must see it now. My wife is innocent,

except she know a whore when she see one.

SOUND ㉓

GO

DANFORTH

(Turns to Abigail)

X's US TO R OF Abigail

You deny every scrap and title of this? A + GIRLS RISE

DAN

Courtesy of William Ball, General Director, American Conservatory Theatre

Figure 65. Page from Act III of *The Crucible* showing diagrammatic recording of blocking, and exact moment when sound cue 23 is to be taken.

unrestricted. Additionally, if a new and desirable interpretation is found during rehearsals, it can be implemented without destroying a preconceived network of blocking. The qualification "in theory," however, must be kept in mind, for occasionally the very opposite results occur.

There are now few extremists in the directing trade, however. Even the most dedicated of the "old school" directors (who are considered the most authoritarian) have come to realize the value of improvisational blocking, at least with experienced actors, and even the most dedicated improvisationalists have bowed to the pressure of production deadlines and the actors' inherent desire in many cases to be told what to do or which action is better than another. Today the director we would call authoritarian still directs from a promptbook, but he discusses his blocking with his actors and probably changes it when they suggest something better. And the director we would call improvisational usually works within a predesigned set and at a certain point in rehearsals begins to help the actors choose among the various improvised actions they have attempted in rehearsal. So most plays, once they reach the stage, are fairly well formalized into a set blocking pattern, no matter how they arrived at it. Both systems, for that reason, have to find methods for achieving spontaneity as well as precision and polish.

Which method works best? There is no answer to this question; excellent directors work both ways. There are many determining variables: the play, the set, the actors' experience with each other, the director, the director's self-confidence, the number of called for actions, the number of people on stage, the length of the rehearsal period, and so forth. Obviously a beginning director working on a complex set with thirty beginning actors in what is to be (hopefully) a new interpretation of *King Lear* (with two weeks rehearsal time allotted) had better do some preblocking before the rehearsals begin, or he will be swamped. In that extreme case, as a matter of fact, he had best preblock the entire show. On the other hand, if you are Mike Nichols directing Alan Arkin, Eli Wallach, and Anne Jackson in the three-character comedy *Luv*, you might very well come to the first rehearsal and say, "Well, let's see what this play is all about," and proceed from there. Nichols apparently did just that and won every directorial award in New York that year.

Ordinarily beginners are cautioned to preblock. First, the rehearsal time is limited. Until a director is fast enough to come up with blocking spontaneously, much time could be lost in pondering blocking decisions while the actors cool their heels. But a more important reason is that the successful attainment of directorial objectives takes careful creative thinking, which may be impossible for the beginner (or anyone else) under the pressure of rehearsals. An inexperienced director who comes to rehearsal without some fairly firm planning may find himself unable to generate ideas on the spot. The rehearsal is chaotic and the blocking is put off for another day, and then another. Actors tend to lose patience with, and confidence in, a director who does not seem to know what he wants, and even though that may be the director's privilege, he is foolish to exercise it wantonly. Most directorial goals require a good deal of directorial homework, and if the blocking is to achieve clarity and telling effects, the director almost certainly has to plan it.

Experienced directors tend to do much *gross* preblocking, often in their heads with a note or two in their promptbooks. Entrances and exits are plotted, key scenes are diagrammed, certain effects are planned, and suggestions for behavior at various moments are at the ready. The scene is blocked roughly and then refined, changed, and supplemented during the course of rehearsals. This is probably the most common method of blocking in use today.

Improvisational methods in blocking are also widespread today, especially as a modification of gross preblocking. Old-school directors usually sat in the middle of the house and dictated the movements authoritatively. Many contemporary directors sit in the first row, or on the stage itself, and continually engage in dialogue with the actors at this point in rehearsals. Such directors suggest movements ("Why don't you move to the bar and get a drink?") or ask the actors to suggest them ("What do you think he would do here?"). They may ask some actors to suggest placements or movements for others ("Where would you like her to sit when you say that?") or they may put the actor on his own ("Block yourself in this speech"). Some directors remove themselves entirely from the blocking of certain scenes (such as between two characters) and ask the actors to go to another room and work out the blocking for the scene, then come back and demonstrate it on stage. All these methods have been used successfully, even within the framework of a grossly preblocked show, and may be recommended to those who wish to try them.

Finally, however, the director must take responsibility for the blocking. Only he, sitting in the audience (and he should sit in every possible area of the theatre during rehearsals), can judge whether the blocking objectives of clarity and dynamic communication are being met.

Recording the Blocking

No matter how it is derived, the blocking is usually set (fixed) at a certain point in rehearsals. This can be immediately, in the case of a minutely preblocked production, or in the final dress rehearsals of an improvised one. Some directors prefer never to set the blocking, to let it change ad lib each performance, but this is rare except in the case of totally improvised shows, where the dialogue and action change night by night as well. The time-honored way of setting the blocking is to record it in a production book. This is ordinarily done by the stage manager, who keeps a book of the play which includes all technical cues (sound, light, and scene shifting) as well as a detailed notation of the blocking.

Blocking is recorded for two reasons. First, the director and actors might work very hard at selecting the best blocking for a moment, and then forget, the next day, what they had arrived at. Ordinarily this does not happen (most directors have total recall of their blocking, even years after the production), but rehearsal fatigue should not be overlooked as a reality of play direction. Unusual and intricate blocking patterns should be carefully noted so that if the director forgets, perhaps in a late rehearsal, what he set up, he need not reconstruct the entire scene in his mind to recall it, and so that he will not resort to a less interesting blocking pattern because he is too tired to remember the original. The second reason for recording blocking is to establish a workable production book for the play. This proves invaluable when in late rehearsals or during the run of a show a new actor is substituted for another, or a stage manager has to be replaced. The production book is also necessary for understudy rehearsals, and in Broadway theatre for rehearsing road companies. Finally, when the production has closed, the production book can be filled with photographs, reviews, and set and costume designs and bound as a book. It becomes the director's only tangible record of his production, and a possible asset to him in getting future work.

Blocking is noted by a set of conventional symbols. X is used for "cross" and *DL, UR, DC* for down left, up right, and down center, for example. Other abbreviations and stage managerial shorthand may be used, together with symbols drawn on a ground plan. For example, "Cl xdr, sts ch 5" might mean "Claudius crosses downstage right, and sits in the number five chair"—a chair numbered on an accompanying diagram. Any method of shorthand is acceptable as long as it is coherent and can be readily passed on to a replacement stage manager.

7

Lighting

Lighting is the newest of the theatrical arts, and its sophisticated use since the discovery of electricity has paralleled the rise of the director. This has not been accidental. The development of incandescent lighting which could be regulated by remote control gave the director one of his most powerful tools, and much of the history of modern directing has been shaped by men who made important discoveries in lighting: Adolphe Appia, Gordon Craig, and Louis Jouvet. Some well-established contemporary directors, most notably Peter Hunt, began their careers as lighting designers.

Besides providing illumination and establishing locales, lighting can be used to create and maintain focus, to establish and change mood, and to amplify the rhythm of a performance. Lighting is a fluid, multicolored, four-dimensional medium that can work with or against the composition, acting, and interpretation of a play, and a director is well advised to understand its possibilities before he begins a full scale production. The

experienced director rarely makes a decision regarding scenery or blocking without considering the lighting consequences, and he frequently designs his composition specifically for certain lighting effects. In practice,
the director often finds he must make concessions in his blocking to get
the lighting he wants, or vice versa, and the more he knows about the
technical scope of the light designer, the more he can anticipate both the
artistic possibilities and the adjustments that lighting may dictate.

Sunlight was the most common form of illumination for plays until
the past two or three hundred years, and it is still a viable source, used
in outdoor daytime productions. Sunlight is notoriously unregulatable,
and if the production is to be lit by the sun, all the director can do is to
orient the theatre so that at the time of day of the performance the sun is
at the audience's back rather than in their eyes.

While oil lamps, calcium lamps (limelights), and gaslights were in
use before the twentieth century, today virtually all stage lighting is provided by incandescent electric lamps, occasionally supplemented with
carbon arc spotlights. Incandescent illumination can be remotely regulated as to intensity, focused and aimed in a variety of lighting instruments, and colored via gelatin filters, and it provides steady illumination
for hours without monitoring. Carbon arc lights are occasionally used today as followspots in large theatres; they can generate more illumination
than ordinary incandescent instruments, but they require the continuous
attention of an operator (to advance the carbon) and cannot be dimmed.

Lighting Instruments

A lighting instrument consists of a light source (ordinarily an incandescent or a quartzlight bulb), a reflector, a lens, a housing, and a
clamp; all lighting instruments are designed to get the most light possible
to the desired place, and the least light anywhere else. Each type of lighting instrument focuses light differently.

The ellipsoidal reflector spotlight, commonly known as a Leko,
throws sharply focused beams over long distances. The Leko beam may
be shuttered or "goboed" (both processes involve the insertion of metal
plates) to any shape desired, and if tightly focused, will throw a sharp circle, rectangle, or trapezoid of light on stage with clearly defined shadows.

The Fresnel light (named after its lens) throws a more diffuse beam
and is ordinarily used for short throws. In a proscenium theatre, Lekos
ordinarily provide illumination that comes from the house so that there
will be no "spill" of light into the audience, and Fresnels provide most or
all of the spotlighting originating from the stage itself.

Striplights (including footlights and cyc lights) are groups of lights arranged in a row to provide a band of even illumination. They are ordinarily wired in three or four circuits, so that three or four colors can be mixed to provide differing tonal values to the stage.

Beam projectors, "scoops," "wizards," "P-C's," and a variety of trade name instruments and specialty instruments are also used by the lighting expert, but the vast majority of lighting instruments fall into the three categories above.

Practical lights are ordinary household lamps or chandeliers that, in realistic sets, can be turned on by the actors and used for their illumination.

Lighting Control

Lighting designers and directors look for maximum control in lighting, with the ultimate goal being independent control of every instrument used in the production. In practice this is rarely if ever accomplished and never absolutely necessary. Control is provided by the circuitry of the theatre and the dimmers in the control room. The more circuits and dimmers, the more control.

Circuits are simply numbered wires. One end leads to the lighting instrument, and the other to the dimmer board, usually through a "patch panel" which makes the proper connections. The dimmers are operated manually (in which case there are usually arrangements for operating several at a time), electronically, or in some modern installations, by computer. Electronic and computer dimmer boards afford the most control with the fewest operators, since a single move of the master switch can make literally a hundred (in a 100-dimmer board) intensity changes, some up, some down, precisely and simultaneously—a feat that is impossible manually without fifty sharp technicians.

Effects of Lighting

The director is interested in lighting techniques not as ends in themselves, of course, but as mechanisms of achieving his directorial goals. Providing illumination is simply one of these goals, but it should not be too briefly passed over.

Illumination of what? Illumination of the action is the first but not the final answer. The action of a play must be illuminated to achieve visual clarity. In the illusionistic pictorial theatre of the early part of our century, it was considered equally vital to keep light off the audience.

The second position, however, may reasonably be questioned today. Until the days of English director Henry Irving, toward the end of the nineteenth century, the audience area was always as bright as the stage; in fact, records indicate that expensive and awesome chandeliers in the audience were lighted precisely as the play began, and not before! In other words, only recently have we abandoned the idea that the audience is part of the show. Some directors today feel that that idea is worth reviving. The Berliner Ensemble productions of Bertolt Brecht, for example, are performed in a nineteenth century theatre which is never fully darkened, and which is filled with gilded cupids, cherubs, and rococo elaborations that remind the audience that they are in a theatre, not lost in a romantic imaginary fable. This, of course, was Brecht's intention. Arena staging makes the spectators aware of each other because the action takes place among them, and there is usually enough general illumination in the house to make that awareness part of the overall aesthetic effect. Modern playwrights occasionally "turn on the houselights" (for example, in Paul Foster's *Tom Paine*) to engender audience participation, and the directors of environmental productions frequently light their theatres evenly to disavow the "imaginary line" between actor and patron. The new all-black interiors of some proscenium theatres, such as the Ahmanson in Los Angeles, which were touted as light designers' dreams, have become for the most part audiences' headaches, since constantly peering at a brightly illuminated set from the back of a pitch black auditorium is, after a while, like staring at the sun through a telescope. Lighting design should not *automatically* be directed to leave the audience in the dark.

Lighting the Action

Besides providing adequate illumination for the set and the actors and creating credibility for the time and locale, lighting can be controlled to support the action in creating effective focus, mood, and rhythm. These interests are not always parallel, of course, and what might create effective focus might also destroy the credibility of the locale, so all lighting decisions must be coordinated at the directorial level, either by the director himself or by the lighting designer.

The director's prime decision is specifying the *amount* of moment-to-moment control: the amount of visible light shifting (cues) during the course of the action within a single continuous scene or act (that is, while the curtain, if there is one, is up). There are three basic ways of working with lights during a scene or act.

Static lighting. The lights come on at the beginning of the scene and do not shift, except to go off at the end of the scene. Traditionally this form of lighting is used for naturalistic plays (although practical lights may be turned on and off, and characters may let sunshine in through windows and doors), since it generally copies the lighting of everyday life. It is also used frequently for tight, fast farces and comedies, and for realistic dramas. It is also useful for Brechtian "epic" theatre, which seeks to downplay the magic of the theatre and to give straightforward productions of didactic lecture-like plays. Static lighting, of course, was the rule for many centuries, and many directors today swear by it for everything. "If you don't have to change the lights, why do it?" asks one, and a director who calls for light cues should be able to explain why.

Imperceptible light cueing. The aesthetic of cueing lights imperceptibly is virtually the same as that of not cueing them at all—the creation of a natural stage action that does not call attention to itself or its theatrical contrivances. By imperceptibly shifting the lights, however, the director can have his cake and eat it, too. He can acquire mood changes and focal changes by very slowly shifting lights to emphasize new areas of the stage and perhaps new background coloring. A blue sky can redden over a five-minute period, so slowly that no one notices the change except by subliminal registration. An area in which principal characters are sitting can imperceptibly grow brighter, and background characters can be deftly faded out, as an important scene localizes in a small area. This sort of cueing, if done very subtly, can retain credibility and gain flexibility, and it is frequently used in realistic plays of great subtlety and/or atmosphere, such as those of Chekhov or Tennessee Williams.

Bold theatrical cueing. The director can call for highly focused lighting effects to produce a nonnaturalistic style. Blackouts, single spotlights, followspots, color shifts were originally considered expressionist in their serious theatrical applications. They create a theatrical effect that must be justified on its own terms. The overall effect of theatrical lighting, of course, is to emphasize the theatricality of the presentation; no attempt is made to disguise light changes as if realistically occurring by some natural process. Rather, the lighting changes are the director's and designer's interpolations into the script to enhance its inner action. A famous example is Fritz Erler's *Faust* (Munich, 1904), in which the walls turned red at the entrance of Mephistopheles.

Bold theatrical cueing is common today in multiscene plays like *Antony and Cleopatra,* or Ibsen's *Peer Gynt,* that demand many locale shifts. It is also widely used on Broadway, particularly in the opulent Tom O'Horgan productions of *Hair, Jesus Christ Superstar,* and *Lenny,* and in Hal Prince's musicals, *Cabaret* and *Follies.*

The Effects of Controlled Lighting

Lighting controls what the audience sees. Major differences in lighting intensity totally control the audience's "picture." For example, lighting the stage while keeping the house black directs their attention to the stage, and blacking out the stage altogether terminates their attention just as a falling curtain does. Used more subtly, lighting operates totally independently of other compositional tools, for no matter how many focal principles may be at work, a major lighting change will always overrule them and is *never attributable to the actor or character upon whom the focus rests.* This principle may be extremely valuable when a director wishes to draw attention to a character who must in all other respects be nonattractive and noncharismatic. (Imagine, for example, a scene in which a character is dreaming, and his dream is being acted out for us— but we are asked to be aware of the dreamer as well. One way to stage this is to let the dreamer sleep in a pool of light, while the "dream" is performed on another level, in a slightly dimmer area, the rest of the stage being black.) The director guides the audience's attention with his lighting, just as the film director does with his alternation of close-ups, long shots, and two-shots. While many-cued theatrical lighting that tries to imitate film editing is an obvious contrivance, it can also be said that as in film, many-cued lighting tends to promote naturalistic acting, since the actor need do nothing out of character to attract the audience's attention when that attention is necessary. Thus, boldly expressive lighting, though it may create inconsistencies in an otherwise totally naturalistic *play,* is not at all inconsistent with the most naturalistic *acting.*

The Director Works on Lighting the Play

Depending on the resources of the theatre company employing his services, the director works in conjunction with a lighting designer and/ or lighting technicians, or does the design and work himself. If he collaborates with a lighting designer, however, he has more to do than just approve the designs. At the very least, a director is invariably held responsible for deciding (either in collaboration or not) what style of lighting will be used (the amount of control) and what actual cues will be taken. One way of doing this, of course, is to let the lighting designer come to rehearsals and prepare a suggested cue sheet. Another, more professional solution is for the director to plan at the blocking stage which light cues will be needed, which might be desirable, and which might be worth thinking about. In either case, the director should come to his first lighting rehearsal with a prepared cue sheet including all cues he thinks possible or desirable for inclusion in the production.

Lighting cues are set during special lighting rehearsals. During the lighting rehearsal, each cue is fixed, including notation of which instruments are patched to which dimmer, the intensity readings of each dimmer, and the manner of executing each cue. Manner of execution means which technician is to move which dimmers, how fast, and (where applicable) in what order. Cues are listed by number; on the sheet a characteristic cue would list all dimmer readings which are to change, who will change them, the cue for "taking" (either a visual cue, if the operator can see the stage and hear the dialogue, or a cue from the stage manager conveyed over an intercommunication system), and the "count" on which the cue is to be taken. Since there are literally hundreds of "items" per cue, and sometimes hundreds of cues per production, the lighting rehearsal may take many hours or days. The lighting and technical rehearsals for new Shakespearean productions of England's Royal Shakespeare Company can take not days but weeks, and the college or community theatres that try to squeeze complicated lighting rehearsals into a single afternoon or evening usually betray their amateur standing on opening night.

The full participation of the director during lighting rehearsals is essential to the artistic integration of the production. The director's participation at this stage of the production is similar to a film director's participation in editing his film. In both cases the director works with trained artists who presumably know more about the actual technical workings than the director, but only the director (again presumably) knows the total content and intended effect of the play or film. The stage director is responsible not only for working out with his technicians exactly what is required or desired at each point; he will also invariably remain on the scene to approve the nuances of each cue. Lighting rehearsals can be highly creative sessions, with suggestions flying back and forth from the director to his staff, and a director who leaves these decisions up to his technicians leaves some of his directorial responsibilities up to them, too.

8

Audial Composition

Stage composition is usually studied in terms of its visual effects alone, but this is only half the picture. The audience has eyes, but it also has ears, and the term *composition* applies to both senses. In fact, composition is also a musical term (a musical writer is a composer), and in theatre usage it can indicate the orchestration of sounds the audience hears as well as the sights it sees.

There are many sounds in a play. Primarily, in most cases, there is spoken dialogue. Many plays also contain music, in the form of songs, background music (what in films is called "theme music"), on stage or pit orchestras, and sometimes *a capella* group singing. In more and more contemporary plays—for example, *Subject to Fits* and *Lenny*—perhaps in the tradition of Brecht's epic theatre, music is intrinsic to the production, yet these plays are not considered musicals. This tradition is as old as Shakespeare and the Greeks. In addition to music, there are sound effects, either on stage or recorded, such as thunder, telephone rings, horn beeps, rainfall, and wind. Sound effects need not be realistic; for example, the last scene of Edward Albee's *Tiny Alice* is played against the amplified sound of a heartbeat. Then there are the sounds the actors make: footsteps down a corridor, the tinkling of icecubes in a glass, the ad lib screams and grunts of a fight, the cutting of a coconut with a machete. Finally, there is the sound of the theatre air conditioning, the hum of amplifiers and lighting instruments, the fidgeting while the audience gets comfortable after intermission. With the exception of unpredictable sounds (subways rattling underneath Broadway theatres, airplanes flying over outdoor ones), these are the audial components of a play.

Except for some attention to pace and rhythm, the goals of audial composition have usually been ignored by directors. They have felt that if the visual action is carefully worked out, the composition of sounds will be acceptable. But making audial composition more than just "OK" is a valid goal. We shall discuss various aspects of audial composition serially.

Rhythm

Speech is naturally rhythmic. Someone excitedly telling a story tends to speed up his delivery; someone speaking of a difficult subject to sensitive listeners tends to speak slowly. Ordinary conversations are punctuated by expletives and interjections, like "No!" and "Right on!" (or whatever is in fashion). We can describe any spoken sentence in terms of pitch, inflection, volume, tone, and the pauses that surround and punctuate it. The delivery of speeches creates the major rhythm of a spoken play.

Rhythms affect the communication level of the content of a speech. Listen to a television newscaster delivering a standard news item. He invariably begins rapidly, with an unusually high pitch on at least some of the first few syllables:

In Chi ^{ca} go today, $^{twenty-}$ seven men were found guilty of destroying public property. . .

The rapid delivery secures the audience's attention. But by the end of the item, the announcer's voice has slowed and dropped in pitch, so that his final wind-up is more like this:

In all, they were sentenced to one hundred and eighty-six $_{years.}$

[and then] In ^{baseball} today, the Giants . . .

The audience's attention won, the newscaster can now make his points with heavy meaning, potency, and irony. Compare, in this regard, the measured delivery of David Brinkley or Eric Sevareid commenting after a regular newscast.

Directors also use rhythms to engage their audience's attention and to make points, but they must ordinarily justify their usage of rhythms by realistic means. Ordinarily this is not too difficult—characters simply play the intention of engaging each other's interest, and they will engage the audience's. The attention to rhythms in stage speech should not only provide an orchestrated sonic pattern, it should also reveal the workings of the inner action of the play.

A useful image of the rhythms of speech is provided by the roller coaster. Imagine the three phases of a roller coaster's course: chugging slowly and with great power up the initial ramp, coasting at medium speed around the first curve, then plunging freely and furiously down the glide. The speed of the roller coaster is inversely proportional to the power expended in moving it. Speeches are similar. Those that take the most inner energy to deliver (such as a difficult confession, for example) can be delivered at the most ponderous (uphill) speed; those that are easiest to say (Undershaft's political philosophy in Shaw's *Major Barbara,* for example, which we imagine he has rattled off a hundred times before) are like the roller coaster hurtling freely down the track. And just as a roller coaster ride achieves its greatest excitement by a rhythm of ups and downs, so does a play become truly interesting when it has a changing, up and down rhythm.

Rhythm in speech is directly connected with the difference between inner and outer action. If a character has a line like "Well, I have to go now," and his intention is simply to go home because he has something to do (and his presence is no longer particularly desired), his inner action, outer action, and internal monologue are virtually identical. He can say the line rapidly and leave. If, however, he is a father leaving his son for perhaps the last time (he is going off to war, for example), then his outer action and inner monologue are quite different (he is probably thinking, "Will he miss me? Will I see him again?"), and he presumably gives the line slowly. However, if in the identical situation he wishes to disguise his feeling so that his son will not see that he is upset, he will again speak rapidly—probably too rapidly—to imitate the behavior of one whose inner monologue and outer action are the same. So there are at least three rhythmic possibilities of delivering that line, and for that matter, any line:

1. Rapidly—he has nothing particular on his mind
2. Slowly—he has a lot on his mind
3. Too rapidly—he has a lot on his mind but is trying to hide it

A director varies rhythms to create the greatest possible sonic texture. He punctuates his play with pauses the ultimate of (2) that are filled with internal conflict and inner monologues, and interjections which are the ultimate of (1) and (3). Again, even a blind person listening to a play in a foreign language should be able to note the character dynamics merely by listening to the rhythms of speech. The French theatre, as a matter of fact, is noteworthy on this score; French directing is perhaps more a matter of audial composition than of anything else.

Pace

Pace is the overall dynamic of the play. Most "minor league" drama critics seem to consider directing as no more than pacing, and fast-pacing at that, and frequently mention the director only by way of saying that the play was "too slow" or "well paced" (by which they mean "fast"). For this we must simply blame the ignorance of such drama critics, while recognizing that *subtle* pacing of a play is indeed a concern of the director.

Bernard Shaw said that if a play seems to be going too slowly, the director should slow it down some more. What he meant was that the director should slow the play down to examine its internal rhythms and inner action; that if a play seemed slow it was because it was improperly understood and directed to begin with. The problem in pacing a show, as Shaw correctly observed, is that inexperienced directors too often work for a fast result. Realizing that scenes in fine plays they have seen were performed at a rapid clip, such directors instruct actors from the first rehearsal onward to speed everything up. One old school director of our acquaintance does little more than sit in the back of the theatre during rehearsals and shout "Louder and faster!" at the actors, sometimes beating out the pace with a stick. Obviously, this can lead to very superficial results.

Undeniably, action which is loud and fast is initially more exciting than that which is low and slow, but masterpieces like Lindsay Anderson's production of *Home* stand in direct contrast to this principle. In *Home* the actors never raised their voices, never spoke rapidly. There is no absolute rule on pace. The only thing the director must always remember is that slow outer action must be exquisitely filled. If the characters speak slowly and monotonously, and if the audience can see nothing going on in their heads either, then the play is sunk.

Most directors try to break a play down, during the rehearsal period, into its separate beats, playing them slowly until the actors are fully comfortable with their moment-to-moment intentions and actions. Then, in the last week or two of rehearsal, the play is "paced up" to performance level, the fastest level at which all the beats can be clearly played and at which the rhythms are not hurried into a muddy merge. There is a final premium on speed: the audience does not want to waste its time, and the director should not let time elapse without some information going to them. *The real pace of the play is not the pace of sounds or movements, but the pace of information flow from the stage to the house.* In a badly paced play there are great information silences where nothing is going on, or the information comes across too fast for the audience to understand it or for the actors to play it.

Directors almost always find that naturalistic actors are more comfortable at a slower pace than is theatrically desirable. This is natural for actors—just as a dancer feels rushed if the orchestra ups the tempo on him, as a secretary feels rushed if she must type ten letters before lunch. Actors like to have time enough to play all the things they want to and are instructed to, and of course they are getting information flow from each other even if the audience is not. In pacing a show, therefore, it is sometimes necessary for the director to push his actors a little, just as it is sometimes a choreographer's job to push his dancers, or a boss's job to push his secretary. No director should feel that his primary responsibility is to keep his actors comfortable and happy. The director's primary responsibility is to his show and to the audience for whom it is intended. If in his judgment the information flow to the audience is too slow, he must take measures to increase it or speed it up, while ensuring that the credibility of the show remains intact.

Even the best plays include dull passages that must be gotten through quickly. In his stage direction for the opening scene of *Henry IV*, playwright Luigi Pirandello even cautions the director, "This scene should be played very rapidly." The scene consists of necessary, but rather boring, exposition, and Pirandello does not want the audience to leave the theatre before the fireworks begin in Act Two.

The audial and visual composition of a play work hand in hand, but they are not parallel. A character can be pacing the floor slowly and speaking rapidly, or he can be racing around and saying nothing at all. Imagine the orchestration of sights and sounds in the examples that follow.

In Anouilh's *Antigone*, Antigone sits awaiting death in a bare stage prison. The guard walks back and forth behind her, his heels beating a steady rhythm on the floor.

In Dürrenmatt's *The Visit*, the semicircle of townspeople silently converge and cover Anton Schill. After a pause, a piercing scream is heard.

In *Hamlet*, the king leaves the stage while Polonius shouts for lights. Forty people, all ad libbing and yelling, leave the stage by five different exits. Suddenly there is silence and Hamlet is alone on stage.

In *King Lear*, Lear is told while eating with his cohorts at a huge oaken table that he is to be denied his hundred knights. After two moments of silence he screams, "Darkness and devils!" and overturns the giant table. The table crashes to the floor along with a dozen pewter mugs, which clatter and tinkle for several seconds.

In *Measure for Measure* the curtain rises on about thirty nobles facing the duke, who is upstage. As the duke raises his hand, all the nobles simultaneously fall heavily to their knees with a huge "thud." After a pause, the duke begins to speak.

In Ionesco's *The Chairs* an orator ceremoniously walks onto an empty stage, unrolls a speech, gazes out to the audience, and squeaks, because he is a mute.

Music

Music has long been used to create excitement and to enhance the emotional empathy of films, television, and radio shows. Early silent films were played with a "live" musical track provided by the local organist. Today theme music in films is developed by specialists who create splendid effects, such as the underlying theme music of *Love Story* or the pseudo-Scarlatti which enlivened *Tom Jones*. Radio and television shows use music extensively to add excitement and to punctuate key scenes; few of us have forgotten the Lone Ranger riding into the distance to the strains of Rossini's William Tell Overture and Liszt's Preludes. Soap operas often use music (which, in fact, is why they are called operas) to cover the virtual absence of plot and characterization.

Music is accepted in film, television, and radio partly because these are by definition technological media. In dealing with projectors, celluloid, and wave transmission, it is only a simple step to add a phonograph and a sound system. In the theatre, however, music is not immediately justified as an acceptable convention; it must be justified by style. For example, naturalistic plays which use live actors portraying true-to-life situations seem to resist the intrusion of recorded sound. There are, however, many ways to integrate music into stage productions.

Recorded music can be conventionally used in a naturalistic play when it is part of the play's natural environment. Countless American plays feature scenes in which an actor turns on some music—as in Arthur Miller's *A View from the Bridge,* where Rudolfo plays the phonograph, or in Saroyan's *The Time of Your Life,* where Joe plays the jukebox. Chekhov was the master at integrating off stage musicians into his plays, and the farewell scene of *The Three Sisters,* which is accompanied by an army band in the distance, is incredibly poignant. Even when music is not specified by the playwright, nothing prevents a director from having a character turn on a radio (which plays, of course, some preselected music timed to the action of the play) during the course of a scene. The effect of the music might be extremely helpful, and the effect of another character turning it off, suddenly, can also be telling.

Recorded music can be used without an apparent natural source in a play not tied to the strictures of realism. Tennessee Williams's *The Glass Menagerie* is described by its author as a "memory play" in which "atmospheric touches and subtleties of direction play a particularly important part." Williams calls for the use of music "to give emotional emphasis to suitable passages." Sample musical directions in that script are:

> *Music: "The Glass Menagerie" under faintly.*
> *Dance music: "All the world is waiting for the sunrise." The Dance*
> *Hall music changes to a tango that has a minor and*
> *somewhat ominous tone.*
> *The violin rises and the stage dims out.*
> *Waltz music: "La Golondrina"*
> *Music changes*
> *Music swells tumultuously*
> *A tender waltz*

Some of this music is justified realistically (a dance hall is presumably across the street), but most is not. As Tom, a character in the play, says to the audience, "The play is a memory. . . . In memory everything seems to happen to music. That explains the fiddle in the wings."

Stylized plays[1] in general can be effectively integrated with music. In William Ball's production of *Tiny Alice* for the American Conservatory Theatre, Julian made his final, futile escape attempt to the cataclysmic sounds (hugely amplified) of the *Dies Irae* in Verdi's *Requiem*. When Verdi's fanfares climaxed, Julian fell down the giant stairway he had been attempting to climb, while red banners streamed from the doorway he could not open. Directors frequently turn to heroic scores to accompany scenes, grand entrances, and key moments of Elizabethan plays, or to Mozart for Restoration comedies. Mendelsohn wrote a rather famous score for *A Midsummer Night's Dream,* as did Sibelius for *The Tempest;* these are often played along with the dialogue, where they can be successfully integrated. Electronic music was successfully used to accompany Herbert Blau's production of *King Lear,* and rock music is used today (as will the contemporary music of any day be used) in nearly any play which admits musical additives.

---

[1] *Stylized* is a vague but accepted term used to describe departures from naturalism. See Chapter 10 for a fuller discussion.

Live music performed by a visible source[2] was a feature of original Greek and probably Elizabethan staging. It is still used in the Kabuki and Nō dramas of Japan. In such productions the playing of the musicians is a conventionally accepted aspect of the visual production. Some modern plays have copied these models; *A Taste of Honey* (English) and *Subject to Fits* (American) have both used on stage orchestras of three to five pieces to accompany the action, with both underlying theme music and musical punctuation. Many other plays, not written to include an orchestra, are produced as though they were. Many plays include songs to be sung (for example, *The Good Woman of Setzuan*), in which case it is the director's option where the musical accompaniment should originate, and what it should consist of. In other plays or productions, the actors themselves play musical instruments (as in Tom O'Horgan's production of *Tom Paine*). Finally, there are full-scale musical productions.

In all productions featuring live music, great attention must be paid to the integration of the orchestra's (or musician's) presence with that of the rest of the show. Seemingly inconsequential details like the need for music stands and lights to read music by can cause giant problems in dress rehearsals. Because a violinist executing a virtuoso cadenza can draw focus, just as can an actor scratching his jawbone, problems of visual composition are vitally affected by musicians. Decisions on where to put the orchestra are matters not just of acoustics, but of visual concern as well.

In general, the use of an on stage orchestra declares to the audience, "We wish to entertain you" or "We wish to make sure you get our points"; the former merely by the natural enjoyment most people derive from music, and the latter by making the stylistic admission that "We (the director, actors, and musicians) are openly and directly *presenting* our play to you; we are not trying to pretend that we are simply copying life." Brecht, for example, used songs to stop the action and present didactic pieces of commentary (some would call them propaganda) evolved from the play's dramatic content. The use of an on stage orchestra would certainly enhance that effect, which is one of intentional intrusion into the story. The use of a live orchestra on stage throughout Joan Littlewood's production of *A Taste of Honey,* an otherwise naturalistic play, could have been counterproductive; however with sensitive direction Littlewood was able to use the music with minimum intrusion and maximum enhancement.

The out and out musical play, such as *My Fair Lady,* presents a wide variety of directorial options in the artistic integration of music with plot. This is even more true when the theatre is equipped with a flexible or-

---

[2] Music played by a live but hidden orchestra is considered in this chapter as though it were recorded. The effect is the same in both cases.

chestra pit which may be raised or lowered automatically (ordinarily by hydraulic lifts). The orchestra can be lifted to stage level, as it is occasionally for an overture, or lowered completely, or it can be lowered so that only the conductor is seen. The possible combinations multiply when there are both a pit orchestra and an on stage orchestra, as in Hal Prince's production of *Cabaret*. Music in the all-out musical can range from entirely presentational (as in a "production number") to hidden background to the "realistic" scenes in the play.

A final type of theatre music is incidental or intermission music, played while the curtain is down before the play begins, during intermissions, and after it ends. Occasionally incidental music can "bleed" into the beginning of acts, recommencing as the lights dim at the end of acts. Incidental music does more than divert the audience while the stage is dark; it can be used to set the emotional tone in the play, to revive key themes played during the action, and to "set up" an audience for a theatrical opening at the beginning of the show.

The director's decisions regarding the use of music are broad in scope, as the following possibilities show.

• Should music be used at all? Silence is often effective where music is not. Music can be intrusive in a naturalistic play; if over-used, it can be offensive in a stylized play.

• What is the music to do? To set the period? Mozart with Molière might establish a classical ambience, while John Cage with Molière might indicate a modern production and keep the audience alert to modern implications of the seventeenth century play. Should music set the emotional tone? Convey excitement? Suspense? Jarring internal transitions? The effect of memory? Of time passing? Should it play against the emotional tone, as the bright marching music plays against the sadness of the departure of the soldiers in *The Three Sisters,* heightening the poignancy?

• What kind of music should be used? Classical? Pop? Jazz? Rock? If classical, what period? Should an original score be composed?

• From where does the music emanate? A sound system? Orchestra pit? On stage? In a stage box in the audience?

• Do we see the musicians? The conductor? How much? At all times? Does the orchestra move?

• How is the music timed? How is it integrated with the action? Are the characters supposed to be aware of it? Do they play with it or against it? Is it just for the audience's benefit, with the characters oblivious of it (as in most films)?

These questions must all be answered, and in practice, not in theory. Music must be chosen carefully and timed perfectly. A speech that is to be spoken to music must be rehearsed with great precision, so that it ends when it is supposed to, generally at the same time the music ends, night after night. Recorded music, inflexible in performance, must be matched to the behavior of live actors (sometimes flexible) and to the situation. For these reasons music cannot be effectively added at the last minute to "beef up" a scene that was planned without it; it must be integrated early in the rehearsal period if it is to be a valuable part of the play's overall composition.

Sound Effects

Sound effects are both functional and creative. If the script calls for a telephone to ring or a horn to beep, the sound must enhance the telling of the story of the play. In such cases, in realistic plays, it is desirable to imitate the sound as closely as possible. If when the phone rings it is clear that a stage manager is playing a sound effects record off stage, the effect does more harm than good. "Realistic" sound effects must be just that, and it takes good equipment and good technicians to make realistic effects sound real.

Realistic sound effects need not be limited to functional ones. Sounds can be used to underline, much as music can. Continuous sounds such as wind or the falling of rain are often called for in scripts; if not called for, they frequently can be added. The sound of traffic can be used in a play that takes place near a busy street (for example, *My Sister Aileen*), both to set the locale and to underline the action. In such a case the sound effect can be modulated to be louder at certain moments, quieter at others, and even totally silent. If the effect is to be realistic, the modulation of continuous soundtracks must be subtle. Sounds can also punctuate action; for example, Tennessee Williams asks for a passing locomotive during certain abrupt moments in *A Streetcar Named Desire*. A character can sometimes put an "exclamation point" on a sentence by pounding a table or hitting a wall; if it can be safely done, he can throw a glass against a wall and let the sound of the crash be a counterpoint to the dialogue. Such sounds can come across as gimmicks, or they can be successful adjuncts to a play's audial composition, depending on the artistry with which they are handled.

Nonrealistic sound effects are rarely used, but they can be enormously effective in plays which admit a high degree of stylization. William Ball began his production of *Tiny Alice* with an ear-piercing siren blast. Drumbeats have been used to intensify fight scenes. The cadence of actors stamping their feet was effective in the Open Theatre production of Jean Claude Van Itallie's *The Serpent*.

We might mention at this point the amplification of stage sounds and speech. Most musical plays today are produced with electronic sound amplification, ordinarily with microphones placed at the footlight positions and hung from the flies. The sound is then projected into the audience by speakers located over or around the stage or even in the far reaches of the theatre. Sometimes the actors even carry hand or body mikes. More and more spoken plays are using microphones and amplification. The use of such technological equipment simply to make the sound audible is generally undesirable if unnecessary. It sets up an intruding factor only to compensate for the actor's weakness; it makes softly spoken dialogue sound unnaturally loud, and loud dialogue tinny. Since it is vital that the actors' words reach the audience, the intrusion, if necessary, is better than the confusion which would result otherwise, but it is never preferable to nonamplified projection. The exception to this is when hand mikes are used by the actors as props, as in the rock opera version of *Othello, Catch My Soul,* or in *Hair;* there the mikes are part of the overall style of the performance.

Integration of Sounds and Sights

The use of sounds is as vital a part of overall composition as the visual effects. The compilation of sounds and sights is complex. In one production of *The Night of the Iguana,* for example, the second act closed with an amalgam of the following sounds:

1. The actors' voices (live)
2. Bursts of thunder accentuating certain words of dialogue (recorded)
3. A marimba band in the background (recorded)
4. Wind (recorded)
5. Rain (recorded)
6. A broadcast in German coming over the portable radio (recorded)
7. Parrot screams (recorded)

and sights:

1. The lights blacking out as the power goes off
2. Shannon and Hannah illuminated by flashes of lightning
3. Maxine lighting a candle behind a slatted door, watching
4. The Nazis seen in the tiny light from their portable radio
5. Moonlight illuminating the foliage, bending in the wind, and the hanging lamps, swinging
6. Rain glistening in the moonlight
7. Shannon's hand, spotlighted (followspot) as he reached for rainwater to cool his head

Almost all these production elements are called for by the author (Tennessee Williams) himself, who, however, warns that despite these elements, the director must avoid an "effect curtain," seeking instead to portray the human values of the moment rather than the purely theatrical. This is sound advice.

In every style and kind of play, composition must remain subordinate to and supportive of the explication of the human actions, which are the stuff that all theatrical dreams are made of. Composition is never the play itself; it is only the outward manifestation of a production. But effective composition can make a strong play stronger, a funny play funnier, and a tragic play a searing theatrical experience. No director has ever had much impact in the theatre, no matter how brilliant his interpretation of scripts or his work with actors, without having an innate sense of composition and a conscious ability to use that innate sense. The goal of Part II of this book has been to define that innate sense and to explore the possibilities of its use on stage.

III
Acting

9

Directing Actors

The Actor-Director Relationship

The most obvious function of the director is to supervise the rehearsal and performance of the actors. In some cases this function is only modestly creative, and in others the creative options are enormous; in all cases, however, the actual day to day work of the director in supervising the acting is massive in terms of time and energy. A Broadway production is rehearsed for a minimum of three forty-hour weeks and previewed for another two weeks, giving the director close to 200 hours of rehearsal. The great European directors, particularly Stanislavski and Brecht, were known to spend more than a year on a single production, amassing well over 1000 rehearsal hours. By contrast, the typical university production, using amateur talent, is put together in under 100 hours, making one wonder how university students can be expected to attain proficiency so much faster than lifetime professionals.

The goal of rehearsal is primarily to put together an ensemble of successful acting performances. In a typical rehearsal schedule, the early rehearsals are set aside for blocking, the final rehearsals for technical rehearsing, and the great middle portion of the rehearsals are for the benefit of the actors and their problems. What is the director's connection with the actor's work? Just as he collaborates with the designer, the director works with the actor to stimulate his best effort toward a certain vision, interpretation, style, or theme of the production. He discusses with the actor the play and its meaning, each scene and its meaning, each reference and its meaning, and he helps the actor assure that these meanings are finally conveyed in performance. He seeks to integrate the actors not only with the text of the play and the style of the performance, but with each other's behavior and performances. A director who succeeds in achieving all these interrelated goals is very successful indeed. If, beyond this, he succeeds in inspiring his actors to excel themselves, giving brilliant performances, he has done a truly creative job.

A PERSON-TO-PERSON COLLABORATION

No one would suggest today that the actor-director relationship is a terribly formal one, but it was in past decades. Although the soap opera concept of the tyrannical director shouting commands and reading lines from the back of the house is still prevalent in popular fiction and in a few rear guard community or college theatre situations, it is rare in professional theatre today, either in America or in Europe. Actors are seldom considered puppets, and directors are rarely responded to as infallible gurus. The turn of events and philosophies which has brought this about is part of the growing complexity of modern life, which has influenced the entire nature of the theatre. Plays are no longer so rigidly classified as in the past, and characters have greater flexibility of action and are less one-dimensional. Modern acting places a greater premium on the many-faceted personality; audiences seek such human qualities as vitality, intelligence, and sympathy from the credible performance. The director must, therefore, seek to liberate these qualities in his actors and not to confine them within rigid boundaries, if the collaboration is to be truly creative. A maximum of freedom within complete yet understated control is the ideal.

General Directorial Methods

How does a director work with actors on the personal level? This question cannot be answered with a generalization, since the chief factor involved is the personality of the director himself, and the other factors also vary: the personalities of the actors, their talent and experience, the length of the rehearsal period, the nature of the play and the production, the director's experience working with the actors, the impression (if any) he wants to leave on them, and the impression (if any) he wants to make on the producer.

The last two factors are really extraneous. The objective of artistic and creative play direction should be the final production. While it may be desirable for the director and actors to form a loving and harmonious ensemble during the rehearsal period, this must be considered simply a pleasant by-product of the final goal. If the director earns the hatred of the cast and the personal enmity of the producer, it is still his final product that will be judged, not his methods of achieving it. Being in a play is often fun, and it is often desirable that it should be, but this is not a rule. Play production is not socializing, nor is it group therapy; it is the creation of art, and the artistic impulses must have overriding concern. No worthwhile study of directing could ever put a director's popularity with his actors over his creation of an artistic product.

The director-actor relationship is ordinarily one of give and take, with the director doing somewhat more giving and the actor somewhat more taking. If the director is widely experienced and the actors considerably less so, the director's authoritative function will increase. Similarly, if the play is to be rehearsed in a very short time, as in many summer stock productions, the actors will be less inclined to question or challenge the director's authority. But the overall considerations are ones of personality, and no textbook principles can overrule a director's innate psychological makeup. If he is naturally assertive, he will probably seek to exercise immediate control; if he is naturally less dominant, he will probably be more inquiring and suggestive.

PSYCHOLOGICAL ASPECTS OF DIRECTING

A director cannot ignore the psychology of his actors, who are, after all, people. Some actors work better when bullied, others when coddled. Some actors resent being bullied, or resent your bullying another actor; others resent your coddling another actor, particularly if they feel they are doing a better job and being bullied for it. These situations always arise, no matter what style of directing the director uses.

Coddling an actor means supporting him to build his confidence and self-esteem. This technique is not restricted to use with novice actors; some of the greatest actors in the American theatre frequently need their egos boosted, particularly after a time away from work. Coddling can make an actor secure and comfortable, which may be essential to his performance. The value of building an actor's security and confidence should be obvious: it reduces his rehearsal tension, permitting him to concentrate on the beats of the play. It allows his characterization to come forth powerfully, without tentative quirks and aborted gestures. It gives him the flexibility to experiment without worrying that he will be slapped down by the director if he is a bit out of line. It gives him the freedom to project, knowing (or thinking) that what he is projecting is essentially in the right direction. Conversely, an actor whose ego has been sufficiently bruised can easily grow apathetic or hostile during rehearsals—normal defense mechanisms—which results in a disastrous performance. But beware of over-coddling, especially if it derives from directorial timidity or laziness.

Bullying, on the other hand, may be used on the actor who confidently goes off in all the wrong directions. Just as it takes some force to stop a freely rolling automobile, it takes a similar amount of force to get a strong performer off one track and onto another. Bullying does not bother an actor who has great personal confidence (unless it goes too far, or unless the actor is only using a show of confidence to mask his basic insecurity), and some actors thrive on it. Unfortunately, bullying can sometimes be a cover for the director's insecurity, and as such it can be a needless and even dangerous aberration in the rehearsal procedure.

Suggestion is the overwhelmingly desirable way of working with the actor, according to most directors. A suggestion is neutral; it neither praises the actor nor criticizes him, it simply opens up an alternate form of playing a given moment or scene. An actor not open to suggestion is generally undirectable, and unless his performance alone can guarantee the success of the show, he should be avoided. "Try to seduce her with that line," a director might offer; "Why don't you try sitting on the couch when you say that"; "Suppose you are worrying about her feelings on this line?" In answer to suggestions like these, the actor will come up with voluntary responses which he will perform better than if they had been summarily handed to him. Coddling, after all, may not help an actor get across his points, and bullying may do little for his internal character development. Suggestion, mixed with a pinch of correction and a peck of encouragement, is a fine way of achieving results.

RESULT DIRECTING

Results, we reiterate, are the director's objective. To some "method" actors, "result-directors" are anathema, yet the director must remember that in the long run a result is what he is working toward, like it or not. It is certainly self-defeating to demand immediate results from actors (this is usually what is meant by "result directing"), but the actor should be coddled, bullied, or given suggestions so that results eventually occur. The results may remain in the director's private thoughts during rehearsal—and he is frequently well advised to keep them private and to work instead on his actors' moment-to-moment intentions and behavior —but in the end results must surface in the production. Ideally, the actor is coached to achieve the director's preplanned result, but when the actor reaches it, it is as a complete (and happy) surprise to him, and he approaches the director with an exclamation like, "I finally figured out what that scene was about." The director simply smiles in thanks and congratulates his performer.

A director achieves his greatest results, particularly in a naturalistic or seminaturalistic play, when his work is invisible in the final performance. When a reviewer praises a play and its excellent acting and does not even mention the director, the director should feel the greatest personal success. Directors should rarely, if ever, compete with actors for final attention. Whatever feelings, interpretations, and compositions of the play he has in mind at the beginning of the rehearsal period should be completely integrated into the performance by opening night, or eliminated from the production as unplayable (at least by the actors he has chosen to play them). A direction that cannot be convincingly executed by an actor is an embarrassment to the production; if the director insists that the actor go through with it anyway, that is a directorial error, not an acting one. Finally, a director should have the humility to realize, when he cannot achieve a desired effect through his actors, that it was possibly a poor effect from its inception. No director alive has not made poor decisions in the prerehearsal period; the good directors recognize them and stop pursuing them.

SPECIFIC DIRECTORIAL METHODS

In addition to the matter of psychological attitudes in directing, a director can work with his actors in several technical ways. These may differ from play to play; experience shows that working with actors in a play by Miller or Williams may be different from working with them in a play by Congreve, Brecht, Beckett, or Megan Terry. To accomplish his ends in differing situations, the director will need several approaches toward acting. We shall discuss various approaches in historical order, from the methods of the nineteenth century actor-managers, to Stanislavski's "system" of naturalism, to Gordon Craig's "antinaturalistic" system of the actor as puppet, to Brecht's system of actor alienation, to contemporary methods of game playing and improvisation. The director should become aware of the approaches open to him, and to some of their virtues and inherent dangers.

Directing in the Nineteenth Century

From our vantage point in the 1970s we can see an almost infinite spectrum of possibilities for use of actor potential in interpretive forms. The nature of the theatre today is so all-encompassing as to deny the application of rigid criteria and to make intensity of communication the true test of a performance (if any test is admitted!). However, this has not long been the case. It is a function of this century and particularly of the past twenty years, during which the impact of democratic psychology and technological sophistication has broken down critical preconceptions of the nature of art. In the nineteenth century the concept of a "proper" way to perform a given role tended to hold sway. American actor Mark Smith was praised in 1869 for his "most unexceptional Brabantio," the implication being that he had in all ways fulfilled the normal expectation of how the role should be performed, and was therefore excellent in the critic's eyes. This attitude is consistent with acting manuals (still being published in the 1940s), which stated that one should always kneel on the downstage knee, enter on the downstage foot, and pause at the door before exiting.

The actor has not always been subject to such rigid critical criteria and managerial disposition. Left to himself, he is essentially an individualist; we date our western histrionic tradition from a highly individualistic act on the part of Thespis some 2500 years ago. Being for much of his existence beyond the social pale has enabled the actor to preserve his independent way of life and his ability to entertain society, often at the expense of its cherished beliefs and mores. Two factors—a need for material and a need for protection—have tended to limit this independence, subjecting the actor to playwrights and patrons. But playwrights, as Shakespeare ruefully observed, cannot control the actor once he is on stage, and the right patron, as Molière had reason to know, can preserve the freedom of the actor as well as limit him. Possibly the freest actors were the ones we know least about, the Jongleurs, Skops, and similar itinerant entertainers of the middle ages, and the commedia dell' arte troupes of the sixteenth century. Without playwrights or patrons, they had, finally, only their audiences to please. Actor and audience—the two basic ingredients of theatre.

The academic, aesthetic, and commercial limitations on the actor's freedom, which led to the stifling situation at the end of the nineteenth century, can probably be traced back to the eighteenth century growth of an urban, middle-class, industrial society with bourgeois attitudes. As theatre became one of the commodities of this society, entrepreneurship became more important than art, and performance meant copying an original that was known to sell. From time to time a genius would effect a change in interpretation, which could then become a new stereotype, but for the most part the Boulevards, Broadways, and West Ends evolved as centers of mass-produced entertainment based on safe formulas which catered to the desire for sensation, wish fulfillment, and hero worship of its middle-brow audiences. Little was left to the creativity of the individual actor. The star system, a product of easier travel and cheap newspapers, led to the domination of the actor-manager, with productions geared to the exhibition of his unique traits. Add science and sophisticated stage technology to the actor-manager's overall control, and the director evolves, standing outside the scene to arrange all the elements which now form the theatre's technical vocabulary.

Throughout this process the nonstarring actor had gradually come to play an increasingly subordinate part in the creative process of theatre. Subject to the repetitious requirements of formula plays, removed from the audience behind a proscenium arch while economic hostage to their taste, subordinated to the ego of a star performer and the increasing gimmickry of staging techniques, it is little wonder that the actor in the latter half of the nineteenth century had denied his creative function in favor of the facile employment of certain well-tried mannerisms calculated to produce a Pavlovian response in the audience with the least amount of effort on the actor's part. Any sense of the protean quality of the actor's art, of the exploration of a dramatic text by an ensemble to arrive at its true nature, or of the communication of that truth to an audience in a manner which illuminated for them part of their experience of life had been lost beneath a welter of commercial exploitation, egotistical self-display, and technological trickery.

To counter this theatrical atmosphere at the end of the nineteenth century came the art theatre movement which led to the formulation of perhaps the most influential approach to the craft of acting in this century: the Stanislavski system. With this system and its extension into the Strasberg "method," we shall begin our exploration of how a director can work with his actors to achieve their joint aim.

The Stanislavski System and Naturalism

Konstantin Stanislavski acted at the great flood tide of "Naturalism," and the ideas and approach to acting which he incorporated into his system were to a considerable degree a function of this timing. The attempt to perform "naturally," to base the art of acting in nature, was hardly new. It had been the pursuit of actors for many centuries, but to each century it had meant something different: to the seventeenth century French actor, balance, form, and perfection of verbal utterance; to the eighteenth century English actor, a more prosaic, heavy, and stilted glamorization of bourgeois attitudes; to the Romantic actor of the early nineteenth century, an extravagantly physical and dynamic exercise of emotional pyrotechnics. All these forms of "natural" acting were attempts to communicate by external means the immediately recognizable elements of a role, always within a consciously theatrical framework. It is of course very possible in the societies to which these actors catered—societies for the most part geared to a hierarchical order, strict form, and stereotypical social codes and manners—that stage mannerisms based on these manifestations could communicate meaning with facile accuracy, if without depth of understanding or feeling. However, by the end of the nineteenth century new social and philosophical approaches had rendered these codes and attitudes obsolescent. Human existence was becoming increasingly sophisticated and far less susceptible to simplistic impersonation. In France, Émile Zola and his interpreter André Antoine were engaged in minutely accurate portrayal of the seamy side of life. The dawn of psychology brought with it the concept that behavior is by no means comprehensible from its external attributes, that its true meaning and significance can be determined only from an understanding of the thoughts and feelings, sometimes unconscious, of the individual.

Against this background, more human than histrionic, Stanislavski looked for ways of exploring, and creating on the stage, the natural and organic expression of the individual's deep-seated feelings, eschewing facile mannerisms which impersonated the form of emotions without including their content. The impact of Stanislavski's system was nowhere greater than in the United States, because of the visit of the Moscow Art Theatre to America in 1923. After the visit, Richard Boleslavsky and Maria Ouspenskaya remained in New York to teach Stanislavski's system, and the adoption by the Group Theatre of their understanding of the system led ultimately to the evolution of the "method" of the New York Actor's Studio under Lee Strasberg. Then came the publication, in English, of Stanislavski's three major works. It is likely, therefore, that any director working in the United States will have in his company actors whose approach to their craft is to some degree determined by an acquaintance with the Method. (This is true to a lesser extent in other parts of the world.) Thus, it is important that directors be aware of the method approach to acting, and the virtues, expectations, and limitations of method-trained actors.

Stanislavski's system requires an actor to bring his understanding and imagination to every moment of the play. It enables the actor to discover within himself what his part requires of him. It is for the director to see that the right questions are being asked by the actor, and the relevant stimuli being employed. The director refines and shapes the results of the actor's explorations, without either imposing upon them or repressing their spontaneity. There are three basic tools for creating inner truth and believability in a performance: knowledge of the objective, understanding of the given circumstances, and affective or emotional memory. Together they form a complete approach to a role: the actor must know what his character is trying to do or achieve on the stage; he must know where his character is, relative to time, place, personal circumstances, preceding events, and attitudes of the other characters; and he must be able to use his past experience of life to help him recreate the present action, filtered through the circumstances and determined by the objective.

To illustrate this process, let us construct a somewhat skeletal hypothetical outline of how director and actor might work on a play. Several readings of the play will take place. The first will be introductory, so that the actors can get the story and catch the flavor. The second reading will clarify the text, so that actors and director reach the same understanding of ambiguities and foreign or unfamiliar words or phrases—the surface value of the text—before work on its interpretation begins. At this stage the director may want to share with the actors some of his research into the play's background, especially if the play has a historical context or specific locales with which the actors are not familiar. The director's exposition will lead to questions from the actors and a discussion of the general background of the play, which helps to flesh out its given circumstances. It can also lead to actors doing further background research along lines agreed to by the whole cast.

Subsequent readings of the play will be concerned with objectives. The director and the actors will break the play into units, each with a specific objective defined in terms of an active verb—to do, to achieve, to attain, to wish for. Each of these individual objectives should relate to the main objective, "through line," or idea of the play. One of the director's most important tasks is to see that the actors understand clearly the main idea of the play and how each unit and objective contributes to the communication of this idea. After the play has been analyzed in this manner, each actor may then divide his role into smaller units, or beats, careful searching of which will reveal different facets of the larger objective and add color and variety to the larger unit. In this way the complex and sophisticated character is constructed and the simplistic one-dimensional caricature avoided.

When rehearsals on the stage begin, the actor already has a clear outline of his character's function within the play, and of the circumstances that will determine how the function is pursued. During the rehearsal period, the director works closely with the actor to help him maintain this understanding, deepen it, and find within his resources the emotional and physical means of communicating his intentions. The di-

rector will probably do this by questioning and reminding. Questions can
be very simple: "Why did you make that entrance?" If the answer is, "To
see Fred," then the next question will be, "Why do you want to see Fred?"
If it is to borrow money, then why does the character wish to borrow
money? and so on until the actor is fully aware of all the ramifications of
an apparently simple action: the character—let us call him Bill—wants to
borrow money from Fred to pay a hospital bill for his wife, who has to
have a serious operation. Suppose that Fred's wife used to be Bill's girl-
friend, but dropped him in favor of the richer Fred, while still in love
with Bill. In such circumstances, the way in which Bill approaches Fred,
his manner of saying, "Hello, Fred," will reflect the unspoken or subtextual nuances of the Fred-Bill relationship. The director, by questioning
and suggesting things the actor may have overlooked, helps him discover
how Bill would make the entrance and say those two apparently simple
words.

The "Magic If"

Understanding the circumstances and the objective of a particular
action does not of itself necessarily lead to the truthful performing of it,
although it is impossible to portray it truthfully without such an understanding. In addition, the stimulation of the valid inner activity on the
part of the actor which is communicated through an honest physical action is needed. Stanislavski talked of the "magic if" as a means toward the
creation of this state. The actor asks himself, "What would I do if I
were . . . ?" This question stimulates the actor's emotions in the context
of the character's problem; it is a function of the process of emotional
memory or recall. The theory behind emotional memory (which has become one of the more controversial elements of Stanislavski's system) is
that the human being is a reservoir of innumerable experiences, emotional moods, and psychological states which an actor has at his disposal, to
conjure up and inform his work on a role. Thus in a given stage situation
the actor evokes his emotions by remembering an emotional experience in
his past which was analogous to that required by his role.

Improvisation in the Stanislavski System

The director can greatly assist the actor, initially by helping him explore his resources and past experiences, and then, should the actor find
he is still unable to discover the necessary emotional response within himself, by creating circumstances which will lead the actor to experience the
required inner activity. Improvisation was the rehearsal tool Stanislavski
employed to help his actors experience the emotional response required

by their roles. Of course, improvisation was by no means an invention of Stanislavski; it had been the basis of perhaps the most virile theatrical art —the Commedia dell' Arte—in the sixteenth and seventeenth centuries, but it had become a lost art until Stanislavski revived it as a rehearsal instrument. Since Stanislavski, improvisation has come to play an increasingly important part in theatre; we shall discuss it later as both artifact and art in its own right. One form of improvisation is more nearly the living of the actual circumstances; for example, Stanislavski, working on *The Lower Depths,* actually took his actors to Moscow's skid row, so that they could soak up through their pores the experience of living in dirt and squalor. The other form employed by Stanislavski is the creation of a situation analogous to that in the stage action, but more directly relevant to the actor's life and circumstances. Improvisation around the circumstances of the play's action, but not limited to the actual text, helps the actor discover nuances and minor details which all add to the richness and lifelike nature of his performance.

In all these ways the director can assist the actor in their joint search for the goal of the Stanislavski system: the honest portrayal of real life on the stage. Stanislavski focused acting on the existential—what it is like to be alive, the feelings and choices involved in living. His system gives the actor freedom to make discoveries about himself and the character, but this freedom should always be exercised within the structure of the requirements of the play and the director's overall concept, as discussed with the actors.

CONTROVERSIES AND MISUNDERSTANDINGS OF STANISLAVSKI'S SYSTEM

For various historical reasons, misunderstandings, misuses, and abuses of Stanislavski's system have become part of the commonly accepted currency of the theatre.[1] The director may find himself working with a self-styled Method actor who has simply taken the aim of naturalness and spontaneity as an excuse for egotistical self-indulgence and the eschewing of all craft disciplines.

The greatest theatrical sin still committed in Stanislavski's name is the result of a historical accident; really, of two related accidents. The first is that Stanislavski began to study acting when it was at the peak of technological gimmickry. Because the most famous actors of Stanislavski's day were given to taking downstage center, full-face positions and orating

---

[1] For a good discussion, see Erika Munk, ed., *Stanislavski and America* (New York: Fawcett World Library, 1966), and Robert Lewis, *Method—or Madness* (New York: French & European Publications, Inc., 1958.)

and gesticulating in arrant disregard of any conceivable form of what we now call acting honesty, Stanislavski tried to right the balance by stressing, in his first studies, the internal reality of characterization rather than its external manifestations. Similarly, because Stanislavski pioneered in the area of internal reality in acting, his book on that particular subject, *An Actor Prepares,* was translated into English long before his technique study, *Building a Character,* which was intended as a companion volume. *An Actor Prepares,* then, received perhaps an unbalanced share of attention in America at that time, while the equally important studies of voice, diction, makeup, costuming, and movement were generally still unknown. Actually, of course, Stanislavski was fully aware of the necessity of craft in acting. His favorite actor was the histrionic Italian, Tomasso Salvini, who once declared that the three principles of acting were "Voice, voice, and more voice." Stanislavski's productions, which can still be seen in Moscow Art Theatre revivals today, are masterpieces of craftsmanship, as well as fine examples of internal reality.

The true Stanislavski "system" therefore represents the sum of Stanislavski's thinking about acting, highly balanced between the actor's internal and external work. When we speak of the Method, however, we are really speaking of the first half of Stanislavski's system, the internal half, introduced to American actors by, among others, Lee Strasberg at the Actor's Studio in New York. To be sure, Strasberg has now elaborated his teaching to include the wide range of aspects covered by the Russian master, but American so-called Method actors are usually marked by a major reliance on private moments and self-examination (some would say self-exploitation) for their acting technique. Much of that technique is useful, but it is not enough to produce the complete actor.

One of the great controversies surrounding the Stanislavski system is its early use of a technique known as "emotional memory." This technique asks the actor to remember personal experiences which affected him and to recreate that remembered emotion on stage in a similar situation. Emotional memory is used today, but it is noteworthy that Stanislavski abandoned it in mid-career, favoring instead his theory of physical actions, a much more Pavlovian concept. The danger of emotional memory, and the reason Stanislavski eventually abandoned it, is that it can cause the opposite of the intended effect: instead of creating the illusion of spontaneity, it can make the actor appear to be pushing, trying to summon an emotion that does not come naturally from the situation. Being essentially a borrowed emotion, it is not spontaneous to begin with. Ordinarily it is preferable that emotion come from within the situation of the play rather than from a situation the actor experienced previously. Frequently the use of emotional memory produces little but self-indulgent, irrelevant emotion; it can lead to a kind of blindness if the actor tries to work with an emotion generated by a recall exercise and then finds it impossible to absorb and create the author's life going on in the scene. The actor should start from the play's intention, not from his desire to emote.

A second controversy over the Stanislavski system concerns this latter point: the amount to which an actor can successfully "use" himself in the character he is playing. This is so far from being a contemporary subject for debate that it is the central argument in a host of eighteenth and nineteenth century acting disputes, beginning with Diderot's *The Paradox of Acting*. It is certainly true that many film and television actors simply play themselves; unquestionably, an actor who truly plays himself (this is easier said than done) will achieve honesty and spontaneity if nothing else. In film, a highly naturalistic medium, playing oneself is frequently all that is required; Strasberg has stated, "The simplest examples of Stanislavski's ideas are actors such as Gary Cooper, John Wayne, and Spencer Tracy. They try not to act but to be themselves, to respond or react. They refuse to say or do anything they feel not to be consonant with their own character."[2] His statement has some validity. A director seeking to create honesty and spontaneity, and blessed with actors who can play themselves and who also resemble closely the characters they are asked to play, may try to emulate the self-projection acting of a Gary Cooper. The problem arises when the actor tries to extrapolate the film technique to the stage. On stage an actor has no cameraman, editor, or sound engineer to do his work for him, and an effective technique in terms of character projection, timing, and audience relationship is necessary. While superannuated football stars may be passed off on the uncritical film public, on stage they would be nonstarters.

We are not saying that an actor does not use himself as substance for his character, but the "magic if" that Stanislavski noted as a bridge from actor to character is too often omitted by Method actors who use the character to play themselves, instead of the other way around. They frequently try to turn the playwright's words into their own vernacular. Robert Lewis tells of an actor he once directed who said "y'know" before every line. "I said 'why?' He said, 'Well it makes it real for me—that's the way I talk.' I said, 'Well you're not going to be able to say: y'know to be or not to be.' "[3] No director could improve on that succinct reply. The director must be on his guard for the Method actor who uses the stylized "naturalism" of broken speech rhythms, and is lost in private moments that never leave the staging area. The audience must be part of the given circumstances of any theatrical production, and the director should know that lines must be heard and actions must have meaning and clarity.

Accepting these caveats, directors are of course free to use whatever

[2] *The New York Times*, 2 September 1956, Sec. 2, p. 1.

[3] Lewis, *Stanislavski and America*, p. 22.

techniques work for them, whether or not they are correct interpretations of Stanislavski. Emotional memory, for example, can be used judiciously with an actor who seems to resist exploring the emotional depth of his part. It can break through superficial playing of a scene, as Stanislavski originally employed it to overcome superficial playing by his too-technical actors. It is a useful rehearsal technique to remove the cliché physical response an actor can place between himself and a true emotion, and to discover a uniquely original way of approaching a situation. Such personal techniques are frequently used in film and television, where a natural response is sought more than the creation of a specific "character" emotion or response, and personal techniques are successful within the terms of these media. But the stage director must observe the caveats about the Method actor and his technique. They have been stressed here because they have received too little attention elsewhere. The misguided, uncontrolled use of the Method can produce extraneous action and irrelevant emotion, suitable perhaps for a therapy session, but having little or nothing to do with the playwright's purposes or valid theatrical action.

Later Naturalistic Techniques

Later naturalistic techniques have focused on the nature of emotion and how it may best be brought out in realistic acting. Even Stanislavski, toward the end of his career, realized that emotion on stage was not an end in itself, and not something the actor "worked up" by artificial means. It is clear from an examination of daily behavior that people do not *try* to be sad, to grieve, to be afraid, or to be overcome with joy. Emotions are emotional, in fact, because they are *not* intended; they may even run counter to our intentions. Everyone has experienced a feeling of empathy when someone else cries, but invariably the empathy will increase if the person is obviously trying *not* to cry, but cries nonetheless. An actor can play a crying scene trying to laugh, but failing; this practice is called "playing the opposite," and it may be considered applicable to all natural emotional behavior. Most modern directors and acting instructors have concentrated, as did Stanislavski later in his teaching, on actions rather than emotions, or, in the words of French actor-director Jean-Louis Barrault, on "deeds":

> If emotion is a state, the actor should never take cognizance of it. In fact we can never take cognizance of an emotion while we are in its grip, but only when it has passed. Otherwise the emotion disappears. The actor lives uniquely in the present; he is continually jumping from one present to the next. In the course of these successive presents he executes a series of ac-

tions which deposit upon him a sort of sweat which is nothing else but the state of emotion. This sweat is to his acting what juice is to fruit. But once he starts perceiving and taking cognizance of his state of emotion, the sweat evaporates forthwith, the emotion disappears, and the acting dries up. . . .

The actor shouldn't look on his character's emotions as "states" (just as he should not think about the sweat beading his body during the performance), but he should attach great importance to emotions seen as "behavior," as last-resort actions. If he does this he will be able to convince himself that characters never arrest the action in order needlessly to display their feelings; no, they are continually in action and reaction. They reason, they plead, they argue, they fight with or against others, even with or against themselves. They dispute, answer back, deceive others or themselves with greater or less bad faith; but they never stop. The audience is at liberty to distinguish between these actions: actions proper, feelings, emotions. For the actor who is right within the drama there is only "behavior." Only Deeds.[4]

Barrault's point, of course, is that emotions can never be played; only actions can be played, and if they are played truly and with intensity, emotions will flow from them. This is a reversal of the more traditional concept that actions occur because of emotions, but the reversal is echoed in modern psychological studies which tend to support the James–Lang theory, that emotions tend to follow actions. According to the James–Lang theory, if a man sees a bear in the forest and runs, he does not experience fear which causes him to run away; he runs away, and the act of running away causes him to experience fear. An American study succinctly analyzes acting in terms of this theory:

If we adopt the external or physical symptoms of an emotion, the internal fullness of that emotion will grow within us. . . . This is a useful attitude for the actor since his script provides him with a wealth of external details to be utilized in achieving an internalization of the life of the character. A play script contains not only specified actions, but a whole range of implied externals embodied in its rhythms, emphases, meanings, and overall structure. By participating physically in these externals, we imitate the character. By understanding and respecting the character's dramatic function and style, we can help ourselves develop identification with him. Finally, by mastery of the techniques of stage performance, we can communicate this fully expressed characterization to our audience.[5]

[4] Jean-Louis Barrault, *Reflections on the Theatre* (London: Rockliff, 1951), pp. 126, 129.

[5] Robert L. Benedetti, *The Actor at Work: An Introduction to the Skills of Acting* (Englewood Cliffs, N.J.: Prentice-Hall, Inc., 1970), p. 43. See also Duncan Ross, "Towards an Organic Approach to Actor Training," *Educational Theatre Journal*, 20, No. 2A (Aug. 1968), 225–68.

Benedetti quotes William Ball, director of the American Conservatory Theatre, as espousing the dictum, "Do the act, and the feeling will follow." This is not, of course, a return to "external" acting (the outward action without the response of a supporting emotion). It is an acknowledgment of modern philosophical and psychological attitudes toward human makeup which recognize a *Gestalt* in which mind and body are considered completely interrelated, not separate entities. Emotion and its muscular symptoms are therefore virtually identical. In terms of theatre, the givens are not the character's emotions, but his actions, and if the properly valid activity is performed, the appropriate emotion will accompany it. This process becomes self-generating and leads to fuller actions and a true physical extension of the script.

To conclude our discussion of the achievements of the naturalistic school, let us say that without question the discoveries of Stanislavski have been a most influential contribution to the art of acting, and to the nature of the actor-director relationship. Until recent times the teachings of Stanislavski were heralded by acting coaches, actors, and directors as almost divinely inspired. The Actor's Studio in New York was the most celebrated school of acting in America from the time of its founding (1947) through the early 'sixties, and its principal teacher, Lee Strasberg, is still the best-known acting instructor in the country today. No director can begin to work in America without at least taking cognizance of the discoveries and teachings of Stanislavski and Strasberg, and nowhere in professional or advanced community theatre is he going to work with actors who, for better or worse, are uninfluenced by Method discoveries and techniques. Many of these techniques, even those we have disputed, retain tremendous hold on the acting community, and the decision on whether to accept them will be determined by the director's purposes.

Antinaturalism Techniques

Of course, the Stanislavski system is not the actor's only inheritance from the early part of the century. Befitting the cyclical nature of human activity, a very few years after Stanislavski's efforts to humanize the actor, to make him appear as like-life as possible on stage, there was a reaction against the whole concept of naturalism in the theatre. Stanislavski himself acknowledged certain limitations of his approach. In *My Life in Art*, speaking of his success with plays which were near to the lives of his actors, he admitted less than success with plays in the grand and heroic manner: "Apparently it is not the inner feeling but the technique of expression that prevents me from doing in the plays of Shakespeare, what we are able to do in Chekhov." His production of *Othello*, for example, was concerned with "psychological pauses" (with unfortunate effects on the rhythm and poetic sense of the line) and heavily naturalistic settings— gondoliers, canals, and so on—to create the atmosphere which he could not trust his actors' presentation of the text, and the audience's imagination, to supply. While Stanislavski was on solid ground in insisting to his actors that art must be based on natural law and human truths, he perhaps ignored the desire of the artist to express the inexpressible, to create a world larger than the earthbound one. Gordon Craig, who was to be a prime mover in the reaction against naturalism, said, "An artist is one who perceives more than his fellows, and who records more than he has seen." The antinaturalists, of whom the first was one of Stanislavski's protégés, Vsevolod Meyerhold, were aware that certain works of art were so all-encompassing that a narrowly naturalistic approach could only diminish them. To act the great Shakespearean roles, for example, the actor must merge his spirit with the text—not reduce it to psychological or sociological compartments—and the structure, images, and rhythms of the text must be the stuff of the actor's playing. He must be transported by an imaginative existence, not anchored in the mundane.

Gordon Craig: The Actor as Über-Marionette

Gordon Craig, like Antonin Artaud some twenty years later, was one of the great prophets, poets, and inspiritors of the theatre. Again like Artaud, he left no practical or coherent system by which his idea of theatre might be achieved. The actor or director who reads *On the Art of the Theatre* or *The Theatre and Its Double* might find great excitement, inspiration, and encouragement; he will not find one element that is of immediate practical use to him on the stage. It was for the Meyerholds, Copeaus, Barraults, and Grotowskis to attempt to come to plain theatrical terms with the immortal intimations of the fevered geniuses.

"To train a company of actors to show upon the stage the actions which are seen in every drawing-room, club, public-house or garret must seem to everyone nothing less than tomfoolery."[6] Thus did Craig dismiss naturalism and the efforts of actors to carefully recapitulate life's minutiae. In its place he would put the *Über-Marionette*. This concept of Craig's has been misinterpreted, mainly because of Craig's lack of explicitness, to mean that the actor should be no more than a wooden puppet, an inanimate object completely subject to the string-pulling of his director. What Craig intended was an actor who was larger than life, befitting

[6] Gordon Craig, *On the Art of the Theatre* (New York: Theatre Arts Books, 1925), p. 36.

Craig's concept of the theatre: "a God-like puppet." The actor who slav-
ishly copied life was not an artist but a hack imitator. If the stage were
rid of the actor as merely a human being with mundane limitations, then
debased realism would go, too; if the actor was no longer a human figure,
then we would not be confused into connecting actuality and art. The actor must be concerned not with the surface of life, but with its spirit and
essence. The Über-Marionette would be unconcerned with the applause
of an audience; the leading lady's ego would be uninflated by bouquets,
her face as solemn, remote, and beautiful as ever. "The Über-Marionette
is the actor plus fire, minus egoism: the fire of the Gods and demons without the smoke and steam of mortality."[7]

How does the actor achieve this, if he wishes to? In modern parlance,
the actor is externally "cool," in an almost trance-like state, while inter-
nally possessed by a visceral commitment to the action he is playing.
Essentially it is a function of discipline, almost superhuman concentration, and a spiritual relationship with the essence of the text. Craig was
concerned with the great myths of man, those primal, archetypal concerns
which Jung hypothesized as being a part of the human makeup. For
Craig, puppets were the descendants of ancient images and totems, made
in the likeness of primitive gods and incorporating these primitive essences of humanity. The actor as puppet is the medium through which
the godhead speaks. It is possible that Craig was trying to make of the actor something which is impossible of achievement. Craig himself was not
a successful director, declaring Shakespeare to be unactable and blaming
audiences for his failure to communicate at their level.

For the director who aspired to the pale fire of Craig's theatre, the
process of working with actors would possibly be akin to the meditative
disciplines of yoga, achieving a spiritual oneness with the text. The spirit
of the play, its supervening essence, would have to be extracted from each
action, thought, and sound. Actors would work with outsize masks which
incorporated the elemental essence of the characters, and possibly with
kothurnoi to give them both a feeling of remove from busy humanity and
a sense of the size required by the absolute nature of their acting. The
Bread and Puppet Theatre is perhaps the nearest contemporary equivalent of Craig's ideal, although Craig wished the actor to become the puppet, not to assume the outward trappings of puppetry. The size, aloofness,
composure, and unmoving concentration of the Bread and Puppet's images has at times an almost spiritually hypnotic effect. The appearance of
one pearldrop tear on the cheek of a sightless, unemotional, madonna-like
puppet can convey more about human emotions than the warmest flood
down the face of the most romantically transported actress. It is the actor

[7] Ibid., pp. ix–x.

who could maintain the outward aspect of that puppet while inwardly conscious of the spiritual implications of the action, that Craig wished to introduce to the theatre.

Vsevolod Meyerhold: The Physical Actor and Space

Meyerhold, a contemporary of Stanislavski, did his most important work in the 1920s. Moving away from the naturalism associated with Stanislavski, Meyerhold went not in the somewhat metaphysical direction of Gordon Craig, but toward an emphasis on the dynamic communication that could be made by the movement of the actor's body in space. For example, in his famous production of Nikolai Gogol's *The Government Inspector,* at the point where the mayor and Khelestakov are sizing each other up, Meyerhold had the actor playing Bobchinsky fall through a door (at which he had been eavesdropping) on the landing at the top of

Theatermuseum, Munich

Figure 66. A Vsevolod Meyerhold set using swings, ropes, and pulleys on which actors performed their biomechanics in a gymnastic style of acting (1927).

the stairs, hurtle down the stairs, and disappear through a trap in the floor at the bottom. Although this occurrence terrified the mayor, Kheles-takov watched impassively, breaking the mayor's nerve and giving Kheles-takov dominance.

To train his actors to accomplish such feats, Meyerhold evolved his theory of biomechanics, based on what he took to be natural laws of movement, which taught the actor to use the stage space three-dimension-ally. Gymnastic exercises, tumbling, and circus skills were all employed to help the actor gain a complete sense of the relationship of his body to space, time, and rhythm. Meyerhold's aim was to make the actor a plastic part of a rhythmically harmonious whole in which other actors, proper-ties, stage furnishings, and scenery were all coordinated. In *The Govern-ment Inspector* Meyerhold had Khelestakov, at the climax of the scene in which he overawes the officials with his fantastic lying, indulge in a wild, incoherent, yet perfectly controlled dance. Using the whole stage, and in strict rhythm with both the accompanying music and the delivery of his

Theatermuseum, Munich

Figure 67. Meyerhold's production of *Turandot* in Moscow (1925). The total use of the stage and the choreography of the actors created a fluid, plas-tic, rhythmic picture.

monologue, the prancing of Khelestakov followed the lines of the set. The patterns of the dance arose from the shapes in the environment and gave it a form of dynamic expression, so that the whole stage picture was an integrated manifestation of general abnormality.

Meyerhold achieved another integrated effect in the same production in the scene in which the officials bribe Khelestakov. Meyerhold staged this scene wth eleven doors, in each of which stood one official. At the same time and with the same gesture, they held out little packages to Khelestakov while they chanted their lines in unison, like an eleven-part fugue. The movements were the stylized ones of robots, and the whole effect was to create a gigantic bribe machine, to which Khelestakov responded with the mechanical movements of a clockwork doll, picking off packets in rhythmic sequence.

Such effects required a tremendous physical discipline and flexibility of actors. A director would be unwise to attempt such a style unless he were working with an ensemble of physically adept actors with a great consciousness of dynamic use of space. Given these ingredients, tremendously exciting theatre can be created by the discovery of those physical actions which, by their dynamic and symbolically integrated effect, communicate the vital sense of the script through the total shape and rhythm in the scenic space.

Jacques Copeau: The Spiritual Ensemble

The movement away from naturalistic detail toward poetic plasticity was continued by Jacques Copeau. Three fundamental elements composed Copeau's work: the script, the actor, and the space. Copeau placed great emphasis on the creation of a spiritual ensemble, that growing together of a group of actors that enables them to intuit each other's life rhythms, emotions, and philosophies, and consequently to act on the same wave length, not as a collection of individuals each locked into a separate, impregnable compartment. To achieve his ensemble, Copeau spent several months with his company in a private retreat in the country where they could play games, read poetry, discuss religion, and otherwise become familiar with each other and with their texts. It is unlikely that many directors can afford the luxury of a three month "getting to know you" period. However, the importance of actors' relationships with each other should not be disregarded, and even one weekend out of a four or five week rehearsal period spent in a common living environment can achieve the kind of mutual intuition and reciprocity that enormously facilitates later rehearsals.

To achieve the fluidly rhythmic performances that were Copeau's ideal, the director must work to obtain from his actors the physical and verbal gesture that expresses the essential nature of the text. This is a process which requires careful analysis and assimilation of the structure, rhythms, and images of the text, and the physical capacity on the part of the actor to communicate these in fluid and poetic gestural equivalents. Many months of careful training and physical exercise are required to equip the actor for this task, and it would be courting disaster for a director to attempt such a production with ill-prepared actors.

One way of helping the actor to appreciate the physical and verbal essences of a text, to get behind the face and normative value of the words, is to take words away from him. A simple exercise in this connection is to give two actors some information they must communicate to each other within the context of some relationship. The actors then work out a scene in which the information is relayed using only physical gestures and nonverbal noises. The movements and noises are not realistic, for they are not intended to be simply a substitute for words, but a means of communicating an essential idea. Masks can also contribute toward the achievement of communication by physical gesture. The use of a non-character mask in an exercise such as the above takes from the actor the expressiveness of his face and forces him to use the rest of his body to communicate his idea. Or a character or emotion mask can be used. The actor dons the mask and observes himself in a mirror, absorbing the essence of the mask. He then improvises and communicates with his total body the sense of the mask. Several actors can exchange masks during the improvisation, adding variety and challenge to the exercise.

Of course, before the actor can use his physical capacity to communicate a text, the director must show him what the values of the text are, in terms of rhythm, melody, and imagery. A director should not approach a play in verse without having some sense of scansion, how variations between foot patterns, placement of caesuras, and the use of line endings to form larger rhythmic structures all contribute to the character of the line, and thus to the speaker. Alliteration and onomatopoeia add color to the line and should be used by the actor for this purpose. Rhythm and color can convey much of the emotional sense of the line, even without help from the content. Imagery is a further element of the poet's palette which contributes to mood and atmosphere. A director must bring all these elements to the actor's attention, so that he will steep himself in the text and be able to bring it to a complete physical (including verbal) realization. Again, having found the values of the text, it is a useful exercise to have the actor convey them in purely physical terms, acting out the images and the essences, stretching his imagination beyond the narrow limits of the words.

Antonin Artaud: A Theatre of Cruelty

A contemporary of Copeau, whose influence on theatre has come to fruition only within the past decade, is Antonin Artaud. With Artaud's concept of a Theatre of Cruelty, the physicalization by the actor of the most primeval, organic essence of man has reached its peak:

> Whereas most people remain impervious to a subtle discourse whose intellectual development escapes them, they cannot resist effects of physical surprise, the dynamism of cries and violent movements . . . used to act in a direct manner on the physical sensitivity of the spectator.
>
> Carried along by the paroxysm of a violent physical action which no sensitivity can resist, the spectator finds his over-all nervous system becoming sharpened and refined, he becomes more apt to receive the wave length of rarer emotions and of the sublime ideas of the Great Myths which through the particular performance will attempt to reach him with their physical conflagration—like force.[8]

Like Craig, Artaud wished to use the great absolutes of man's existence, the archetypal elements underlying his rituals and myths, as the stuff of theatre. Similarly, we acknowledge Artaud's importance for his inspiration, the sweep and dynamic of his ideas, not for any practical techniques he bequeathed to actor or director. Unlike Craig, however, Artaud emphasized super-heated human passions, those elemental feelings of violence and ecstacy which Artaud believed to be contained within man's primitive soul, although repressed beneath his social mask. Artaud's texts were Senecan tragedies such as *Thyestes* and their Elizabethan and Romantic equivalents such as *Arden of Faversham* and *The Cenci*. By conjuring the lusts and passions of these plays, Artaud sought to purge the audience of them; the cruelty of his theatre inhered in this complete possession of the audience, as if by a plague which feverishly explored their innermost senses before passing to leave them whole and at peace.

To create the effect he desired, Artaud sought a stage language based primarily on gesture and sound. For his idea of gesture he was indebted to his understanding of Oriental theatre, especially Balinese. Artaud extolled the precision of the language of gesture of this theatre, in which every movement communicated an exact effect heightened by the coordinated rhythmic sounds, both vocal and instrumental. But how is this translatable into occidental terms, to be conveyed to audiences whose cultures have become contaminated and who are removed by the sophistication of technological societies from the roots of their existence? Artaud

[8] Antonin Artaud, *Oeuvres Complètes* (New York: French & European Publications, Inc., 1956–67), II, 187.

did not really say. The sense of his theatre can be felt from his writings; the method is wholly another thing.

Peter Brook and Jerzy Grotowski

Two important contemporary directors follow, to some extent, Artaud's goals. One is English director Peter Brook, who spent an entire year running a "Theatre of Cruelty" workshop with selected members of the Royal Shakespeare Company, and then produced, with that group as the nucleus cast, Peter Weiss's *Marat/Sade,* which had an enormous critical and commercial success. Brook has subsequently gone on to other forms of theatre and film, but Artaudian traces remain in his work today and possibly always will. The other contemporary director in this framework is Jerzy Grotowski, director of the Polish Laboratory Theatre in Wroclaw. Grotowski's actors approach Artaud's "holy actor" and Craig's "actor in a trance," and his company, in existence since 1960, demonstrates a monastic dedication to the art of acting. To produce theatre in the Grotowski manner one has, essentially, to be Grotowski; it would be ridiculous for us to pretend to interpret to other directors his manner of working. It must be experienced; but at second best we refer directors to *Towards a Poor Theatre,*[9] which contains a series of exercises and explanations of Grotowski's method of working with actors.

ARTAUDIAN EXERCISES

For the less ambitious we suggest the exercises and improvisations that follow, aimed at further exploration of the actor's physical and vocal capacity outside the range of the accepted human expression of emotion. These examples are intended as starting points from which the director can explore his actors' potential, with a clear idea of the kind of theatrical statement he has in mind. Without such an idea, attempts at producing an Artaudian form of theatre will never result in more than uncoordinated and disoriented exhibitions of limited physical and verbal contortions. The discipline required to sustain complete freedom of expression is the greatest challenge that actors and directors can meet.

Because sounds and rhythms are so fundamental to this form of theatre, an exploration of their potential and relationships as means of expression is a good starting point. The director can give the actors various objects with which to produce sounds—sticks, stones, tin cans, boxes,

---

[9] Jerzy Grotowski, *Towards a Poor Theatre* (New York: Simon & Schuster, Inc., 1970).

and so on. The actors then explore the complete sound range of the instruments, muting them against the body, suspending them in the air, laying them in various positions on the ground. Then the director can introduce rhythms, enormously varied in pace and intensity. Groups of rhythms can be formed and complete conversations held by exploiting the sound and rhythmic range of the instruments. Scenes can be played using the vocabulary of sounds the actors have discovered to convey the sense of the text. The purpose of this exercise is to let the actors experience the possibilities of rhythm and sound. This experience can then be transferred to the actor's voice and body, the voice producing sounds different from those of the normal human vocabulary, and the body expressing a language beyond the accepted psychological or social clichés of everyday behavior patterns.

As extensions of this basic exercise, improvisations can be performed which require the completely nonnaturalistic expression of emotional states. For example, a scene can be set up on a completely naturalistic basis, but at a certain point an incident can be introduced, by way of a message or a new character, which creates an emotional state in the actor. The actor is required to express this state using sound and movement which are completely nonnaturalistic, but which communicate to the audience the essential quality of the emotion. Scenes can be created to give the actor more assistance in finding and using essential sounds and movements. For example, say that two girls have been roommates for many years. One has a boyfriend who has developed a secret attachment for the other, and finally the first girl has to be told. The boy must tell the girl, but he wants to avoid hurting her or destroying the relationship between the two girls. The girl tries desperately to keep the boy, wants to maintain her pride, but cannot disguise her bitterness at her roommate. The scene can be improvised naturalistically at first, then played again using only the essential words which convey the idea. Finally, the actor chooses essential sounds which reflect the sense of the scene, and the scene is replayed using variations on these sounds. When the scene is reduced to a basic impulse, the sound and movement it creates convey its organic essence.

Another approach to an Artaudian form of theatre which is used increasingly today is to start with the breath. Breathing and the heartbeat are the two fundamental human rhythms, and both affect and are affected by emotional states: a deep breath, for instance, can quiet a state of nervous tension. The actor can be shown how the manipulation of breath affects his body. Short, irregular, rapid breathing affects the muscle impulses and rhythms of movement, resulting in certain expressive qualities. Breath patterns also affect facial expression. The actor should explore the potential emotional responses of a variety of breathing rhythms and depths. Breathing can then be given vocal extension, creating nonverbal sounds supported by and communicating verbal states. Scenes can then be played using only breath and its physical and vocal extensions to convey the essential quality of the scene.

The actor in an Artaudian form of theatre has to grasp the fundamental, non-Stanislavskian point that it is not the truthfulness of his own feeling that is important, but that of the feelings created in the spectator. One of the dangers of the Method was the actor who throbbed with inner intensity but conveyed none of it to the audience. A pure feeling can be far less dynamic, in terms of theatrical communication, than an essential stage image, a gesture, a movement, or vocal impact. The stage image must be charged with emotion, but that emotion does not have to be "felt" in terms of the actor's personal psyche. It is a form of surface truth which, because it is inspired by and relates to fundamental human passions, touches the raw nerve of the audience. It is not limited to rational motivation, but explores the irrational core of humanity. There is danger inherent in Artaudian acting, too: actors can easily slip into nonnaturalistic sounds and gestures which are effective in themselves but not truly related to the essential, emotional quality of the action. Thus, unless the director is constantly testing, proving, questioning, and encouraging exploration, he will find himself with a practiced, cliché-ridden, basically soulless production.

Alienation: Bertolt Brecht's System

One of the most significant parts of the modern theatrical repertory is the "epic" form of theatre associated with the name Bertolt Brecht. Brecht's putative aim was to create an alienation effect with his theatre, and to this end he worked for a calculatedly presentational style of acting. The purpose of the alienation effect was to avoid the emotional empathy between actor and audience that leads the audience to identify with the character—that suspension of disbelief which Coleridge believed a fundamental element of theatre. Brecht wished to replace such visceral communication with an atmosphere in which the audience was fully aware of the theatrical (that is, nonnaturalistic) nature of the event; thus the spectators could sit back and make intellectual judgments about what was being presented to them. Brecht's theatre had a fundamentally political and sociological bias, and was geared to the instruction of the audience. It was to appeal to the mind rather than the emotions.

Brecht called his theatre anti-Aristotelian, in that it was not aimed at the production of any kind of catharsis in the audience. But in one sense it was more Aristotelian than the naturalistic theatre which preceded it, for it returned the primary emphasis to plot—in the sense of the total action of the play—and away from character. The actor trained and accustomed to performing in naturalistic theatre will have difficulty performing as a Brechtian character and will need help from the director.

Alienation has nothing to do with direct attacks on the audience or with deliberate attempts to make the audience physically uncomfortable. That would be counterproductive to Brecht's whole intention, because it either makes the audience retreat into a protective attitude and reject what is being presented to them, or it angers the audience and stimulates a visceral, emotional response which clouds their intellectual capacity. To achieve his alienating effect, the actor must take the audience with him through the story, while presenting his character in such a way as to clarify and comment on the action, so that the audience recognizes the issues at stake, rather than feeling the emotions being generated.

Obviously, to be able to present the issues and comment on them, the actor must first be clearly aware of the playwright's intention and point of view. The starting point for a director will be a discussion of the issues and the clarification of the playwright's idea. This idea will be discovered in terms of the total action of the play; motivations will be external—social and economic—rather than psychological. More rehearsals than usual may be held around a table, because there is no pressure on the actor to start "living" the role. Instead, he should be encouraged to read the play more or less objectively. The actor should confront, rather than assimilate, his character, weighing and intellectually grasping all the events of the play and the part his character plays in those events. His acquaintance with the character should result from the process of looking for its contradictions and deviations; what the character omits is as important as what it does.

In a sense the actor is in the position of the director who employs what is often disdainfully referred to as "show and tell" methods of working with actors. When such a director shows an actor how to perform certain actions, he does not transform himself into the character—it is not, after all, his character—rather he underlines the technical means of producing the effect and has the attitude of someone making a suggestion. This is the situation of the Brechtian actor in creating his character. The director should discourage his actors from any conscious attempts to generate a naturalistic atmosphere (such as the use of broken speech rhythms), and should help the actor discover those specific gestures which clearly show the audience the nature of his character in relation to its part in the action. At times the Brechtian actor speaks directly to the audience, not as in a classical soliloquy, in which the character voices his thoughts aloud but intends to communicate only with himself, but in a conscious effort to make the audience understand the implications of the situation.

The actor has an empathic relationship with his character to the extent that anyone who was describing a series of events to another person would "put himself into the situation." Brecht himself suggests that the actor should adopt the attitude of a witness describing an action that has taken place. Human beings are constantly showing each other how people behave in certain circumstances without attempting to create an illusion of reality. One simply takes on enough characteristics and portrays those actions which display the character and the event. Speaking dialogue as witnesses would in court, clarifying and underlining the important facts, is a useful rehearsal tool for the actor. Other rehearsal devices the director may employ are the adoption of the third person "he" and "she" instead of "I," which helps distance the character from the actor; the adoption of the past tense—historification works against empathic relationship; and the speaking of stage directions. All these means help alienate the text in rehearsal, and the actor will retain the quality in performance. For example, instead of simply performing the action of crossing from another character to a sofa and sitting down, the actor would say, "He gave X an angry look, walked to the sofa, hitched up his trousers, sat down and said '. . .'." Direct physical motivation can also be included in this technique: "Because he hadn't eaten, X felt faint, clutched at a table to support himself, and said, '. . .'."

The Brechtian actor never presents the emotional situation, only the unbiased narrative. Brecht's approach to directing was constantly to adjure his actors to present the plot events and the business; the mood and feeling would follow automatically. The action of the play was paramount, and the actor should always be conscious of this action as having taken place in the past. The actor presents his character to the audience from the point of view of his function within that historical context—a standpoint of social criticism. The performance is essentially a colloquy with the audience about social conditions.

The preceding historical descriptions of acting, the actor-director relationship, and the theories of Stanislavski, Barrault, Craig, Meyerhold, Copeau, Artaud, and Brecht are not presented merely for reference. They are obviously valid and in widespread use today. Nor are they limited to certain classes of plays. Conventionally, of course, a director may be expected to apply Stanislavski's techniques to *The Three Sisters* and Brecht's to *The Caucasian Chalk Circle,* but there is no absolutely compelling reason why he should do so. The plays of Harold Pinter can be rehearsed with Method techniques, and probably with Artaudian ones. Shakespeare and Samuel Beckett have been produced in every way imaginable. Even Chekhov might be refreshed by a nonnaturalistic approach, and an expressionist play by George Kaiser might be seen in a new and clear light by the use of Stanislavski's early experiments in emotional memory. Techniques are the director's choice, cognizant as he is of his acting company, the time schedule of his production, and the style he wants to achieve.

Theatre would be a dying art indeed if we were limited, in our search for means of working with actors, to the teachings of men who have been dead for many years. We have seen how Brook has used Artaud, but he has also gone beyond Artaud, and so has Grotowski. Naturalistic directors today use techniques that Stanislavski never considered and presentational directors following Bertolt Brecht expand old theories and invent new ones. We should, then, examine several entirely modern approaches to acting and directing.

Game Theory and Acting

The movement away from direct identification with character toward mimetics and display of social mask, which was given impetus by Brecht's approach, has become an attitude toward theatre in its own right with the evolution of the game theory of theatrical structure. On a psychological level this approach hypothesizes that human intercourse is a series of transactions by which we seek to maximize our pleasures; the interpretation of pleasure is wide, including what some individuals would regard as pain. These transactions are in the nature of games we play with those with whom we come into contact, and conflict arises only if the other individuals do not play by the rules.[10] An obvious example of this in theatrical terms is the scene in Albee's play *Who's Afraid of Virginia Woolf* in which George publicly kills off the imaginary son, completely altering the rules of the game and the relationship between himself and Martha that the game had helped to perpetuate.

At a more directly physical level, the understanding of play scripts as a series of games has led to the use of games as rehearsal exercises through which the actors may experience the physical nature of their actions. Because many games can express a similar action, actors can explore relationships in physical terms from many angles; this prevents their going stale from the constant repetition, within the limiting framework of a script, of the same blocked action. Through the physicalness of the games the emotional content of the action can also be reached. This, of

[10] For an examination of the psychological basis of these transactions, see Eric Berne, *Transactional Analysis in Psychotherapy* (New York: Grove Press, Inc., 1961). For a popular discussion of them, see Berne, *Games People Play* (New York: Grove Press, Inc., 1964). For an examination and illustration of the applicability of this theory to analysis of character motivation in plays, see Arthur Wagner, "Transactional Analysis and Acting," *Tulane Drama Review*, XI, No. 4 (Summer 1967), 81–88.

course, relates to Stanislavski's later theory of physical actions and the inducement of supporting feelings by playing these actions.

Some very simple examples can be taken from Oscar Wilde's *The Importance of Being Earnest*. In the first act Algy has John's cigarette case, in which is inscribed the name "Cecily." Algy refuses to return the cigarette case until John, who is loath to do so, tells him who Cecily is. Instead of arbitrarily blocking the scene and having the actors repeat the same chase again and again, the director should get at the nature of the action, exploring many physical possibilities by playing various games. "Tag" is the most obvious, with John chasing Algy around differing spatial arrangements. Then there is "Donkey in the Middle," which would involve other cast members, with John in the middle trying to catch a ball, or another object, tossed around by the other actors. "Hiding the Thimble" and "Blind Man's Bluff" would also lend themselves to this action. To add a further dimension, that of John trying to maintain his dignity during the chase, the belt could be removed from John's pants so that he would have to play the games while trying to keep his pants up.

Later in the same act, John is cross-examined by Lady Bracknell as to his social suitability to marry her daughter. The essence of this action is that John is never certain how to answer the questions, or how his answers will be taken by Lady Bracknell. A simple game which gets at the physical sense of this scene is to have John try to catch balls thrown haphazardly by Lady Bracknell and return them into a very small box. John might balance precariously on a narrow bench while playing this game. Or each time Lady Bracknell asks a question, she might hold up two cards, on one of which there is an X; if John does not guess the X card he must remove an article of clothing, or pay some similar forfeit. The lengths to which this game is taken would depend entirely on the relationship between the actors and the discretion of the director.

Ensemble and Games

The creation of an acting ensemble was the goal of the early naturalists, Stanislavski and Antoine, and also of those directors, such as Copeau, not tied down to naturalism. The concept of an ensemble is a vital one in the theatre; it suggests that the best sort of theatre is created by the intimate working together of persons who share not only professional expertise, but genuine affection, a unity of social or metaphysical philosophy, and even love for one another. Not only Copeau, but also Antoine, Stanislavski, and the American founders of the Group Theatre[11] spent entire weeks at country retreats with their acting companies to achieve this

[11] See Harold Clurman, *The Fervent Years* (New York: Hill & Wang, Inc., 1957).

purpose. Some acting companies today accomplish the same goals by living communally (or at least closely) in one form or another, and fine acting ensembles have been achieved by the Living Theatre (a traveling company under the leadership of Julian Beck and Judith Melina), the Combine Theatre of Texas, and the Company Theatre of Los Angeles. Brecht's Berliner Ensemble Company was also a group of actors bound together by social and political philosophy as much as by reciprocal individual desires or career goals.

Lacking the time, money, or will to create the kind of ensemble that can be achieved only over long months or years, the director may work to achieve it in ordinary rehearsal time. The results may possibly be as profound, although they are more difficult to achieve. One of the best methods, used by Copeau in the summer of 1913, is through the use of games. Why games? The major obstacle to the creation of an ensemble is the "adult" human reaction to emotion, which is one of suppression and repression. Even the relaxation of former puritanical attitudes toward the human body has not, as yet, entirely freed people of their inhibitions and moral phobias, and a certain amount of work with any group of actors can probably help make them aware of and free with each other, so that they can approach any relationship or action required of them within the rehearsal or performance situation with complete frankness and flexibility. These are, of course, the essential attributes of the child before social contact with the adult world teaches him to hide behind a series of masks and build defensive barriers around his imagination and emotions. The child's capacity for inventing games and play is unbounded. Part of the philosophy behind the game approach to theatre is, then, geared to the rediscovery in the human being of those capacities for human relationship and interaction that were his birthright. The actor can then become a marvelously free and spontaneous instrument, capable of responding to all the requirements of the game, with all its pleasures and utilities, which theatre essentially is.

The use of games and exercises can of itself help create the ideal ensemble of actors. We present a brief outline approach below.[12] How the games are used with actors depends somewhat on their maturity and experience. The director may encounter resistance from experienced professional actors who are used to doing things their way. In a recent production we were associated with a seasoned professional actor who told the direc-

---

[12] It is impossible to acknowledge exactly the sources of all the games and exercises, some of which are our invention, and some of which have become part of the vocabulary of acting coaches everywhere. We must, however, acknowledge the inspiration of Viola Spolin, to whom we and those of our colleagues with whom we have discussed this approach to actors owe a great debt.

Don Hamilton

Figures 68–71. Falling into the Circle

tor that he *was* experienced and "didn't need his kiddies' games." This may have been true; directors should avoid using games as an end in themselves. A professional repertory that has worked together for many months is less likely to need ensemble games than a scratch cast of university students coming together for the first time. However, if imaginatively and purposefully used, games are always interesting rehearsal tools for approaching difficult actions from a new angle. They are also, in most instances, a good way of bringing a disparate group together. Some games we have found useful follow.

Machine Game. One actor begins a physical action and is joined by other actors in turn, each relating his action to what is already happening. This game helps produce physical relationships and establish a joint rhythm. It also helps actors explore their potential in bodily movement. Use it until tendencies toward linearity and perpendicularity disappear and interesting, varied machines are produced.

Falling into the Circle. This game should be played when the director feels the group is beginning to come together. A circle is formed of about eight people standing very close together. One member stands blindfolded in the middle of the group. With his body straight and firm, he falls backward into the circle. He is then passed around and across the circle for perhaps two minutes and finally lifted and carried horizontally by the group before being returned to earth and having the blindfold removed. This is, of course, a trust exercise in which the actor is literally in his fellow actors' hands. It also gives the actor a sense of bodily freedom in space. It is excellent for bringing a group close to each other.

Melting Architecture. The actors number off. Numbers are then called and the numbered player adopts any physical posture which has some dynamic tension. Each succeeding player joins the gradually developing sculpture until all players are in contact and together form a dynamic but immobile piece of architecture with their bodies. When the last player has joined, begin the numbers again and repeat the process as No. 1 now joins with the actor who completed the first structure. The game can be continued at different speeds and with different structural orientations.

Leading Blind. This is another trust exercise in which members of the group lead each other blindfolded across a number of obstacles and let them physically explore their environment. Apart from its ensemble utility, it can give actors a new sense of props, stage furniture, and the space they are working in.

Painting with Fingers. This game helps actors lose their fear of touching each other. Using his hand as a palette and his fingers as a brush, one actor first paints his partner plain white and then, on this blank canvas, paints in a character. The partner, his eyes closed, tries to sense this character from the finger touch and then adopts the characteristics he has

Don Hamilton

Figures 72–75.   Melting Architecture

Don Hamilton

Figures 76–79. Mirror Game

sensed. With good concentration from both sides, a remarkable degree of accuracy can be achieved with groups of twenty or more.

Other good group games can be used for warm-up purposes.

Streets and Alleys. The group forms several parallel lines, members an arm's length apart. When the game leader calls "Streets" all turn to the right and hold out their arms horizontally; when he calls "Alleys" all turn left and do the same. Meanwhile, two members of the group chase each other in and out of the changing lines.

Numbers Change. The actors sit in a circle and number off. One member, in the middle, calls two numbers. Those called must change places before the caller reaches one of their positions.

Slap. The group sits in a circle, in the middle of which are an empty bucket and a three-foot length of rolled newspaper. One member takes the newspaper and walks outside the circle, tapping everyone lightly and then striking someone harder. He must then return the newspaper to the bucket and get to the "slapee's" place before he himself is slapped with the newspaper by the "slapee."

All the games described above may be used in early rehearsal periods, to warm up a cast before performances, or to bring change of pace to rehearsals that are becoming boring. Their use will depend on the director's sense of the needs of his cast, and the progress of rehearsals.

Certain other games and exercises are especially useful to a director when group concentration slackens.

Mirror Game. Members face each other in twos (or in groups of four or more, but it is simpler to begin in twos). One actor is to be a mirror image of the other's actions and reflect all his bodily and facial expressions. The level of concentration can be observed in the precision of the imitation. This game can be extended to the repetition of common actions, and finally to improvisations based on the actions discovered.

Maintaining Your Argument. Two actors sit opposite each other and talk about separate topics of their choosing. The aim is to maintain one's line of reasoning without being overborne or drawn in to the other person's argument. A variation is to have members of a small group whistle different tunes, each maintaining his tune against all others.

No Motion. An excellent physical concentration exercise is to have the group "explode" out of itself into any physical pose, then alter pose imperceptibly while concentrating on not moving. This game is also excellent practice for control of bodily movement in the case of physically undisciplined actors.

Improvisation

Discussion of the ways of working informally with an ensemble leads directly to our last method, that of working with actors in a totally

Don Hamilton

Figures 80–83. No Motion/Explosions

improvisatory manner. Improvisation was the basis of one of the most exciting acting forms in the sixteenth and seventeenth centuries—the Commedia dell' Arte—and then was lost until redeveloped by Stanislavski at the beginning of the twentieth century. Stanislavski used improvisation as a rehearsal tool for penetrating a difficult action by allowing the actor to exercise his personal approach on an analogous situation. The actor's experience was then channeled back into the action contained within the text. Today the use of improvisation has been extended in two directions: creating a play entirely from improvisations on ideas, and improvising around a text without imposing any external form or preconceptions on the actors. We shall explore the contemporary use of improvisation at some length because it is an increasingly common technique which can, however, if improperly applied, lead to misunderstandings between actors and directors.

Improvisation without a text makes the greatest possible demands on an actor's imagination: ability to give and take with his fellows and to play actions with immediacy and spontaneity. The director's job is to maintain a free, open, creative atmosphere, to stimulate the imagination of his actors, and to select and refine the work from the many possibilities which are evolved. All improvisation sessions should start with games and exercises (such as those outlined for ensemble work) which are calculated to relax the group and start them working together as a responsive unit, heightening their concentration. Improvisation can evolve from the exercises themselves; the mirror game can lead to the discovery of an action which can ultimately be extended to a completely improvised scene. The director should always have a definite starting point in mind for a rehearsal session. If improvisations are not to be extensions of games or exercises, then some theme should be the focus for the actors' exploratory improvisations.

Exploratory Improvisations

Themes are extremely varied. They can be taken from an exploration of a particular human sense: touch, for example, can start with exploration of different textures and can lead to scenes involving the buying and selling of goods, surgical operations, creating sculpture, and various tasks around the home—making cookies, cleaning rooms, and so on. Smell can be developed from a simple concentration on a particular perfume, flower, or gas into scenes situated in beauty salons, fashionable soirées, parks, zoos, or coal mines. Scenes can also be built around pieces of music, items of news taken from the papers, or photographs and paintings.

Beware of having preconceived notions of where an improvisation should lead. One of the great virtues of improvisation is the new light it can shed on apparently clichéd situations. This is particularly valuable when working on a play text. The director should have a fine sense of when an improvisation has, in fact, broken down and when the actors are simply taking their time to explore the situation before coming up with fresh actions. The director can stimulate and influence the course of an improvisation by sending a new actor into the situation to play an objective which will produce a new conflict, or by introducing new props, or by changing the climatic environment—rain, snow, boiling sun, and so on. What the director should not do is alter an actor's character or objective in mid-improvisation. The challenge to the actor should come from outside circumstances and actions which allow him to originate an honest response.

Improvising on a Text

The approach to improvising to create a new theatrical event and improvising on an already-written text is fundamentally the same, the ostensible distinction being that in the latter instance the actor will ultimately communicate to the audience the playwright's words and actions, not those he has originated. In fact, the playwright's words and actions should have so totally become those of the actor that there is no difference in the spontaneity of the two events. This is the goal of the use of extensive improvisation on a text.

Spontaneity is often blocked by tension. Tension can arise in many ways: by an actor's being pressured to perform before he has a visceral sense of his part; by his consciousness that he is in artificial "stage circumstances"; by his being physically hampered by holding a script; by his being imaginatively circumscribed by reading a playwright's words without feeling the actions they arise from; and by his being blocked into rigid patterns of movement by a director who has a firmly preconceived idea of the only way to produce a play. Freeing the actor from these inhibitions is part of a director's responsibility, and a method which is increasingly employed is that of the non–script-holding, non-preblocking improvisational exploration of the text.

The text is the reduction into words of the flesh and blood action visualized in the author's imagination. In producing a play we have to rediscover that organic action, but not by learning the lines by rote and moving through spatial patterns which, however sensitively and honestly thought out, arise from the imagination of one man, rather than from the total experiencing of the text by all the players. Improvisation brings the actor a feeling for the author's text and the character's thoughts, actions, and moves, which in turn bring out the playwright's words, because now the actor feels and understands that no other words would serve his exact intention.

The actor's learning process should assimilate the idea behind the text, not just the lines. It involves his understanding the text with his whole person, physical and emotional as well as intellectual. Some say that this is hopelessly idealistic, that professional theatre allows no time for such extraneous activity. Indeed, in the old weekly repertory system in which the actor was performing one play, rehearsing another, and learning a third in any given week, he could do little more than to pull number 21 from his bag of tricks and hope that he remembered enough to get by (in itself this is a game of some improvisatory potential!). But today the average three or four week rehearsal situation permits exploration and improvisation. Even so, some actors and directors feel that learning lines is boring. "Get them out of the way, and then get down to the play." They ignore that the lines are their only indication of what the play is, and that they cannot learn lines in a vacuum—a character attitude is learned with the lines. Such an attitude, then, tends to circumscribe further exploration of the possibilities beneath and around the lines. Nor does it allow free character interaction in a rehearsal situation.

IMPROVISING IN REHEARSAL: A POSSIBLE MODEL

During the first stage in improvising around a text, the actors gain an overall grasp of the play. Every cast member should be fully aware of every aspect of the text so that he may play his part not as an isolated series of actions, but in relationship to the rest of the play. Actors too often have no interest in scenes in which their characters do not appear, and only marginal interest in characters to which they do not directly relate in their scenes. The first reading of the play should, then, be geared to gaining a sense of it as a whole. Actors should not read the parts they will ultimately be playing, and parts can be changed frequently as the play is read through.

During the second reading of the play the same principle as to the distribution of parts can hold, but the reading will be interrupted by discussion of how the play works. This discussion is an examination not of psychological attitudes and subtextual motivations, but of how the playwright has built the play: why certain scenes follow others, what the crucial actions are, on how many levels the play is operating, how the climax and denouement are achieved. Attention is concentrated on essentials, and notes should be kept, perhaps by the stage manager, of the points agreed on by the group. The actors should also keep notes of the progression of the play; key words will often suffice. The notes will help the actor in later rehearsals by marking the significant actions, conflicts, and tensions in the text as they create the flow of the work. Each actor should take notes on the whole play, the nature of the notes depending on his individual preference, except that the significance of the actions should be generally agreed on.

Rehearsals can now begin without scripts in hand, the actor having his simple key outline to refer to if necessary. Scenes are worked through with improvised dialogue and movement, again, at first, with no actor playing exclusively his final part. It is also interesting and useful to break the cast into groups, each working separately on the same scenes, which they later present to each other. In this way enormously varied possibilities can be found for any part of the text. While the actors should be encouraged to rely as much as possible only on their key outlines, there will at first be times when the actors stray too far from the textual skeleton, or get lost and dry up. At such times the text itself should be consulted, not in terms of what *lines* come next, but what *action*. The actors should approach the text with questions such as, "Why are we in this situation? How do we get from here to such and such a climax?"

When the actors are reasonably familiar with the flow of the play and can run through it using their own words with only brief reference to their key outlines, improvisations should be undertaken to create the general atmosphere of the play and of actions which relate to but do not occur within the text. For example, with a play such as *The Importance of Being Earnest,* which requires truthful representation of social manners and conventions, a general discussion of these, based on period research into upper-class life, would have taken place during the first readings. Now improvisations can be played out to create the atmosphere of tea parties (with cucumber sandwiches), dinners, soirées, and formal balls. More specific improvisations could include Miss Prism creating the circumstances of her loss of the baby John Worthing (which will make her final speech much more real for her); Canon Chasuble preaching one of his "unpublished sermons" at his country church; and John and Algy on a night out at their club. In these specific circumstances the actors who are actually to play the characters would adopt their roles.

As work on character begins, animal improvisations can help provide a physical and gestural sense of the characters. Again, this can be done jointly by the group and then discussed so that many possible facets of all the characters are revealed. Another group game useful for character exploration is "Essences." The characters are discussed in terms of nonhuman objects: what cloth texture, fruit, color, precious stone, or the like is closest to the essential nature of the character. This produces interesting insights and physical images which an actor working alone on his character might ignore, for each person involved sees the characters from slightly different perspectives.

By this time rehearsals may be one-third over, depending of course on the director and the structure he is creating: how far he is manipulating the progress of the rehearsals and driving them along as opposed to having no preconceptions and working totally from what is discovered in rehearsal. Both methods are valid, but experience seems to show that actors work more efficiently if each rehearsal session has a general sense of guidance from the director and a specific focus. This does not mean that the director refuses to alter his original ideas; it simply means that he should have some basic but flexible attitudes toward the play. At this point the director should tell the cast when he expects them to be thoroughly conversant with the playwright's lines. While the improvisatory sessions have been taking place the actors have been reading the text on their own time, so that their physical and emotional understanding of it, gained from improvisation, is channeled into the playwright's lines as they are assimilated, rather than committed to memory, by the actors. For the next rehearsal period more specific work on character is done—concentration on smaller units of the play at greater depth. Actions are still being explored improvisationally to discover their most organic and truthful spatial representation, but increasingly the scenes will take a specific form as the actors fall comfortably into the movements and relationships arising from their now visceral understanding of the action.

Problems continue to arise during this period and questions are asked, and the text must be constantly searched for answers. The director, too, asks questions to make his actors clarify their understanding of motivations, actions, and physical responses. The actors may come up with answers which differ from the director's understanding of the circumstances. Then the director decides whether the actors' natural responses have given them a correct intuition, or whether they have misunderstood the situation, in which case further questioning may correct their approach. Letting the actor find the answer by asking him pertinent questions is always preferable to giving him a solution which he may perform but not understand.

The last third of the rehearsal period is devoted to running through the play for continuity, flow, and pace, and to introducing the final settings, properties, and costumes. It is important, however, that fairly accurate simulations of these final elements have been employed throughout the rehearsal period. The same principle applies to lighting and sound, which should be integrated gradually, not suddenly lumped on at a mammoth "tech" rehearsal a few days before opening night. If possible, members of the stage management and technical staff should have been involved in early improvisations so that they too will have had the experience of discovering the play's needs, as did the actors. The technical elements of the play should then be built into the production in the same rhythm and flow as are the actor and the text.

If the organic assimilation of lines with actions has been complete, there should be no need for prompting during the last rehearsals; in fact, there should be no prompter. The company should know that when a difficulty arises, all the actors must help the one whose concentration has lapsed. Their complete knowledge of the play will facilitate this, but if a complete blank occurs, then the run should be stopped and the action—not the words—examined to determine the problem.

As always, one of the director's prime tasks in relation to his actors is to maintain a relaxed yet positive atmosphere. One of the dangers inherent in the improvisational approach is that focus on the final purpose —a performance—can be lost. Actors can become self-indulgent and idle if the game sense predominates rather than being used as a tool or structure for a clearly defined purpose. So the director must be sensitive to the working climate, constantly able to relax tensions or to stimulate creativity by introducing new ideas and challenges. The discipline of an improvisatory group is not imposed from without, but arises from the concentration on and enthusiasm for the task at hand. Should there be any tendency toward boredom or repetitive work in the last rehearsal days, when the actor feels the need of an audience but the production is not quite ready for one, then the director can run part of the play in another style: melodrama, operatic, Nō. This freshens interest and often, even at a late rehearsal stage, leads the actor to new discoveries.

Working on a text improvisationally can be said to have the advantages of establishing immediate contact between actors and with the pulse of the play. The holding of texts inevitably hinders physical exploration and eye contact. Words get in the way of the sense. The mechanical process of keeping one's place and watching for cues dominates the organic process of listening, feeling, and responding. Texts which are improvised on should become more vital and fully-fleshed, and actors more aware and responsive. The caveat of this technique is that it is a delicate one which means great responsibility for both actor and director. Actors at first feel the lack of any security—no lines or blocking to hold onto—and the director must furnish that security by creating an open, sensitive, ensemble atmosphere. While establishing this mutual trust and respect, the director must unobtrusively move the rehearsals in a positive direction by producing a wealth of creative challenges to the actors, calculating their responses in terms of the play, and finally being flexible without losing his way and allowing rehearsals to deteriorate into aimless, self-indulgent meanderings with no forward progress.

Auditions and Casting

Unless he has been working with the same company for some time, the first contact the director is likely to have with his actors is at the auditions for the production. It is ironic that the moment of casting, when the director needs to know most about his actors, is when he probably knows least. Each director has a different approach to auditions, but there are some general truths. First, take as much time as possible. Of course, in certain professional situations where time is money, the "cattle-call" principle of two minutes per person means making quick assessments. Presumably agents assist by sending out on call only those who have some chance for a part. But the danger in snap judgment is not so much of missing a real talent who reads badly, as it is of choosing a slick cold-reader who has nothing else to give. One is reminded of the young director who addressed an actress of *un certain âge* with, "It's coming nicely, dear," only to be told, "What do you mean, *coming?* This is it!"

Whenever possible at an audition the director should try to penetrate beyond the actor's prepared reading, by asking him to redo it with a different objective, to work against the text, or simply to physicalize the situation without dialogue. Small improvisations can also test an actor's imagination and reveal his emotional/physical range. Do not accept what you see on the surface, even if it appears perfect. Obvious physical suitability for a part is not enough, by itself. Ours is, after all, a craft of tricks and illusions; things can become other than they seem.

Of course, physical suitability must be a part of casting; it is unlikely that a 130-pound stripling would be cast as Falstaff even though, as the adage has it, in every thin man there is a fat man trying to get out (and John Gielgud, a comparative lightweight, has played the part with distinction). Actual physical attributes should be weighed against actable physical attributes and the actor's essential, *qua* person, suitability for a part. Nor is the director casting any single part in isolation from the others; the total physical and temperamental balance of the cast must be considered. In one production of *The Taming of the Shrew* both Petruchio and Katherina were very small people with enormous energy. Their very lack of stature gave a definition to their relationship in unusual terms—they constantly stood out from the much bigger and calmer actors who surrounded them.

By clever casting a director can add dimensions to his production. However, he should beware of casting decisions which seem amusing at first but finally destroy some of the values of the play. For example, if Petruchio were very small while Katherina towered above him, this would initially increase the farcical elements of certain scenes, but ultimately it would destroy the truth of their relationship in the play as a whole.

It is always safer, of course, to cast by type. In amateur theatre this is nearly always the practice. Certain roles call for visual stereotypes. Stanley Kowalski demands an actor with a strong physique and an obvious sexual animalism. An intellectual, puny Stanley would simply destroy the play. By the same token Jimmy Porter, who projects a similar hectoring dynamism and is obviously attractive to women, should not have a bull-like physique, but is much more effective played as a thin, live electric wire constantly giving off sparks. A director should be aware when he attends auditions of the typical qualities he is looking for in a character, and then he may consciously cast against type in the full knowledge of how it will change the play. This is then his interpretive and stylistic decision, the ramifications of which should be clearly understood from the start.

It is not enough to make atypical choices in the cause of half-baked social experimenting, as did one director of our acquaintance who cast a twenty-year-old girl as a sixty-year-old man, and a twenty-two-year-old girl as his daughter, in a naturalistic production. His spurious rationale was that he believed men and women to be fundamentally the same and it "ought" not make any difference on the stage. He managed to solve his theatrical problem (when he discovered it did make a difference) by playing all the old man's scenes with the man seated, back to the audience—it even acheived an extra enigmatic dimension—but the absurdity of the original choice remained to restrict and haunt him.

One of the most interesting casting problems today is that of multi-color casting in plays written for a particular ethnic group. This raises problems the director must answer according to his sense of life and theatre. He should, however, be aware of the problems and not naïvely pretend that black, white, and brown people are the same color, or that color does not carry associations for an audience. For example, would Shakespeare's *Othello* be the same played by a white Othello and an all-black supporting cast? Does not color have a special significance in this play? The same problem would arise in Leroi Jones's *The Dutchman* if the director chose to cast a black girl and a white man, where the play specifies the opposite. Would not the play suffer? In the Minnesota Theatre Company production of August Strindberg's *Dance of Death* (1966) a brother and sister were played by actors of strikingly different races. Though this may have accomplished a worthwhile social goal, it totally confused the audience, who were left wondering whether the boy and girl were half-siblings, illegitimate offspring, or mutants. Since the play spoke to none of this confusion, the audience was engaged in irrelevant considerations during major portions of the play's action. The play suffered.

It may well be that we will one day achieve a social climate in which color has absolutely no significance, but that time has yet to come, and one wonders if an audience's suspension of disbelief would extend so far as to accept a family of two white parents and a black child, or vice versa. We feel that in the classical plays which are concerned more with human absolutes than with particulars, it is possible to cast almost irrespective of color, as long as the director observes any special premises the play might have (such as *Othello*) and does not run too patently against genetic possibilities. We should work *with* certain human differences, rather than pretend they do not exist. But there seems no reason, for example, why Shakespeare's heroes cannot be played by black actors. That Henry V was historically white is not as important as the poetic statement Shakespeare was making about heroism and kingship.

Given the personal nature of such casting choices, a director can do certain very practical things when auditioning actors, which help limit the areas of uncertainty. First, he should study the actor's portfolio, which will indicate the range of the actor's work and enable him to assess the audition against a wider perspective. This avoids too easy a dismissal of a poor first-reader who has an impressive list of credits. Second, all actors should fill out an audition sheet giving personal particulars including, where applicable, whether they are willing to cut their hair and appear nude. The bottom of this sheet should contain a space for the director's remarks about vocal range, physical movement, and so on, and for a tentative list of roles the actor could play. These tentative decisions can be reconciled on a large casting sheet so that at callbacks the director has a clear picture of his alternatives. Finally, if a director knows and trusts the judgment of a fellow director with whom an actor has worked, it would be useful to consult that director on the actor's creative range and methods of working.

Summary: Working with Actors

When the director has discussed all the alternatives and examined the ramifications of all his choices, he has explored only how he *can* work with actors—not how he *should*. This will always be a personal relationship which cannot be accurately prescribed. Each director's approach will be a function of his personality, as is each actor's. Some actors are quick boilers and the director's problem will be to prevent their going stale while other, slower workers are brought up to their level. A director, always conscious of the final needs of the play, should try to work with an actor in his own rhythm, not forcing him to give a performance before he is ready. The director's main responsibility to the actor is to create the best possible climate in which the actor can build his character in the context mutually agreed on.

Drawing a performance from an actor is always preferable to imposing an interpretation on him. Showing an actor how to perform an action is a last resort, after all other explorations have failed. The director must try to understand the nature of the problems which may be blocking the actor's performance. In a production of *The Bespoke Overcoat* a young actor was having difficulty with an action which involved putting on an overcoat on stage. This action was a triumphant culmination of the character's career, but the young actor could never achieve the sense of fulfillment: his movements were small, jerky, and hurried. Questioning by the director revealed the problem to be that the actor was treating the overcoat as a physical obstacle to be overcome. He feared that it would take too long to put on, that he would miss the sleeves, and so on. Only when he was brought to see the action as a moment to enjoy, when he saw that he could take as much time with the action as his level of enjoyment would support, did he relax and fill out the moment to the size it required. No amount of showing the actor how to put on the overcoat would have been effective; it was the total understanding of the gesture that released him.

Why is a terribly important word for the director. If there is one simple word with which to conclude a chapter on working with the actor, it is *why*. The director should constantly explore and question himself, and the actor when necessary. Only by a complete mutual understanding, which need not always be stated, can actor and director work together toward the final good of the play and the satisfaction of each other's creative aims.

IV
Style

10

Styling the Play

Style in theatre has too often been associated with the given way in which a certain type of play should be performed. None of the terms *Greek* style, *Shakespearean* style, or, more broadly still, *Classical* style means exactly the same thing to any two actors or directors, but all are based on conventions handed down through the centuries as to how the plays were originally performed or have come to be performed in the tradition of the theatre. This element of tradition was especially typical of French theatre; Louis Jouvet tells of the respect paid to a certain director's interpretation of Molière because his umpteenth-great-grandfather had seen Molière perform three centuries before. Told by that director that Molière would have disliked his (Jouvet's) production of a Molière play, Jouvet is said to have replied, "Oh, really, do you have Molière's telephone number?" In English theatre, a Shakespearean style of acting too often meant the adoption of an artificially rhetorical manner of speaking and the striking of heroic poses. All of this is the imitation of a form without relationship to its content. It is nothing more than the use of empty, calculated mannerisms—and it is not "style."

This is not to say that Greek, Shakespearean, and French neoclassical theatre had no style. It is likely that each had a clearly recognizable style, compounded of certain fixed elements. Theatre and the society it depicted during those periods were very homogeneous, and the combination of a fixed set of social and moral attitudes with a given dramatic form and theatrical configuration is likely to have produced a clearly defined, consistent style in each period. At best we can make only an educated guess about that style; our world is very different from theirs. Style may have been a given in those structured, conventional, homogeneous theatrical periods, but it is no longer so in our faithless, fractured, highly variegated existence. Although it is conceivable that, at a sufficient remove in time, certain general characteristics of the mid-twentieth century may be defined as its style, we who live in the mid-twentieth century have the impression of a disjunctive and highly differentiated social ethos.

In theatre today all is open to choice. Few speak of "the" way to do a play, and the concept of a definitive production dwells in the realm of Platonic fantasies. Unlike the Elizabethan or Greek playwright, we can choose from a variety of theatrical spaces. A wide repertory of plays from many periods and countries is at our disposal. Our age rejects rather than respects tradition; form is less important than feeling, and intellect is subordinate to impact. To feel that the correct way of producing a play is to recapture the "style" of centuries past is not only absurd, it is now not even regarded as desirable. Style has become an elective rather than a given; the contemporary artist interprets a play from the standpoint of today, combining his sense of the present with his appreciation of the reality of the time in which the play was written. The style he evolves results from his combination of the controllable factors, space, actors, scenic effects, and text, to communicate his interpretation to the audience.

Style should not be confused with form. Form is the recognizable externals; style is the way they are arranged to produce a certain effect. It is said that style is the man himself, the revelation in action of true inner character. We talk of a person's life style, by which we mean everything from the food he eats through the people with whom he associates to the clothes he wears and the moral choices he makes. How people walk, talk, drive a car, and wear their clothes creates their style. It is not the clothes or cars or food by themselves (although the individual's choices reveal something of himself) so much as how they are worn, driven, and eaten or prepared. An old song says, "It ain't what you do, it's the way that you do it." A woman with a given body (form) can project erotic, athletic, or motherly qualities depending on how she clothes and uses her body. Her sense of self, the expression of an inner essence, is enhanced by the externals—clothes, makeup, and hair style—and she reveals her feelings about herself and her relationship to the world through them; but it is the essence that animates the externalities; they do not create the essence. Two women with similar bodies and clothes can have completely different personal styles. Again, this is all contingent on the acceptance of continually changing conventions. The erotic woman of the 1950s projected her quality by wearing tight clothing, heavy makeup, and bouffant hair styles, while her equally erotic sister in the 1970s wears flowing garments lightly emphasizing her body's freedom, an utterly simple hair style, and a face bare of makeup but aglow with vibrant health. The basic quality of the two women is similar, but we need to understand the conventions of the two periods to appreciate the true essence of each.

This leads us to suggest that, as with interpretation, there is an intrinsic and extrinsic style for a given play. The intrinsic style comes from the text, the extrinsic from the director. The intrinsic includes both fixed and flexible elements. The fixed are what we know of the original theatrical architecture, the size of the audience, the sophistication of lighting and scenic devices, the costuming, and the technical presentation of the play, all of which affect its style of production. The flexible are those subjective elements which rely on human interpretation: the social, political, and moral attitudes of the playwright's day, the acting style, and the text itself, which, as works of dramatic criticism indicate, can mean many things to many people. The distinction between historical periods and dramatic forms is often broad enough to be useful in determining intrinsic styles of plays.

Intrinsic Style

Let us take as an example the difference between the performance style of a Shakespearean play and one of Jean Baptiste Racine, a neoclassical dramatist. Shakespeare wrote in flexible yet powerfully controlled blank verse; his concern was to take a broad look at life with many scenes and sweeping movement. His plays were performed out of doors, between heaven and hell, surrounded by teeming humanity. The occasion was full of noise, color, smell, and movement. A Racine play was performed before a small, highly select audience, in a wooden auditorium in which the spoken lines had the quality of chamber music; all-important were the tone and pitch of the voice and the economy of movement and gesture, so that nothing should trouble the air but beautiful sound and rare motion.[1] Nothing could be more different than the intrinsic styles of

---

[1] Michel St.-Denis, *Theatre: The Rediscovery of Style* (New York: Theatre Arts Books, 1969), p. 21.

the worlds of these two plays. The director need not be hidebound by this knowledge, but he should be aware of it before he produces Racine in an outdoor amphitheatre with actors whose experience is restricted to naturalistic dialogue.

In speaking of intrinsic style we are not suggesting that a play can "speak for itself," or that one should "play the lines." Today the words of any classical play are no more than ciphers on a piece of paper. They cannot tell us how the play was brought to life. And if we allow the text to speak, it will say different things to different actors and directors. The words are simply the end of the dramatist's creative process, which was itself a function of a need to express himself about certain attitudes and situations of his experience. We need to understand something of those attitudes, of the theatrical environment of his day, and of how the words sound, with pitch, tone, and rhythm, in the mouths of living actors. Then we can get a feeling for the intrinsic style of the play, which reflects the playwright. We do this not because we wish to repeat this style—time and attitudes have moved on; the audience, though it has a common humanity, has a different set of expectations, and the actors, though they have a common artistic sensibility, have different standards and techniques. We do it because it is important to start with an understanding of what a play *has* said, its essential quality in its time, before moving on to what it might say for us. To ignore this intrinsic element is to run the risk of a warped, meretricious, or hollow production.

Extrinsic Style

What a play might be made to say, of course, is part of its extrinsic style. The creation of extrinsic style begins with the assumption that the theatre is a living thing, its function communication in the present, not embalmment and preservation of the past. Certain elements are constant and certain fundamental truths are present in all dramatic activity, but at the same time, life is constantly moving and fluctuating, and the actor and audience are subjected to the influence of their day: the amending of moral postulates, the alteration of social attitudes, and the influence of technology on art, in television, cinema, and other media. No director can be entirely uninfluenced by the period in which he lives, and even a conscious attempt to re-create the original style of a play must inevitably contain subjective elements. If this were not so, then directors would not be necessary, for it is a director's function to use his creative faculties, and he expresses his sense of his world in the choices he makes while doing this. The creative director does not resist this subjectivity, but examines it and uses it in achieving his play's style of presentation.

Extrinsic style is the manner in which the director projects to the audience what he wishes to say through the vehicle of the play. It is *interpretation in action*. Through the style of a production a director communicates as completely and immediately as possible his sense of what the play has to say for his audience and his time. It is not in any sense arbitrary; it relates to the intrinsic values of the text without being bound by them and projects, in a vital and contemporaneous manner, what the director feels is of interest and moment in the play.

Creating Style

To make a clear statement through style, a director must have a consistent idea of what that style is to be. He does not simply break eggs into a bowl, whip them up, and pour them into a pan without knowing whether he wants an omelet, a soufflé, or plain scrambled eggs. A clean, effective style is achieved only by the consistent interrelationship of the world of the play, the world of the audience, and the world of the stage. The world of the play is its intrinsic style. To understand the world of the play, the director must know something of its historical background and the background of the author. The research should cover both the time in which the play was first produced and the period in which it is set. It should cover not only the nature of the stage at that time—costumes and physical plant—but also the social, political, and philosophical attitudes of the day. Research will help the director gain a sense of the playwright's background; knowing something of his personal tastes and feelings will be useful in gaining a sense of how and why the play was written. Works of criticism can be useful by suggesting levels of interpretation that may not be immediately apparent. They should be used discriminatingly, however, and rejected if they appear to be imposing, rather than deriving, interpretation. Criticism can also help the director understand the structure of the play: whether it has a dynamic build, with a series of short scenes all driving toward a climax, as in *Macbeth;* or whether the tendency is toward circularity, as in *Waiting for Godot,* with steady, repetitive, harmonic progression. The director can reflect this essential quality of the play's form in movement patterns, creating a part of the style of performance.

Another part of the world of the play which must be explored in any attempt to derive its intrinsic style is the actual content: what the text tells us. The characters' mode of life is indicated by the environment suggested by the playwright; this can be very explicit, as with Shaw and Ibsen, or simply implicit in the historical period and social stratum of the characters. The language of the play may be naturalistic or poetic, as may the action, which can depend on the amassing of detail or the creation of symbolic effects. The language of the play may be more important than physical action (as in Racine). The action itself may be inherently comic, tragic, or melodramatic. A director must at least be aware of all these factors if he wishes to gain a sense of the intrinsic style of the play. Just as the nature of a production depends on a series of choices made by the director, so the intrinsic style of the play is the result of a series of choices, conscious and unconscious, made by the playwright. The unconscious choices result from the playwright's reaction to his society, and we may determine them through research; the conscious choices appear in the play and must be derived from analysis of all its components. No matter when the play was written, the process for gaining a sense of its intrinsic style is the same. Once the director understands or has a feeling for this essence, he can translate it into whatever style he believes will best relate it to the world of his audience.

The world of the audience is partly a given, but there are certain variables. The givens are that set of circumstances and attitudes which compose the contemporary social character, in the broadest sense. In the United States in the 1970s this might be a complex of concern for the state of the economy, antiwar sentiment, increasing desire for self-definition on the part of ethnic minorities, examination of long-accepted values of "Americanism," and a sense of despair at the hollowness of existence. It will also reflect the physical mode of living: houses and furnishings, clothes, extensive use of cars, omnipresence of television. Aside from these givens there will be variables depending on the more or less esoteric nature of the specific audience attending the play. For example, attitude toward war is likely to differ between a middle-aged, middle-class, Republican audience and a youthful, draft card–burning student audience. A black ghetto audience is likely to find different values in *Othello* from those which move an all-white audience. As he determines what sort of impact he wishes to make, and thus the style of his production, the director must consider both the given and the variable circumstances in the world of his audience; otherwise he may find that his result is contrary to his intention.

The director can create a style which relates to both the world of the play and the world of his audience, and reveals the statement he wishes to make, not by warping the text, but by translating its intrinsic essence into terms which will be readily understood, and assimilated by his audience. His means of translation is, of course, the world of the stage.

The world of the stage includes all the elements which physically constitute a production: the scenic space, the settings, the lighting, the costumes, the music or sound effects, and the actors' bodies, voices, and gestures. The director's task in molding all these elements into a production is to see that they are all consistent with each other and with the style he has chosen to convey his idea of the play. Any inconsistency makes a specific statement of its own. A director may wish to depart from the consistent pattern, in which case the aberration becomes part of his style, and he must be consistent in creating inconsistencies!

Unwitting inconsistency will work against the impact and the success of the production. For example, suppose the director of a Shakespearean production has chosen to play up the poetic values of the verse, and all but one of the actors are achieving a Gielgud-like, mellifluous flow. If one actor attempts to turn the verse into prose with "natural" breaks and nonmetrical intervals, he will obviously stand out from the rest and break the style. Even if his deviation were intended to make a character statement, it is a very crude way of doing so. We do not mean that one cannot choose to give a "natural" flavor to Shakespeare's language—Nicol Williamson did just that in a 1969 production of *Hamlet,* and was highly acclaimed in some quarters—but the director should know what impression he wishes to make by this means.

Style Informs the Whole Production

Once determined, style should inform the entire production, down to the manner of accomplishing scene changes and whether the audience is allowed to leave the play for a ten-minute cup of coffee. The director cannot work from scene to scene and from element to element, hoping for the best. He cannot achieve the best without a clear sense of what he wants to say and how he proposes to say it. A rigid concept and style need not be determined before rehearsals begin and imposed on the production. Sometimes the style evolves from exploration of the text by actors, designers, and director working in concert. Assuming the luxury of unlimited rehearsal time, this would be a way of ensuring a highly integrated production; but the exploration would still take the path of discovering the intrinsic values of the text and relating them to how the actors and production staff feel about *their* world, and what they wish to convey to the audience. The procedure is different but the purpose is the same, whether one is putting on *King Lear* in three and a half weeks, or *The Room* in three and a half months. The director must discover the intrinsic values of a play and communicate them in a manner to which his contemporary audience can relate and respond. To do this with clarity and dynamic impact requires the consistent relationship of all the elements of production in the creation of the style which has evolved from all the other considerations.

Historical Styles

Let us now discuss various stylistic possibilities and attempt to show the results of various directorial choices in the creation of style.

THE PERIOD IN WHICH THE PLAY IS SET

Setting Shakespeare's *Julius Caesar* in Roman times, or Racine's *Phaedre* in ancient Greece, means that the intrinsic style of the play would not be the same as that chosen for its production. Shakespeare's play was written for an Elizabethan stage, for performance in Elizabethan costume (possibly with minor "Roman" accents), by actors who were observing the vocal and gestural conventions of their day. The values of the play are Elizabethan, and no attempt would have been made to achieve any realism of Roman effect. Thus a director who attempts a production of *Julius Caesar* set authentically in the first century B.C. has a great deal of extrinsic work ahead. We presume that he has a clear idea of the values he wishes to enhance by setting the play in a chronologically exact period; to do this merely as a historical exercise is to do little more than present the costume designer with a limited challenge, and to court a boring production. Perhaps the director feels that the poetry of the play is weak, that greater realism will enhance and project the action of a physically dynamic play, and will make a stronger statement, for a contemporary audience, about the nature of political power.

To create the authentic effect he is seeking, the director will need to explore the architecture, sculpture, music, clothing, weapons, food—in short, the whole social climate of the period—as well as its moral and political attitudes. Knowledge of the tastes and feelings of the historical Caesar, Brutus, Anthony, and Cassius will help the director flesh out both his characters and his action. The acting style for such a production would probably attempt a seeming naturalness within the costume and scenery; the actors should appear at home there. This would be different in nature, but not in effect, from their seeming at home in a contemporary living room; they would forgo heroic pose and rhetorical delivery, for after all, in their day Caesar and his contemporaries were men, not legends inflated by the passage of 2000 years.

As he makes stylistic choices in terms of costume, setting, acting style, and so on, the director knows that he is emphasizing certain elements of Shakespeare's play to the exclusion of others. In our Roman *Julius Caesar*, he is likely to lose poetry and an absolute sense of stature for his more immediate, physically dynamic, and solid impact, but he does it consciously. He is not ignoring the intrinsic nature of the play; rather, he seeks to add historical depth and clarity and by his choice of style to project the import of the play in fuller and more immediately recognizable terms.

THE PERIOD IN WHICH THE PLAY WAS WRITTEN AND PRODUCED

Consider *Henry V* as it might have been produced at the Globe Theatre in Shakespeare's day, re-creating as nearly as possible the conditions of Elizabethan performance. This involves an attempt to illustrate and project the intrinsic style of the play, presumably in full knowledge of the obstacles occasioned by the passage of time. The director who takes this approach has probably chosen to discover what the impact of the play might have been in original production. This is perhaps a historical experiment, but it can have interesting results and audience appeal if there is a wholehearted attempt to carry the audience back into the atmosphere of a theatrical experience in Shakespeare's time. The director is trying to project what he believes to have been Shakespeare's purpose in writing the play. Interpretation is involved, of course, for there can be no neutral production, and two directors adopting Elizabethan style might have different ideas of what Shakespeare was saying. But with a sense of the play's intrinsic values, by creating an extrinsic style the director hopes to cross the gulf in time and reach his audience with the impact (in the case of *Henry V*) of the color, pageantry, vigorous action, and heroic patriotism within the play.

Laurence Olivier, in his film version of *Henry V,* made the world of the play so alive and vital that it reached its contemporary audience and swept it along on the flood of events. Summer Shakespeare festivals in the United States, such as Ashland in Oregon and the Utah Festival, take pains to create as authentic an Elizabethan atmosphere as research and scholarship allow. Besides using outdoor stages which are reconstructions of the Elizabethan stage, with direct actor-audience contact, these festivals entertain their audiences with Elizabethan dancing and music, and suitably clad "wenches" sell oranges, horehounds, and other Elizabethan delicacies. When such effects are executed sincerely and with artistic purpose, as is usually the case at Shakespeare festivals, they can help greatly to set the mood for an audience and introduce them more fully into the world of the play and the style of the total theatrical event. In such cases style is created by the atmospheric adjuncts as much as by the play itself, and the stage and its surroundings should be stylistically consistent.

When a stylistic choice of this nature is made, there is always a danger that the external events will overshadow the play. In a highly acclaimed 1969 production of *The Way of the World* in Los Angeles, the director overemphasized the creation of the atmosphere of a Restoration theatre performance, to the detriment of the intrinsic values of the play. The presumed nature of a Restoration audience was splendidly recaptured. Factions seated in the audience engaged in shouting with each other and with the stage performers; orange girls were ogled and chatted with; fops preened themselves and went on stage to interrupt the performance, attack the actors, and generally display their egos. All this was lively and amusing, but on the stage the unfortunate actors were valiantly struggling through William Congreve's intricate verbal aphorisms and somewhat complicated plot. Perhaps the audience did take away a good sense of what it must have been like to attend a Restoration theatre performance, but they had little sense of the play itself. But this was a conscious choice on the part of the director, who had cast weaker actors in the roles of Mirabell and Millamant than in the roles of fops and interrupters. The director could justify his decision from many points of view, not the least of which was that *The Way of the World* was not a success in the Restoration theatre, but has been acclaimed by contemporary critics, which suggests that in the atmosphere of its original theatre it was too delicate and cerebral to survive. The production could also be justified by its success; the contemporary audience found it exciting and fascinating. However, a director must be aware of the implications of his choices when he makes radical stylistic decisions. To choose a historical representation can lead to a closer communication of the world of the play to a contemporary audience, or it can mean the burying of the play beneath external eccentricities.

Contemporizing the Play

A play can be contemporized directly, by dressing the characters in up-to-date clothes and giving them contemporary mannerisms, speech patterns, props, and so on; or it can be done indirectly by introducing contemporary overtones within the physical world of the play.

One immediate advantage of modern-dress productions of classics is the creation of an environment to which an audience can immediately relate. There is no sense that the play is something from another time, which might create a historical barrier to communication. One problem which does arise, however, with Shakespearean and other plays written in verse, is *verse*. Is it stylistically consistent for actors dressed in contemporary clothes to speak a language that is completely removed from a contemporary form? We emphasize that contemporizing a play requires more than dressing actors in modern clothes and adding a few contemporary gestures and behavior patterns. If a director has a valid sense of the intrinsic style of his play and feels that it has an essential quality that can best be illustrated by translating it into its contemporary equivalent, and if he does this consistently, the language, as a consistent part of the intrinsic style, will become all of a piece with the style the director has chosen for his production.

Classical comedies, perhaps because of the lightness of their content, their conventional structure, and the similarity of lovers' problems through the ages, lend themselves to contemporization. Shakespeare's *Two Gentlemen of Verona,* one of the earliest, slightest, yet most pleasant of his comedies, was given highly contemporized productions by the Royal Shakespeare Company in 1970 and the New York Shakespeare Festival in 1971. Stylistically the productions were very different: the English pro-

Photo by Holte Photographics. Courtesy Royal Shakespeare Theatre, Stratford-upon-Avon.

Figure 84. *Contemporizing Shakespeare.* Sir Eglamour as scoutmaster in Robin Phillips's 1970 production of *Two Gentlemen of Verona* for the Royal Shakespeare Company.

duction was jet-set mod, while the American was New York ethnic. But both were extremely successful in capturing the intrinsic style of the play and relating it to the world of the audience for which it was performed. It is likely that neither production would have been successful in the other environment.

Two Gentlemen of Verona, which deals with young love that comes and goes with the uncertain glory of an April day, is set by the Royal Shakespeare Company on an unlocalized stage of platforms, ramps, and screens which can become a private pool or a lido beach, and costumed in the kind of rich-hippie garb reminiscent of an undatable historical period and seen in Kings Road Chelsea and Greenwich Village. The intrinsic style of the play is brilliantly converted in both set and costumes into contemporary terms, and matched by the characterizations—from the posing adolescent socialites, Proteus, Valentine, and Thurio, to Sir Eglamour (the knight in shining armour who rescues the damsel in distress) portrayed as a scoutmaster complete with bicycle. Perhaps no finer example of stylistic interpretation could be found than the turning of the old, well-meaning but ineffectual knight into his charmingly absurd, good deed–seeking, modern equivalent. In such ways the creative director reveals his sense of then and now and relates them both. The Royal Shakespeare Company took no liberties with the verse, which sat well on the lips of the upper-class socialites, and the production was consistently successful in relating the intrinsic style of the play to the extrinsic style of the production and revealing in a highly immediate way the problems of adolescent friendship and young love.

The New York Shakespeare Festival's production takes more extreme liberties with the text while retaining the plot intact. It is more acutely conscious of the world of its audience, very different from that of Stratford-on-Avon. The cast is a New York ethnic mix; blacks, Puerto Ricans, a Jewish Launce, and a Chinese Eglamour are a no more unhappy mixture than the inhabitants of New York itself. The costumes are exactly what these young people might wear in their day-to-day life, the setting is in the center of New York City, and the effect on the audience is one of instant recognition and relationship. The production has been given extra music and songs, all carrying through the contemporary ethnic-mix style: soul and latin, rock, ballad, and blues all reveal the intrinsic mood of moments in the play, with a direct immediacy to the audience. Lines and allusions have been updated: the duke does not banish Valentine, but has him drafted, and Silvia does not send a message to her lover, she sends him a "hot night letter." Everything is in the spirit of Shakespeare's original, and the play winds up with a party on stage in which the cast plays with yo-yos, skateboards, and bubble machines and throws frisbees with the audience.

The two productions we have discussed illustrate the range of sty-

Friedman-Abeles

Figure 85. The ethnic and athletic *Two Gentlemen of Verona* directed by Mel Shapiro for the 1971 New York Shakespeare Festival in Central Park (and later on Broadway). Notice the contemporary yet timeless costuming, the open scaffolding nature of the set, and the emphasis on physicality.

listic possibility even within the scope of highly-contemporized versions of a play. Both these productions had a keen sense of the intrinsic style of Shakespeare's play and of the world of their audiences. They are excellent proof that externalities do not determine style. Verse, costumes, properties, and so on can vary and yet project to the audience for which they have been selected the same essential quality of production.

Of course, it is not necessary to dress a play in modern costume to contemporize its values. During the 1960s, the Royal Shakespeare Company under the direction of Peter Hall had a fairly consistent stylistic policy of "democratizing" Shakespeare. This was a function of Hall's personal beliefs, of the egalitarian ensemble nature of the Company he created, and of a general social tendency in Britain at that time—the old middle-class establishment was under attack, and the rise of the "meritocracy" was at hand. Hall felt that his audience was very much concerned with the issues of social democracy, and this influenced his interpretation of Shakespeare's plays.

Stylistically Hall achieved his idea by using texture and behavior patterns. Textures in costumes and settings were more mat and realistic than the glossy, meretricious fabrics often employed in plays set in upper-class environments. Costumes actually looked as if they might have been worn more than just the few short hours on the stage. Hall's approach to upper-class characters was twofold: he would either reduce the high-flown language, manners, and social attitudes, as in his 1962 production of *A Midsummer Night's Dream,* in which the young lovers were foolish and clumsy and did not speak the verse musically; or he would exaggerate upper-class characteristics, undercutting the characters by overstressing haughty gentility, languor through lack of occupation, and affected language. In Hall's 1966 production of *Twelfth Night* Orsino is petulant, stupid, and self-indulgent.

The democratic interpretation was especially apparent in Hall's 1966 production of *Henry V,* with Ian Holm as the king. The style of Hall's production was utterly different from that of Laurence Olivier's (see page 227). Gone were the magnificent costumes; Henry dressed in dun-brown,

Photo by Holte Photographics. Courtesy Royal Shakespeare Theatre, Stratford-upon-Avon.

Figure 86. Peter Hall's 1966 production of *Henry V* for the Royal Shakespeare Company. The plain and worn look of the costumes and the simple, unheroic staging create the aura of First World War trenches.

the color common in modern battle dress. The acting was bluff and rugged; Henry was a pragmatic, workmanlike leader who might have risen to his position through the ranks. There was no sense of heroics. The military events were unpleasant, painful affairs, spattered with mud and blood. It was a ragged army led by a tired leader. What was projected was the dogged determination of First World War trenches, the unsung deeds of men following their leader not so much because he is king, but because he is as stubbornly intent on victory as are they. What heroism was present was of a democratic twentieth century nature. No ritual or rhetoric; a play about war, courage, and patriotism for our times.

Because of Hall's acute sense of the intrinsic style of Shakespeare's work, and because of the sincerity of the Company's democratic beliefs, which reflected changing times in Britain, the productions for the most part worked and made an important statement, through their style, to the audience. The occasional aberration does point out the dangers for an unwary director of this kind of stylistic interpretation. For example, while the portrayal of Orsino as a petulant and rather stupid youth makes a possibly valid statment about the idle aristocracy, it does make one wonder how Viola came to love him.

In the late 1960s the British National Theatre made a series of stylistic reinterpretations of Restoration comedy. Perhaps nowhere in theatre is the term "style" more bandied about than in connection with Restoration drama, probably for the following reason. The life style of the rather special and esoteric group of people with whom Restoration drama is concerned is so far removed from contemporary experience that it is extremely difficult for an actor to get a real sense of it; therefore, a tradition has grown which enables actors and directors to avoid coming to grips with the problems of the plays themselves, by perpetuating a group of mannered characteristics known as "Restoration Style." This was forcibly demonstrated a few years ago in a production of William Wycherley's *Countrywife,* given by a group of young acting students and recent professionals. At the first on-stage rehearsal the actor who was to play Sir Jasper Fidget adopted a peculiarly mincing gait and lisping manner of speech which were either a copy of some bad production he had seen, or an illustration of the received opinion that all Restoration characters were fops, and all fops were "queer," so here was his imitation of a homosexual acquaintance. This portrayal ignored some clues that a simple knowledge of the period and the text would have given him: Sir Jasper was a successful city merchant, and as such was neither a "rake" nor a "fop," and Wycherley had supplied a direct sense of his character in his name.

The young actor's approach illustrated what too often happens in a production of Restoration comedy. The play is dressed in velvet, lace, and

Figure 87. *Love for Love* at the British National Theatre, with Laurence Olivier as Tattle (left). Notice the creased, unglamorous costumes, the lived-in set and worn furnishings, and the relative simplicity of the actors' manner. Directed by Peter Wood.

ruffles; it is all bows and curtseys, with no sense that different people bow in different ways; it is, in fact, all froth and surface mannerisms with little sense of the real life of the characters and the substance of the play. In its productions of *Love for Love, The Recruiting Officer,* and *The Beaux' Stratagem* the National Theatre Company eschewed all superficial "Style" by starting from the premise that the plays were concerned with real events, environments, and people. The directors, Peter Wood, John Dexter, and William Gaskill, believed that a contemporary audience would gain a more meaningful understanding of the social behavior and problems with which the plays were concerned from seeing their true reality rather than a mannered, tinsel surface. No longer would costume, manner, and affectation stand between the play and the audience, allowing the audience to view the play as a fantastical pantomime which had no connection with their world.

The problem of style for Wood, Dexter, and Gaskill was not so much that of creating one, but of stripping away an encrusted "Style" to discover the true nature of the play. This they achieved by studying closely the attitudes at work in the play, and their meaning in the seventeenth century. Class attitudes and attitude toward family and inheritance are of particular importance, as they have changed considerably since the seventeenth century. The actors were helped to understand this; their costumes were treated as everyday dress, not as clothes for a fancy dress party; and the actors were placed in environments which appeared to have been lived in for many years. Then they were encouraged to play, as truthfully as possible, the actions given them by the playwright. There is nothing magical in this approach—it is at least as old as Stanislavski—but it produced a remarkable change in the accepted style of Restoration productions. There were still bows, but they had a meaning; there were still red-heeled shoes, but they occasionally had mud on them; and lace ruffles might be a little frayed or soiled. Gone was the brilliant, supercilious, cartoonlike hollowness of "Restoration Style," and in its place were people with problems of love, marriage, and sex that were very similar to those of a contemporary audience, and which they could now appreciate and relate to, because the situations involved real people, not posturing mannequins. The new approach was really a very simple but thorough exercise in play production, starting with a total understanding of the world of the play—physical, social, and moral—but seen from the inside, not through a scrim of accumulated conventions and misconceptions. Then this was translated into a simple style, simple in the sense that it was a truthful projection to the audience of the attitudes, manners, and artifacts of the world of the play, in such a way that the meanings contained within the play were clarified while the intrinsic style was retained.

Setting the Play in an Arbitrary Period

Think of Shakespeare's *The Taming of the Shrew* set in the American "Wild West," or *The Merchant of Venice* in Victorian Italy. The reason for choosing a historical setting which is neither that of the play itself, nor of the time in which it is being played, is that the director believes that there is something in the physical, social, or moral climate of the chosen period that enhances certain qualities of the play. It can, however, be a dangerous choice. The director not only has to reconcile the style of the play with the world of his audience, but he has to reconcile the style of his chosen period with both. An arbitrary setting can give added dimensions to a production, making it an intellectual adventure tour of Western civilization. It can, on the other hand, lead to problems of interpretation for the actors and confusion for the audience, who are asked to look at the play through two separate pairs of eyeglasses.

The National Theatre Company in Britain under director Jonathan

National Theatre Company of Great Britain

Figure 88. Joan Plowright as Portia in Victorian riding habit in Jonathan Miller's 1970 production of *The Merchant of Venice* for the National Theatre Company of Great Britain.

Miller chose to set their 1970 production of *The Merchant of Venice* in the Venice of the late 1800s. Shylock, played by Laurence Olivier, was locked inside an artificially fabricated society, wandering in frock coat and striped trousers through sophisticated salons and elegant restaurants. Antonio and Bassanio, complete with top hats and canes, discussed their financial affairs in calm and quiet against the prosperous background. The British audience immediately recognized in the smug, merchanting values of such a Victorian society the closed, private world that the "City" of London presided over for so many years, complete, of course, with subtle anti-Semitism, caste structure, and ritual snobbery. This is what the director wanted to drive home to his audience; presumably he felt that the play set in its own time would have had too many contradictions

National Theatre Company of Great Britain

Figure 89. A Mafioso-like Benedick, played by Robert Stephens in Franco Zeffirelli's production of *Much Ado About Nothing* for the British National Theatre Company.

Friedman-Abeles

Figure 90. The principals in A. J. Antoon's Edwardian production of *Much Ado About Nothing* in Central Park, New York (1972).

and inconsistencies for his point to be clear. Neither was the social climate of contemporary England helpful to the director's point. Thus the Victorian period, with its hidden taboos and careful prejudices, seemed stylistically right for the director's interpretation. Its inherent problems are evident. First, the leisurely life style of the nineteenth century does not easily accommodate the violent and quickly changing rhythms of Elizabethan drama, which were essentially designed to portray human experience in an open context, not a closed, private world. This fact must inevitably produce some stylistic conflict. Second, having established Shylock as a relaxed and successful businessman in a sophisticated world, the actor meets with problems of text once Shylock comes under pressure and crumbles. The tribal inheritance and animal nature of the man Shakespeare drew come through unless the lines are thrown away, and they do not sit stylistically on the lips of a prosperous pin-stripe–suited businessman. Finally, as always, what does one do with Belmont in late-Victorian Italy, with all the Princes of Levantine myth, and the caskets out of a fairy tale?

Miller's production is an example of an excellent conception which could not entirely work: the three worlds could not consistently mesh together. But the director's main interpretive point was assisted by his chosen style. We quote this production as an example of the conscious choices a director faces, the balancing of pros and cons he must make, and the necessity for him to appreciate the implications of his choices when determining a historical style for his production.

Aesthetic Styles

Productions in aesthetic styles are neither historical in nature nor realistic (a term we shall discuss later); they emphasize ideas or emotions by means of highly selective theatrical effects used to achieve a specific impact on the audience. Among these, perhaps the most significant in the mid-twentieth century has been the Epic style, associated with Bertolt Brecht.

Epic Theatre

It is not our intention to discuss the philosophy of Epic theatre; this has been well covered by John Willett and Martin Esslin in their works on Brecht.[2] To understand Epic style one must understand two Brechtian presumptions. First, theatre is theatre, and it is pointless to try to fool people into believing that they are witnessing a "slice of life." Second, theatre must be more than escapism. It must serve a social function by making people think about how they are governed and how they

[2] Martin Esslin, *Brecht: The Man and His Work* (New York: Doubleday & Company, Inc., 1960); John Willett, *Brecht on Theatre* (New York: Hill & Wang, Inc., 1964).

live their lives. These two basic principles determine the intrinsic style of Epic theatre, and though the framework leaves many choices open to the director, he cannot truly project a Brechtian play or create an Epic style without taking cognizance of them.

The theatricality of the Epic style is captured by the nonuse of realistic settings and the frank acknowledgment of the technological equipment which produces theatrical effects. Locations are created by the actors themselves with a minimum of props and change from scene to scene with absolute freedom. This is reminiscent of Shakespearean staging, but with the distinction that no attempt is made to thrust the action into the audience—it is consciously removed from the audience. There is no attempt to hide the lighting instruments or the means by which sound effects or scenic changes are created. An orange box with a placard above it reading "Bar" is as much a bar as the most realistic of Belasco's creations. The director is not obliged to use all these techniques in an Epic production, but he must be aware of the intrinsic necessity of regarding the theatre as a technological tool kit rather than a box of magic tricks.

The desire not to fool the audience with make-believe is related to the second principle of Epic theatre, its dramatic purpose. Epic theatre should be a tool for social improvement; the audience must ultimately

Courtesy of Berliner Ensemble

Figure 91.   Epic staging in the Berliner Ensemble production of Bertolt Brecht's *The Caucasian Chalk Circle*.

have a cerebral rather than visceral experience. This is achieved by acting, music, media, and content. These are combined, with the scenic effects described above, to keep the audience always intellectually aware of what is being performed on stage, to challenge the audience to think about the play, and to prevent them from becoming so emotionally involved with the action that they lose their objectivity. The acting style of Epic theatre has been discussed in Chapter 9; we will only emphasize here that the remove the actor maintains from his character is in keeping with the total stylistic principle of objectifying the stage events.

Music, media, and content may be used to make a direct statement, or they may be conjoined for ironic purposes. In *Mother Courage* and *The Threepenny Opera,* harsh and grating music give a distinctively sardonic flavor to these productions. Posters and projections may comment directly on the action, for example, to show mangled bodies in a scene deploring war; more often, and more effectively, they make an ironic statement. Joan Littlewood's 1963 production of *Oh, What a Lovely War* included an electric marquee that listed the mounting casualty figures while the characters talked gaily of what a "jolly affair" war is. Littlewood also used music ironically, staging song and dance acts with the thoughtless, insouciant lyrics of the day in front of film projections of the actual horror of war.

The purpose of Epic style is to make a direct social or political statement which will challenge the audience and stimulate them to action. This is really what *alienation* means when applied to the Brechtian method. It does *not* mean that the director makes the audience dislike the play and the actors, or sets up a mutual antipathy; directors who attempt this are stylistically wrong. The aim of the Epic style is to create objectivity, to break the audience out of its accepted way of viewing life, to confront it intellectually with the playwright's point of view. The content of the play may consist of direct preachment, for example, the plays written by Brecht in his middle period—the *Lehrstücke* or teaching plays. The physical and acting style of these plays is in the Epic vein, but there is little employment of irony, and the theatre is treated as a lecture hall in which a direct political moral (usually Marxist) is driven home. In other plays by Brecht and other Epic playwrights, the moral often appears in more of a parable form, the playwright's statement made through an ironic confrontation of the apparent action with setting, music, media, and costume, which combine to reveal a complacently accepted attitude in a new light.

Let us make it clear once more that while the employment of some or all of the artifacts and techniques we have just discussed is necessary to create an Epic style, it is not a sufficient condition if they are not employed with the clear purpose of breaking empathy with the audience and making the audience objectively consider an issue. The artifacts and techniques by themselves merely create the form; the intrinsic intention is necessary to create the style. There have been extremely romantic productions of *Mother Courage* in which an unduly sympathetic performance of the title role has created empathy with the audience, who are bathed in maudlin regrets at her misfortunes and lose the playwright's social statement about war and capitalism.

On the other hand, Joan Littlewood created an Epic style and effect without using an alienation style of acting, and with a much less consciously structured sense of theatre than Brecht, whose training in Marxist dialectic is apparent in his dramatic form. In her production of *Oh, What a Lovely War,* the actors did not need to take an objective approach to their characters because the total form of the production was an ironic comment on its subject, World War I. Littlewood created a vaudeville circus form with a basic ensemble of actors, dressed as Pierrots, who played a number of different parts in a series of olios or circus acts. There was no possibility for the audience to identify with any of the characters, who were distinguished only by hats and props, but the audience did identify with the cheerful actors who played to them as people. This was all part of Littlewood's plan, for the more the audience was emotionally drawn in by the actors, the harder they were then hit by the alienating effects of the projections, posters, and data, not to mention the ironic text. The audience was brought up short and made to see themselves as susceptible to all the chauvinistic superficialities of war—colorful uniforms, patriotic speeches, brave music—while ignoring the horrific realities. This was exactly the point Littlewood wished to make. Thus, the essential point about Epic, as about all style, is the intention behind the form: the intrinsic nature of the impact the director desires. Brecht and Littlewood may have differed somewhat in their employment of elements of form, but their sense of the intrinsic style was the same.

The "Isms"

The "Isms" are those forms of theatre current in the early twentieth century which were to a considerable extent a reaction against naturalism: constructivism, expressionism, surrealism. Our dealing with them under the same heading is partly a reflection of their deriving from the same source, a desire to retheatricalize theatre, and partly an acknowledgment of the difficulty in discussing them as styles. Perhaps more than any other styles we discuss, they must be seen or experienced to be understood.

CONSTRUCTIVISM

Constructivism is perhaps the most concrete of the "Isms." Developed by the Russian director Vsevolod Meyerhold, it reflects man in a

Theatermuseum, Munich

Figure 92. Constructivist set for *The Man Who Was Thursday,* directed by Alexander Tairov.

machine age, and to some degree man as a machine. Settings make use of naked technological artifacts: scaffolding, boards, ladders, slides, wheels. It is a theatre built on engineering principles, affirming the materials and rhythms of a dynamic industrial society. The cast epitomizes machine-like muscularity with its acrobatic style of performance; actions are illustrated by cartwheels, somersaults, and tumbling. For example, in Meyerhold's production of *The Magnificent Cuckold,* the young lover entered by plunging down a slide. At the bottom was his girl friend, whom he crashed into and knocked to the floor while triumphantly shouting "Whee!" By this action Meyerhold wished to convey, in physically dynamic terms, the essence of an eager lover meeting his mistress, a physical illustration of the young man's sense of abandonment to the joy of the moment.

The basic problem for the director, assuming he has assembled a cast that is capable of acrobatic performance, is to discover the physical actions that will convey the emotional content of the text. The danger in this style of production is that the theatricalism will obscure the text, leaving a kind of circus performance that does not illustrate the intrinsic

Joe Cocks Studio

Figure 93. *A Midsummer Night's Dream,* directed by Peter Brook for the Royal Shakespeare Company (1970). Notice the bare staging, the use of levels, and the suspended actors. Compare with the Meyerhold set on page 187.

action of the play. A 1970 production of *A Midsummer Night's Dream,* by Peter Brook for the Royal Shakespeare Company, while not constructivist in the Meyerhold sense, did employ a circus image, using acrobatics, trapeze work, and circus tricks performed by the actors to project Brook's sense of Shakespeare's play for the 'seventies. Brook's production was highly acclaimed; it succeeded because while he had one foot in the circus, he had both hands on Shakespeare's text. The play took place within a bare, brightly lit, white set which, while it did not reproduce the three levels of an Elizabethan playhouse, did have them in terms of acting space. The tricks performed by Puck and Oberon, without in any way losing Shakespeare's language, were consistent with their characters as magic makers, and were a celebration of the total skills an actor should have. Brook succeeded in making his magic fit the intention of the play. At one moment Puck was a friendly sprite; then, with the help of a pair of stilts, he became a frightening demon contemptuous of the mortals beneath him. In such ways a brilliantly creative director can interpret the intrinsic nature of any play into a style of his own.

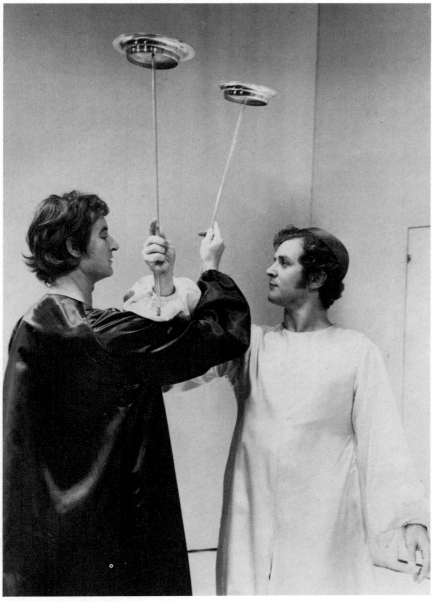

*Photo by Holte Photographics. Courtesy Royal Shakespeare
Theatre, Stratford-upon-Avon.*

Figure 94.   Puck and Oberon performing circus tricks in Brook's *A Midsummer Night's Dream.*

EXPRESSIONISM

Expressionism in theatrical form was a post–World War I phenomenon born of a vehement sense of social indignation. This took the shape of an attack on bourgeois forms and attitudes and a rejection of that "realism" in the theatre which seemed to be a detailed perpetuation of those attitudes on the stage. Expressionism was a revolt against authority and convention in art and life; it was a rejection of "good taste." Its theatrical style was a combination of the distorted, the grotesque, and the bizarre; extremism of emotion, language, and stagecraft was its hallmark. It was an external projection of inner states, but not in any naturalistic sense— rather the world of dreams and psychic fantasy made concrete.

The theatrical style of expressionism was achieved by very specific scenic, lighting, acting, and verbal effects within a structure based on the pattern of the human mind in dream. All of this was geared toward making direct social statements. There are two distinctions between expressionism and surrealism, which otherwise used similar techniques to achieve similar stylistic ends. First, expressionism was concerned with the problems of man and society, while surrealism was not necessarily so concerned; second, surrealism focused on the effect of dreams, the release of the free fantasy of the unconscious, while expressionism made a very calculated use of the structure of dreams to create a specific impression.

Theatermuseum, Munich

Figure 95.   Expressionistic staging **of** Ernst Toller's *Transfiguration*.

Expressionism is theme-centered rather than plot-oriented; its actions are not necessarily causally related. Staging is very fluid, making use of many separate areas, and this feeling is enhanced by the lighting, which picks up now this area, now that, in no seemingly logical order—like the process of the mind itself. This form of staging is of course very Shakespearean or Epic, but with the distinction that there is no logical sequence or progression, and more than one area may be employed at a given time. We do not mean to say that expressionism is formless; however, its form is more a musical, contrapuntal interrelationship of themes which make a total impression on the audience, rather than the logical incremental building of actions toward a climax.

Expressionism creates stage images out of metaphors and figures of speech. The inner workings of the mind become externally represented. For example, in *Job,* by Oskar Kokoschka, a man's head is turned by a woman, and this turning takes place physically on stage. Later, when he is cuckolded by the woman, antlers grow from his head. This literal representation of action breaks down realistic form and replaces it with grotesqueries, often macabre, as when a murderer runs around with his head in a bag. This technique is linked to the return of the theatre to magic and pantomime, and the attack on accepted ways of looking at life—the release of the uncensored working of man's inner conscious—which were the aims of the expressionists. Language is less important to the creation of the expressionist style than is the use of extravagant gesture and mask. The appeal to the audience is visual and emotional rather than conceptual, and the nature of the acting required is almost entirely opposed to the detailed naturalism of Stanislavski, the external manifestation being more important than the inner motivation.

The intrinsic style of expressionism could not be appreciated without a sense of the vehemence of the social feeling behind it. There was an inherent tension between the playwright's sense of the world as grotesquely meaningless and materialistic, and his romantic concept of himself as alienated artist, but missionary and savior. Simply to employ the techniques of expressionism without a feeling for its social fervor would be to produce a possibly clever but inevitably hollow imitation of the style. The distortion of the true values of life, which leads to the distorted stage images, is the catalyst behind this style which has largely been overtaken by or incorporated into the later avant garde of the post-1950s.

Example: Lysistrata

Before we discuss the styles of the avant garde, it might help summarize our discussion so far to look at one play, suggesting possible interpretations, and to show how certain hypothetical styles could be achieved through the exercise of the choices open to a director.

Aristophanes' *Lysistrata* seems to offer both the problems inherent in the production of a play that is 2500 years old, and at least two themes of considerable pertinence for the 1970s. These themes, likely to interest a contemporary director and his audience, are the antiwar sentiment of the play and its concern with the social place and political power of women. The intrinsic style of the play is determined by these factors and by what research and scholarship have brought to light about the physical circumstances of the Greek theatre and the manner of production of a Greek comedy.

From research the director gains a sense of open yet formal staging, use of masks and extravagant costume to delineate character, music and dance as an important part of the action, a vigorously physical and phallic sense of life, and a close relationship between actors and audience in the joint, ceremonial nature of the event. Given these factors plus the themes of antiwar feeling and political activism for women, how does the director go about creating a style which will make a valid contemporary impact on his audience? Suppose first that the director feels that the play's antiwar theme, and the part played in this by the women, are sufficiently broad as to need no special focus for his time, and are best served by a clear and dynamic projection of all the original elements of the play in their Greek form. His style then becomes a recapitulation of the Greek costume, dance form, music, and space. Space is likely to cause some problem—the availability of large outdoor amphitheatres and Greek spring weather is limited! If his theatre is indoors and intimate, costumes and acting style will be affected. He will have to decide whether masks were simply functional, used in an attempt to overcome distance, or a more integral part of character; whether masks are used will affect the size and nature of the acting style. He will also be obliged to choose among available translations, and the degree of formality of the language will again alter the impact of his production. Thus, even when a director attempts to recapitulate as nearly as possible the intrinsic style of a play, he still must make numerous choices which will crucially affect the style of his production.

Another director might wish to make the antiwar sentiments of *Lysistrata* specific in contemporary terms. In the United States in the 1960s or '70s this could mean a direct reference to the Vietnam War. There are many parallels between the length of this war and its impact on American society and the Peloponnesian War about which Aristophanes wrote his play. The director might choose to make the Athenians and Spartans into Americans and Vietnamese, using Marine costumes for one side and Vietcong uniforms for the other. Textual references could be updated to include names of contemporary generals and politicians—after all, this is exactly what Aristophanes did; comedy was a vehicle for social comment. The chorus patterns could be in the form of military drills and marches—again, the Greek chorus was a paramilitary group. The music could be martial and strident, and the acting style geared to portray real people rather than comic characters. The sexual humor could be comtemporized and given a barrack-room slant (there is no more sexually-oriented creature than the private soldier, deprived), and the focus on women could emphasize their general deprivations, rather than the satisfaction of their sexual appetites. The end of the play could become the signing of a peace treaty and a joint victory parade—victory over war. Certainly, some elements of Aristophanes' play would be lost or played down in such a production, but there are enough common intentions so that a careful and consistent implementation of the style would project, for our times, a more serious but intrinsically similar antiwar appeal.

A different way of making an antiwar statement is the employment of an Epic style of production for *Lysistrata*. The play could be given all the intrinsic physical values of the Greek—costume, mask, vigorous bawdy humor—while an ironic counterstatement is made by projections, posters, and sound effects from the Vietnam War, or even a progression through the history of war from Greek times to the present. Bright, colorful lighting and perhaps a puppetlike acting style could produce the effect of a cartoon or silent comic film, in contrast with which the naturalistic display of the horrors of war would create the total satirical sense of the play, giving it the effect of a comic grimace.

A somewhat more difficult but still possible interpretation would be the women's liberation aspect of the play. The problem would be that in Aristophanes' day the idea of women taking such action was utterly absurd to the Greeks and was therefore part of the humor of the play. To make a social point about the potential political power of women, their greater good sense, and their humanitarianism, the director would need to reorient the focus of the play. The play would be physically contemporized in terms of costume, nonuse of masks, and a less formal and gestural acting style. The women could perhaps be a group of militant protesters, and the men a group of old-fashioned "chauvinist pigs." The physical sexuality of the play, the women's use of their bodies as a weapon, could either be underplayed or, possibly more effectively, be made very self-conscious and ironic—the women using the men's view of them as sexual objects, which they despise, in order to prove that they are more than that. The humor of the play could thus be retained and turned strongly against the men through the women's self-knowledge, shared with the audience. The end of the play could be staged to give very strong focus to the triumphant women, associated with the symbolic figure of Peace, leaving the dominant impression that their strength of purpose had prevailed and produced peace through their political skill and good sense.

Perhaps closer to the intrinsic nature of Aristophanes' play might be a production which attempted neither to set it in a specific historical period nor to make a directly political statement, but to contemporize the essential impact of a Greek comedy on its audience. The director would have to determine the quality of the impact in Greek times and then find the means of translating this impact into terms of contemporary experience. While such an approach acknowledges that a contemporary audience cannot have the same experience as the historical audience, it can have a similar experience in its own terms. Suppose that the director decides that the play is neither about women's liberation nor specifically antiwar, but concerned with the more profitable and humane virtues of making love rather than making war. He further decides that the nearest contemporary equivalent to the bawdy, physically active, song-and-dance elements of Greek comedy performance is vaudeville burlesque. The director is now in a position to make choices that will project his statement through his style and relate the world of the play to that of his audience with great immediacy and truth. He could make use of the olio structure of vaudeville—a series of acts interspersed with chorus numbers—which is similar to that of a Greek comedy. A live band might be used to translate the chorus numbers into terms of contemporary music and dance. Costume might be completely contemporized, or the director could choose a basic chiton with vaudeville overtones like hats, props, and masks, which could even pick up the characteristics of well-known vaudeville and comic actors whose manner and attitudes relate to characters within the play: the Commissioner of Public Safety might be based on W. C. Fields, and Kinesias could have overtones of Charlie Chaplin. The translation used with such a style would have to be contemporary and vernacular, and it could be made more immediate by the inclusion of references to the world of the audience itself. The text could be geared to move directly toward the reestablishment of a peaceful communion, underlined by making the end of the play into a party in which the audience would be invited to join.

We have briefly outlined five possible styles for the production of *Lysistrata*. Some were closer to the intrinsic style of Aristophanes' play than others, but we believe all of them to be possible and valid, provided the director knows clearly what he wishes to emphasize, and employs the elements of production consistently, once his stylistic choices evolve from his sense of how his statement can best be projected to his audience.

The New Theatre

No discussion of the art of directing today can be complete without some examination of the aesthetic principles and practices of what is known as "New Theatre." Of course, as we have tried to suggest, theatre should be constantly renewed by the work of creative directors and performers; but there has evolved over the past fifteen years or so (from about the mid-1950s, although it is impossible to give an exact date) a new sense of life and self-expression which has been reflected in a new approach to theatre. This approach is now sufficiently established as to have a determined set of principles, which, though variable, constitute a conscious attempt to break away from what would be termed by this avant garde the "formal theatre." To discuss the New Theatre fully would require a complete book, and various aspects of it have already been chronicled,[3] but we hope in this brief discussion to give the aspiring director a sense of its underlying purposes, and to examine its principles enough to enable him to assess its values and decide how it might relate to his sense of life and theatre. Whatever one's individual opinion of the pros and cons of the New Theatre, it is unquestionably one of the choices on a modern director's theatrical palette.

Stated simplistically, the New Theatre reflects the continuing tendency toward fragmentation of society, our subordination to technology, and the spectacular breakdown of traditional values, especially the linear, logical, and rational approach to life that has dominated Western society since the seventeenth century. There is a return to experience rather than explanation, the rejection of the cerebral in favor of the visceral and tactile, a sense that life should be not interpreted but felt, and that feeling should be a totality of sensations, a rejection of mind in favor of body. Life is the living, and theatre is the performance. There are no masterpieces,[4] as there are no master minds; life is too complex to allow one dominating set of standards. The emphasis is on subjective feeling rather than objective assessment. The director becomes more than ever the creator as opposed to the interpreter, and his style is an uncircumscribed projection of his point of view. Thus his point of view becomes the pretext; but the director is still working with space, performers, and scenic artifacts, and his choice of relationships will still influence the ultimate nature of his production—and there are still guidelines which will distinguish between these choices.

Before we discuss these guiding stylistic principles, gaining some understanding of how they have evolved will help put them and the New

---

[3] See Michael Kirby, *The Art of Time* (New York: E. P. Dutton & Co., Inc., 1969); R. J. Shroeder, *The New Underground Theatre* (New York: Bantam Books, Inc., 1968); and Richard Kostelanetz, *The Theatre of Mixed Means* (New York: The Dial Press, 1968).

[4] Antonin Artaud, "No More Masterpieces," in *The Theatre and Its Double* (New York: Grove Press, Inc., 1958).

Courtesy of Freehold Theatre, London

Figure 96. An emphasis on physicality in the New Theatre, shown in this production of *Antigone* at the Freehold Theatre, London.

Theatre itself into a more total perspective. The oldest influence on the New Theatre is probably that of *Dada*. This form of theatre, and of art in general, originated toward the end of the First World War, when a group of like-thinking artists gathered to give readings, poems, music performances, and dances, all in the same environment and many of them simultaneously. The idea of diverse simultaneous events was joined by the desire to "confront" the audience. The distinction between performing and nonperforming was broken down, as art was not to be removed from life, and performances were taken into the streets where any environment was used. In 1952 composer John Cage integrated various elements of Dada into his work, and in a famous presentation in the summer of that year at Black Mountain College in North Carolina, he combined a lecture, a recitation from a ladder, a piano recital, movie projections, and a dance performance into one fairly simultaneous event which took place in and around the audience. It is said that a dog began to follow the dancer, Merce Cunningham, around the room and, in the spirit of the piece, became part of the performance!

In terms of use of space the Bauhaus experimenters of the 1920s were forerunners of the New Theatre. Walter Gropius and his followers were trying to escape the idea of the physical theatre as a determined space, at that time a proscenium stage, within which a performance took place, with complete separation of audience and performer. They proposed by the use of technology to mechanize all the physical elements of the theatre, so that the audience as well as the performance space could be sculptured. The spectator-actor relationship was to become completely flexible, molded as the director wished for the needs of his production. The efforts of the Bauhaus designers were cut short by political circumstances in Germany in the late 1920s and '30s, but their sense of an all-embracing, flexible environment was revived by the New Theatre.

The changing concept of art exerted its influence on the new concept of theatrical environment. After the Cubists broke down the accepted classical harmonies and created the collage concept, it was only a matter of time before everything that had hitherto been regarded as foreign to paint and canvas would be involved in the creative act. From pieces of paper extending the space of the canvas into three dimensions, the art work reached farther into the space of the room until finally it came to fill it completely and to include not only the artist, but anyone visiting the environment thus created. People as moving, colored shapes became part of the artistic event. Mechanically moving parts were then added, and the created surroundings could be rearranged at the artist's or spectators' discretion. Sound and speech, both mechanical and recorded, became part of the art work/environment. The art work now appeared to many artists more an arena in which to act, so action painting and flexible en-

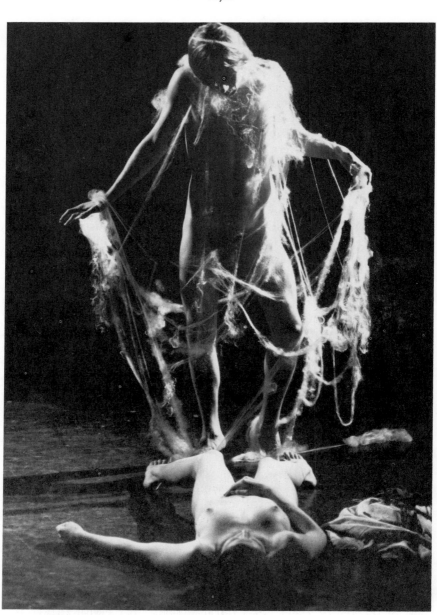

Company Theatre Foundation

Figure 97.   Nudity is another New Theatre technique in service of valid theatrical purpose, here used in *The Emergence,* produced by The Company Theatre, Los Angeles (1969).

vironments took the place of canvas. As art came closer to theatre, so theatre took over its spatial aesthetic.

An important event in the development of New Theatre was the publication in English in 1958 of *The Theatre and Its Double* by Antonin Artaud, a prophetic French visionary of the 1930s who had been influenced by Dada, surrealism, Asian theatre, and opium. Artaud called for a theatre of great physical intensity which would explore and release man's most fundamental and primitive passions and desires. It was to be a theatre which rejected domination by text, totally surrounding and involving its audience with the searing nature of its physical and aural impact. According to Artaud the theatre must create "a language in space, language of sounds, cries, lights, onomatopoeia, the theatre must organize into veritable hieroglyphs, with the help of characters and objects, and make use of their symbolism and interconnections in relation to all organs and on all levels."[5]

The relating of Artaud's desire for a total theatre to current trends in the cultural history of Western civilization was done by a nontheatre practitioner, Marshall McLuhan, who did, however, look at contemporary culture as if it were intended to be total theatre. McLuhan envisaged a "retribalization" of man in a culture which emphasized involvement, physical sensation, and sculptural values. McLuhan based his thesis on the worldwide proliferation of media, which he analyzed in terms of the amount of participation they provided for the user. He suggested that man seldom used more than a limited portion of his senses, and thus failed to gain a satisfactory level of total sensory experience. He particularly criticized the printed word (note the New Theatre's movement away from text) as having limited man's capacity for total experience. McLuhan's purpose is the same as that of the propounders of all-embracing, environmental, participatory theatre in which sensory experience and abstract information are integrated on the level of the hieroglyph, so that we may re-obtain that experience of the world's meaning and perception which has been sacrificed to rational, verbal, and linguistic patterns.

From the confluence of the foregoing ideas and practices at a watershed in theatrical evolution, we derive the aesthetics of the New Theatre, which we shall discuss under the headings of environment, media, and Artaudian effect. Most New Theatre productions are a mixture of all these elements, but this is not necessarily the case; while most media productions are inevitably environmental, they do not have to be Artaudian, and environmental productions do not have to employ media, but strive for at least a partial Artaudian impact.

[5] Artaud, *The Theatre and Its Double,* p. 90.

ENVIRONMENTAL PRODUCTION

The basic stylistic principle is that the space in which the performance is given should be regarded as a totality, embracing both actors and
audience in one continuous whole. The action takes place around, above,
behind, below, and among the audience. (This does produce problems in
terms of focus; one production solved the problems by seating the audience in the middle of the space on swivel chairs.) The purpose of this
technique is to create a totally shared experience, where bodily contact
can occur between actor and audience; spectators are drawn into and become an integral part of the event. Some proponents regard it as a return
to the essence of predramatic ritual in which all participants were both
themselves and actors, and no division existed between actors and spectators.

The definition of space in an environmental production is not predetermined, but organic and dynamic. There are two kinds of space:

Courtesy of Ann S. Halprin

Figure 98. Ann Halprin's improvised "happening," titled *The Atonement*,
presented by the San Francisco Dancers' Workshop. There are no spectators;
everyone is a participant in the total environment defined by a huge newspaper collage. Dress is by random choice.

transformed and found. *Transformed space* is an environment created for the production by the designing of *all* the space, not a separation of the space into an area for performance and another area for audience. Spatial design should arise organically from the exploration of the action and serve its needs. The action should not be made to fit the needs of a predetermined space. Ideally the nature of the spatial definition should evolve with the production itself and be created spontaneously and gradually by the interplay of director, actors, designers, and technicians.

Found space is a given environment which is explored, not altered; the performance adjusts to the environment and copes with its given elements. A production occurs in found space, for example, if it is given in the streets or other public places or taken into a building and performed in the space as given. In both transformed and found space, it is a principle of performance that spectators may, by their movements, unexpectedly redefine the space, and that performers must be prepared to adapt to and take advantage of this flexibility of environment.

Flexibility of environment is related to another principle of environmental production, flexible and variable focus. Unlike "formal" theatre, where one of the director's tasks is to create a specific focus and to ensure that the audience sees what they are supposed to, when they are supposed to, environmental theatre can offer a choice of focuses. More than one event can take place at the same time; indeed, because of the all-encompassing nature of the environment events can occur all around the spectators, who may choose what to look at and in what order. Of course, the director does decide what range of alternatives to give the spectators, and by relating the simultaneous events to one sensory totality he can provide the audience with a greater depth of experience of a given action than is possible in single-focus structure. The range and rate of exposure of the simultaneous events can vary from an intense experience of a single action with informational content—that is, the audience is expected to understand the content of what it is exposed to—to a bombardment of the senses of the spectator that results in a virtually hallucinatory experience with no informational content. A director must consider, as part of the world of his audience, the rate at which the audience can absorb and interrelate the events presented to them if he wishes to convey a specific impression.

The multifocal principle derives from the idea of man as a being who, in his daily life, is surrounded by a plethora of impressions which he absorbs through eyes, ears, nose, and finger tips, and whose experience is not linear—particularly in the modern urban confusion of lights, movements, and sounds, some distinct and some but faintly heard—but an ever-changing totality. The experience creates the impression; "the medium is the message."

This understanding leads to a final basic principle of environmental theatre: that the text is not sacrosanct, but serves the needs of the production. The play is no longer the thing. Nor ever was, suggests Richard Schechner, one of America's leading proponents of New Theatre, pointing out that the famous line from *Hamlet* concludes, "With which I'll catch the conscience of the King." The play was even then being used by Hamlet to further an extradramatic end.[6] Text need be neither the starting point nor the goal of a production, but simply one of its elements—if there is a text at all. The text is "confronted" to discover what values are important in a contemporary situation; it is often cut, expanded, and rearranged to emphasize relationships and attitudes that were, perhaps, less pertinent at the time of its writing.[7] This technique is related to the new dimensions that can be gained from environmental representation of scenes that were written sequentially with an influence on each other but are now played simultaneously or intercut, with interesting results in terms of depth of understanding of an action, or of ironic juxtaposition.

While we have enumerated various stylistic principles of environmental theatre, we hasten to add that the implementation of these principles does not necessarily produce the effects sometimes claimed for them. The director might consider certain caveats when setting out to create a style with environmental ends in view. First, the idea that the creation of one space common to performer and audience will lead to a totally shared experience as in predramatic ritual is not always successful in practice. For one thing, in both primitive and traditional societies where ritual was an important religious and social function, there was an almost complete group orientation, the actions of individuals unconsciously reflecting and furthering the ends of the group. This tends not to be the case in our highly fragmented modern society. Second, as long as there are people who know they are actors, and people who know they are spectators, there will be a division between the two, and the space that is being used by actors at any given time becomes performance space while that occupied by the spectators is audience space. Thus the violation of the audience space by the actor simply becomes a part of the structure of the theatrical event—it does not make that event more free-wheeling and less structured. To put one's arms around a person is not to embrace him in the emotional connotation of the term; to surround the audience with a performance does not necessarily mean that they are touched as human beings at any greater depth than in a proscenium situation.

[6] Richard Schechner, "Six Axioms for Environmental Theatre," *The Drama Review*, XII, No. 3 (Spring 1968), 60.

[7] Charles Marowitz and Jerzy Grotowski have successfully produced such "collages." Refer to reviews of Marowitz's *Hamlet* and *Macbeth* and Grotowski's *Akropolis* and *The Constant Prince*.

Nondefined space is virtually impossible to achieve if there is to be any blocking at all, for to make even the simplest statements in terms of actors and space, the director is likely to pinpoint some actions as happening in certain areas. As Richard Schechner admitted with reference to his production of *Victims of Duty,* at several points in the performance audience members did not want to give up a place in which an action was to be staged. "The performers, in character, had to deal with these people, sometimes forcibly moving them out of the area."[8] Schechner rationalized this as adding to the performance. But what happens when a "sweet old lady" character has to chuck someone out of her rocking chair—does it not permanently affect her sweetness in relation to the audience?

As Richard Gilman pointed out in a review of Schechner's *Commune,* there is no reason to suppose that an audience will have any less rigid a set of expectations about its role than in "formal" theatre environments. Describing a young audience member at the performance, Gilman said,

> He had been reacting the way a Broadway spectator reacts to *his* kind of consolations and exotic presences. He had yakked at dirty words, yelled "Wow!" at a nude scene, twitched with self-satisfaction at hearing Anti-Establishment views expressed, and done all this with beady-eyed attention to what others in the audience were doing, including me, and with that violent determination to have a good time, to belong and be with, that reveals no sort of open spirit or impulse toward the communal but their terrifying absence.[9]

We mention these problems not to criticize the New Theatre, but to provide a balanced view of its possibilities and to discourage directors from the belief that the implementation of certain stylistic devices will automatically produce the desired result. In New Theatre, as in any form of theatre, the honesty and directness with which an effect is communicated—themselves a function of the clarity and consistency of the director's vision—will distinguish between empty and contrived productions and those which unite audience and performer in an illuminating, exciting theatrical experience.

MULTIMEDIA PRODUCTIONS

Multimedia production is the application of contemporary technological artistry to the environmental concept. The recognition of the theat-

[7] Schechner, "Six Axioms for Environmental Theatre," p. 50.

[8] Richard Gilman, "*Commune*: Review," *The Drama Review,* XV, No. 3 (Spring 1971), 329.

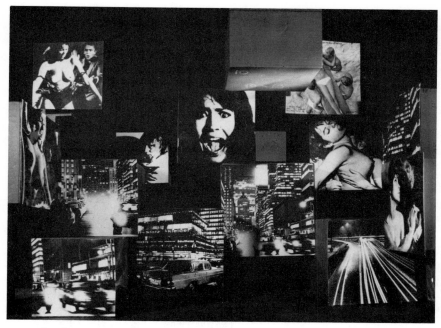

Art Centrum, Prague

Figure 99. A Josef Svoboda montage for Werle's *Die Reise,* produced in Hamburg by Lars Runsten (1969).

rical possibilities of multimedia can perhaps be dated from 1958 when Josef Svoboda produced his *Laterna Magika* at the Brussels Exposition. *Laterna Magika* featured eight mobile screens and five projectors of both slides and film. There was interplay between projections and live actors, augmented by various treadmills, lifts, and other mechanical stage devices, the whole being audially embraced by stereophonic sound. The performance, which had a disconnected revue-type structure, created a pluralistic field of vision and a dynamic montage of simultaneous images much in keeping with mid-twentieth century modes of perception. Multimedia may or may not be employed with live performers and may or may not have an information structure. The light shows which were a popular form of entertainment in the 1960s may be regarded as a form of multimedia theatre, employing amplified stereophonic music and the projection of slides and film of changing colored patterns, together with strobe lights and other visual effects. These were directed, in the sense that a choice of relationships had to be made between the various elements, and geared to the achievement of a particular effect, usually hallucinatory.

A more calculated and informational use of the form can be achieved when a director wishes to make a total statement from his various effects. If it is an antiwar statement, the director could employ battle film, projections of victims of the atomic attack on Hiroshima, flashing and explosive light effects, sounds of bombing and gunfire, screams of victims, and so on, which, without any plot basis, combine to make the required statement. Of course, the director can also employ irony by contrasting some of his elements: playing peaceful music against the war film, or projecting children at play against the sound of explosions. (These not particularly subtle examples are given simply to emphasize the stylistic possibilities.)

The use of media to heighten or intensify the production of a play offers an interesting challenge to a director. The techniques he may employ are essentially those we have discussed in the section on environmental theatre: intercutting, superimposition, and simultaneity. But in addition he must deal with the relationship among film and projections and live performers. Again the question of focus becomes important if he is dealing with a plot-oriented production. Experience suggests that a live performer, other things being equal, will tend to dominate film or projections. But the problem of actor and image competing for attention is probably best solved by having the actor acknowledge, and play with, the images as an integral part of the performance.

Media can have various functions in a plot-oriented production. They can create scenic atmosphere, either directly, as in the projection of church interiors in Christopher Fry's *Sleep of Prisoners,* and the use of film of street scenes to provide background in a scene calling for this, or indirectly, as in the projection of Christian art works to create atmosphere for Fry's play, and the use of a montage of street signs and sounds in the other instance. Media can also illustrate subtext, making visual the actual thoughts of a character, representing past situations referred to by characters and thus creating a denser experience of the action, passing ironic commentary on the actions of a character or recapitulating previous stage action that he might now be working against, and becoming the alter ego when a character is exploring his emotions or motivations.

These are but a few of the possible uses of media. Television brings added dimensions. It can be used directly to overcome the problems of visibility in environment—scenes can be televised as they are acted, and projected on sets around the theatre. It can be used to show the progress of an outside event that comes to impinge on the play's action; for example, if the entrance of an individual is a climactic point in the plot, we can see him preparing for the entrance and approaching the other side of the door, heightening the tension of his arrival. Television can also show another view of action that is taking place—from the rear or above—or it can focus on and emphasize specific detail.

We have in no sense exhausted the possibilities of the use of media, but have attempted to show that they can do more than create mind-blowing effects. Media can be used to produce new rhythms, densities, and associations; they can help a director key audience reactions both intellectually, by visual information, and emotionally, by use of changing visual and aural images. In using media a director should have, as always, a clear idea of the impact he wishes to produce. He must be aware of the need to produce a conjoint focus or impression and to determine the relationship between the audience's receptivity and the speed of his media input, and he must be cognizant of the different effects produced by fundamental relationships between the elements and dissonances between some of them. Finally, especially in classical plays where poetry was intended by the author to do much of the work that media now do, he should take care to support and underline the impression rather than the detail. Just as a physical action on stage should reveal an idea within the text, and not call attention to itself, so should the use of media be to project the implicit rather than the explicit, which would be not the adding of a dimension but useless repetition.

ARTAUDIAN THEATRE: THEATRE OF CRUELTY

Any discussion of New Theatre must make some reference to the stylistic implications of the work of Antonin Artaud and his "Theatre of Cruelty," but because Artaud was more prophet than practitioner it is difficult to be specific, though his general aesthetic is evident. We emphasize first that the implication of Theatre of Cruelty is not necessarily the infliction of pain—beatings, torture, and mangling of human bodies—although these may be used to create the required impact. Cruelty implies, rather, an intensity and severity of emotional attack which is calculated to drain the ulcer of man's repressed animal desires and instincts—the aggressions, lusts, hates, and sadistic impulses which Artaud believed to be held in, suppurating beneath the mask of civilized behavior. Artaud compared his theatre to a plague which seizes man in a raging fever, then leaves him cleansed of disease and peacefully accommodated to his normal existence. The purpose of Artaud's cruelty was to purge, within the theatrical experience, all the primitive instincts which lead to wars and murders and rapes when the thin patina of civilization is broken.

The basic principle of Artaudian theatre is an all-out attack on the senses, geared to bring to the surface, expose, and incorporate within the performance all the passions and instincts hidden within man's archetypal viscera. This is a tall order. It obviously calls for an environmental approach, attacking the audience with sensations from all sides, and it can use media—electronic sounds, lights, and projected images. We have referred to some of the demands Artaudian theatre makes on the actor in

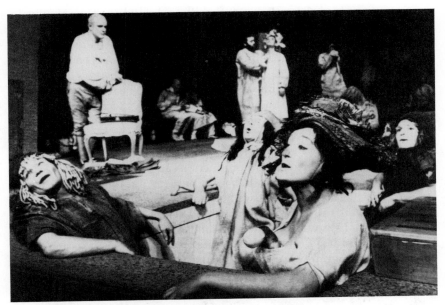

Photo by Holte Photographics. Courtesy Royal Shakespeare Theatre, Stratford-upon-Avon.

Figure 100.   De Sade, and inmates, in stage trap in Peter Brook's 1965 production of *Marat/Sade* for the Royal Shakespeare Company.

Chapter 9. Acting must be intensely physical, the nature of its communication preverbal and prerational. Emotions are projected by grunts, howls, and gestures that spring from an inner primitive energy. Directors experimenting in this mode (and it is all experiment, for Artaud left no model, no handed-down experience), have resorted to such means as simulated sex acts (and in at least one instance actual copulation); orgiastic couplings of writhing nude bodies; the incorporation of the spectators in mutual physical exploration with the performers; acts of pain and torture with the splashing of animal blood on the audience; performers urinating on members of the audience; and, in Peter Brook's famous production of *Marat/Sade,* the performance of the atrocious physical and mental malfunctions of the inmates of an insane asylum.

Creation of an Artaudian style, when the director is working from a text, means the discovery of those elements within the text which implicitly refer to the more primitive instincts, and the heightened projection of these elements by means of the techniques mentioned above. The director's task is to find those actions, images, and gestures which create the kind of hieroglyph and make the archetypal impact that Artaud was seeking. Some texts lend themselves more easily to Artaud's theory; the intrinsic style of Jacobean and Senecan tragedies, and early Gothic Romantic plays (Artaud himself did a production of Shelley's *Cenci*) have been found well-suited to the creation of an Artaudian style, as has Euripides' *Bacchae*.

Just as "When did you last have a catharsis?" has become one of the standard theatrical jokes about Aristotle's tragic effect, so the impact Artaud was seeking is not easy to achieve. It requires a mutual and deeply felt intention on the part of both actor and director, plus the difficult combination of free and uninhibited exposure of self with great discipline and control. Too easily an Artaudian production can become an excuse for self-indulgence, or it can be only an external implementation of the elements, lacking in all passion and impact. We have been witness to both errors. We have seen groaning, sweating, writhing actors possibly having a lovely time and working out all manner of primitive urges, but in complete disregard of the rather glum and frustrated spectators surrounding them. On the other hand, in a well researched and theoretically well presented

Photo by Frederick Eberstadt. Courtesy of Richard Schechner.

Figure 101. Primitive emotion given violent physical expression is another attribute of New Theatre, seen here in Sam Shepard's *Commune,* produced by the Performance Group (1970).

performance of Artaud's version of the *Cenci,* we were subjected to stereophonic aboriginal chants and howls that bore evident traces of their tape-recorded nature, while death stalked very carefully through Gothic mausoleums and maidens were ravished with painstaking precision so as not to disturb their makeup. In Artaudian theatre, above all, disaster awaits the director who is seeking a gimmick and has no deep commitment to the statement behind his style.

In summary, New Theatre is a theatre of total impact which is consciously moving away from preconceived forms. It is nonmatrixed; that is, it does not need a central focus. It does not have to employ an informational structure, and the text may be only a pretext for the performance. Impression is more important than understanding. The New Theatre attempts to exist as an event which is part of, rather than removed from, life itself; to use an all-encompassing environment rather than a stage; to involve the spectator in the enactment of his myths; to eliminate the distinction between actor and ego, between the performed and the experienced. To achieve this it is not enough to be open and receptive and have all the life attributes of a "beautiful person." Like all achievement in theatre, the goal is won by insight, a clear sense of purpose, sincerity, and skill—that combination of talent, technique, and experience which can never be gainsaid.

Realism and Naturalism

We have consciously left discussion of realism and naturalism to the end, because they purport to be closest to life experience and therefore should need least contrivance, and because, as the predominant modes of the twentieth century, they are likely to be the styles most familiar to directors and audience. We shall not, therefore, spend a great deal of discussion on them, and we shall dismiss realism fairly swiftly.

Realism, which can have as many definitions as life itself, is usually the term given to those productions in which all the actions have a more or less naturalistic basis, the settings are a reasonable approximation of a real life environment, the language is not unduly rhetorical, and the director interposes himself enough to keep the actors in open positions most of the time, the characters tolerably believable, and the pace fairly smart and steady. It is closely related to naturalism and has prospered since the mid-nineteenth century, when Madame Vestris started to use box sets to narrow down the theatre's interests into the room in which man lived most of his life. This was followed by the "cup and saucer" realism of Tom Robertson and the middle-class realism of Ibsen, both of whom wanted to bring home discussion of social problems of concern to the average individual in their day by placing the discussion within an environ-

Victoria & Albert Museum

Figure 102. External realism in *The Whip,* London, 1909.

Theatermuseum, Munich

Figure 103. Naturalism in a 1903 Berlin production of Maxim Gorki's *The Lower Depths.*

ment to which the audience could immediately relate and say, "Oh, yes, my drawing-room (or my parlor) is just like that." Realism has tended to become the style in which one produces Arthur Miller, John Osborne, Neil Simon, and most other commercial playwrights.

One of the problems with realism is that life tends to leave it behind, and the realistic artifacts which drew an immediate response from the audience in the 1890s seem a bit archaic if reproduced in the 1970s. The director must immediately decide how far he wishes to update furnishings, props, costumes, and so on, and what this will do to the play, for the discussion of pertinent problems of the 1890s may seem out of place in mid–twentieth century surroundings. The modes and manners of the late nineteenth century or even the first part of the twentieth are also much less realistic to contemporary audiences, and the director must decide how far these manners were an intrinsic part of the play's style and were necessary to make its social points, and how far he can validly update them.

A fairly fundamental distinction between realism and *naturalism* involves the inner workings of character. Realism could be concerned greatly with external detail—such as Belasco's putting Childs Restaurant on the New York stage—but very little with inner truth and valid motivation. While realism worked from the premise that the environment was a theatrical recapitulation of real life circumstances, naturalism took the position that what was happening on the stage was life, or at least a "slice of life," which the audience simply happened to be looking in on; thus, theoretically no concession should be made to the presence of an audience at a naturalistic production.

Some very definite directorial options are involved in the creation of a naturalistic style, and the manner in which they are employed tends to determine where the production lies along the realism–naturalism continuum. Lighting in naturalistic productions should attempt to reproduce as subtly as possible the environmental atmosphere of the given circumstances in the text. Light should emanate from actual sources in the set; general lighting should avoid hard edges and artificial shadows, and the quality should, in conjunction with the textures of the set and the makeup of the actors, produce a completely lifelike effect. The same principles apply to the set: there should be no cut-out trees which wobble when touched, or flats which shake when doors are slammed. Sets should look lived in, not newly built and painted for the theatrical occasion; nor should they be so constructed as to give a completely balanced and formal sense—unless it should happen that the circumstances of the play dictate a formal environment. Costumes should seem well worn (no beggars in clean, pressed rags), and in textural and color terms should belong to the set.

As with the physical environment, so with the staging and acting.

Naturalistic staging is geared to produce the effect that the stage is simply a room with its fourth wall removed to allow the audience to look in. Movement should therefore have the apparently random and casual pattern of life. Stage balance will be informal; there is no creation of stage pictures for their aesthetic effect. Actors may adopt rather closed positions when speaking to each other (which they should do, rather than speaking to the audience off each other), and they may even turn their backs to the audience. (The first great naturalistic theatre, Antoine's Théâtre Libre, was sometimes known as "the theatre of Antoine's back.") There is likely to be a good deal of small business in naturalistic productions—people in real life do not sit still and talk to each other for very long; they smoke cigarettes, drink coffee, swing their legs, turn on the radio or record player, play with their moustache—but the business should not be gratuitous, it should be related to action or character, or a calculated and unnatural effect will be produced.

We have discussed naturalistic acting style at some length in Chapter 9 and will simply mention here some general stylistic options of naturalism. Dialect, rather than pure stage speech, is likely to be used; lines may overlap, and ad libbing is possible. Line delivery is almost certain to have a broken pattern, with lines split up and interjections used. Emotion is generally inner-working and understated.

Naturalism as a dramatic genre, and thus, if we are to respect intrinsic style, as a theatrical performance, is concerned with the sociopsychology of ordinary human beings in ordinary situations. It seeks inner truths and reveals what makes men tick. To project this with truthful stage actions places a director in a challenging situation; yet perhaps the greatest tribute that can be paid a director of a naturalistic play is that it did not seem "directed." Naturalism is theatre, as free from art and artifice as art and artifice can make it!

Summary

Sir John Gielgud once defined style as "knowing what kind of play you are in." This is an excellent starting point. In this chapter we have suggested that in a play there is both an intrinsic style, which relates to Gielgud's point, and the possibility of manifold extrinsic styles. Extrinsic styles can project the intrinsic values of a play in new directions and new guises, suited to changing technology and social, political, and moral attitudes. The director must still recognize what kind of play he is dealing with, but the style of that play does not have to recapitulate the thrust and detail of its first productions.

Style may be varied, but it should not be arbitrary. We have suggested that it is a function of the consistent relating of the world of the play, the world of the audience, and the world of the stage. Consistency is important. Another famous actor, Sir Ralph Richardson, said that he "gives a director three mistakes—then I am on my own." By this Richardson implied that if a director has failed to do his homework and does not understand his play in every detail, then he will inevitably commit inconsistencies and is not worthy of the cast's and, by extension, the audience's confidence.

Peter Brook wrote in *The Empty Space,*

> All the different elements of staging—the shorthands of behavior that stand for certain emotions: gestures, gesticulations, tones of voice—are fluctuating on an invisible stock exchange all the time. Life is moving, influences are playing on actor and audience, and other plays, other arts, the cinema, television, current events join in the constant rewriting of history and the amending of the daily truth. . . . A living theatre that thinks it can stand aloof from anything so trivial as fashion will wilt. In the theatre, every form once born is mortal; every form must be reconceived, and its new conception will bear the marks of all the influences that surround it. In this sense the theatre is relativity. Yet a great theatre is not a fashion house; perpetual elements do recur and certain fundamental issues do underlie all dramatic activity. The deadly trap is to divide the eternal truths from the subtle variations; this is a form of snobbery and it is fatal.[10]

The creative director's challenge and fulfillment is to keep the theatre a living contemporary force. He does this by his insightful understanding of the playwright's work and his honest and imaginative translation of this work into a meaningful and dynamic stylistic statement of his times.

[10] Peter Brook, *The Empty Space: A Book About Theatre—Deadly, Holy, Rough, Immediate* (New York: Atheneum Publishers, 1968), p. 16.

V
Appendix

11

Directing the Play

To this point we have discussed the art of directing from the premise that no single method, avenue of approach, and ordering of concerns can be absolutely preferred over any other. We have suggested various approaches, examples, and exercises, because a director works from a broad range of possibilities and his success is determined by the choices and decisions he makes. If there were a "correct" method of directing plays, as there is a correct method of laying bricks, directing would not be an art at all. Still, we feel that it would be useful in a book of this nature to provide a model detailing definite stages to be followed in the production of a play. A director must, finally, be able to make decisions and organize his options on the many disparate elements of a production in a relatively structured as well as aesthetic manner. Creative imagination alone is not enough; it was once said of Franco Zeffirelli, the brilliant but hardly pragmatic Italian director, that he was the "kind of director who needs a director." Thus, as a direction for directors, we suggest one possible model

273

Friedman-Abeles/Hank Kranzler

Figures 104 and 105. *American directors at work.* The director's rehearsal behavior encompasses many modes. Above, *exploration*: Broadway and film director Mike Nichols, right, leads a coffee-table reading and examination of Murray Schisgal's *Luv* with the cast, Alan Arkin, Eli Wallach, and Anne Jackson, third, fourth, and fifth from left. Below, *explanation*: founding director of the Association of Producing Artists, Ellis Rabb, script in hand, blocks a production of *The Merchant of Venice* for the American Conservatory Theatre.

Courtesy of Martha Swope

Figure 106. *Discussion*: Alan Schneider, leading American director of the plays of Samuel Beckett, Edward Albee, and Harold Pinter, coaches Hal Holbrook and Lilian Gish in the Broadway production of *I Never Sang for My Father*.

Photo by Hank Kranzler. Courtesy of American Conservatory Theatre.

Figure 107. *Suggestion*: William Ball, founding director of the American Conservatory Theatre, issues a directive from the back of the house.

for a production, including a checklist of practical directorial decisions which must be taken during the process of mounting a play.

A Production Model

The model includes twenty-one steps in a production sequence, progressing from the selection of a *property* (the professional term for a new script or script source) to the director's responsibilities during the actual run of the production. In practice many of these steps will be combined with others or even circumvented, but here we shall spell out each separate stage so that the director is aware of their possible consideration. Many of the stages may be the immediate responsibility of someone other than the director, but he must be party to decisions at each stage if the final production is to resemble at all his original conception.

The model is divided into three sequences: a proposal phase, a preproduction phase, and a production phase.

The Proposal Phase

The proposal phase is the period during which the director either initiates a play production or is given one by a producer. Few directors today are in the fortunate position of being besieged with offers. Most play production in the United States comes at the initiative of directors themselves, who are constantly on the lookout for new scripts. In addition to searching out new properties, directors also have mental files of plays they would like to do, given the right circumstances. It is hardly surprising that directors should play a major part in the initiation of productions, for if they are not eager to get things going, they shouldn't be in the business.

1. PROPERTY SELECTION

In our model the director chooses the property, normally a new play to which he has manuscript access, or a previously produced and/or published play which he has read. He chooses the play for one overriding reason—because it appeals to him. Its appeal may be artistic or commercial; we hope that it is both. The play appeals as a work of insight, intelligence, sensuality, theatricality, humor and/or dramatic impact, and these values encourage the director to think that others would be interested to support its production by investing time and money as financial backers, producers, actors, technicians, or audience.

It is neither surprising nor a capitulation to mass taste that the director bears his audience in mind when considering plays to produce. Louis Jouvet, one of the most artistic directors of his or any other time, set the maxim, "In the theatre, there is only one goal: success." This was not crass commercialism, but a simple admission that theatre is collaborative and communicative, and it cannot exist without the successful creation of active communication with a live audience.

The property selected by the director need not be a play. It may be a novel the director thinks would make a good play, a series of poems, an autobiography such as that of Anne Frank, a concept that could be a basis for improvisation, or any other idea that might generate theatrical outcome. In each case the director's primary considerations must be: Does it appeal to me? Will it appeal to those I need to attract to work with me? Is there an audience for it?

2. Acquisition of Rights to the Property

Interest in a property conveys no legal right to produce it on a stage, even in situations where no admission fee is to be charged. Every copyrighted literary work belongs to its author unless and until other arrangements are made, and even works which are not copyrighted may be legally protected in certain situations. Therefore, the legal permission of the author or his representatives will almost always have to be secured for the presentation of any material written within the last fifty-six years, the maximum duration of copyright.

The director must acquire the rights for a *new manuscript* directly from the author or his agent, or find a producer who will do so. The normal means of acquiring these rights professionally is to offer the author a sum of money as an option fee, which will permit the director as the possessor of dramatic rights to produce the play within a certain period of time. At the same time a contract is negotiated which specifies the royalties the playwright will receive during the production, what rights he gives to the producer, and what rights he retains. Contracts of this sort are ordinarily drawn up by theatrical lawyers, and in professional situations they are subject to requirements of the Dramatists' Guild.

In a college presentation of a new play, presumably by a little-known author, a royalty is rarely given, although a cash prize or bonus may be connected with the production. Still, a contract should be drawn up giving the college (the producer) the right to produce the play, for without this contract the playwright has a legal option to withdraw his manuscript from production at any moment—including an hour before opening.

If the property selected is a previously produced play, the technical and legal difficulties of acquiring rights are minimal, particularly if the production is to be an amateur one. Most previously produced plays worthy of present attention have been published and are easily available for examination. Plays may be copyrighted for a period of twenty-eight years, and the copyright can be renewed once only for another twenty-eight years. If the play is, then, more than fifty-six years old it falls into what is called *public domain* and can be freely produced without payment of any royalty. Thus, all the plays of Shakespeare, Marlowe, Sheridan, and Wilde fall into that category, and plays by Shaw, for example, are one by one becoming freely available as the years pass. (It is interesting to note seven or eight productions of the same Shavian play occurring simultaneously in different parts of the country as the play comes into the public domain.)

Previously produced plays that have extant copyrights, *including translations,* are available for professional productions through the authors, their estates, or their agents for royalty payments that are usually negotiated at a percentage of the box office gross. The same plays are usually available for amateur production at fixed rates. Almost all nonmusical American plays and translations produced on amateur (including collegiate) stages today are handled through three leasing companies which have purchased the amateur rights to the plays. These companies are Samuel French Inc. (25 West 45th Street, New York, New York 10036), Dramatist's Play Service (440 Park Avenue South, New York, New York 10016), and Dramatic Publishing Company (86 East Randolph Street, Chicago, Illinois 60601). These companies annually issue catalogs listing the plays they control and the royalty rates for performances. The usual royalty for a nonmusical American play performed in a college or community theatre is twenty-five to fifty dollars per performance depending on the length of the play and its present popularity. That one of the leasing companies has acquired rights to a given play does not mean that the play may be presented anywhere at any time. Frequently plays are made available only after certain professional engagements have terminated, and even after a play has been generally released it may be withdrawn in certain areas, or perhaps altogether, pending a possible professional revival or filming.

Musical plays are handled slightly differently, amateur productions being leased almost exclusively by Tams-Witmark Inc. (757 Third Avenue, New York, New York 10003) at a somewhat higher royalty than for straight plays. This company also rents scripts, scores, and other material essential to the musical play—material which has not usually been made generally available.

Whatever the play, the director should make an inquiry about its availability his very first task, since all production plans hinge on his legal right to the script. Once the property has been selected, a phone call or letter to the author's agent (normally listed in the front of the published edition of the play), or to the leasing company (also listed, when known, in the front of the published script) is necessary. If the leasing company is unknown a letter to Samuel French and Dramatist's Play Service will probably find it. The agent or leasing company will respond with a contract which, when signed, assures the director of the right to produce the play for a stated royalty on given dates. All changes in the contract (extra performances and so on) must be renegotiated, but this is seldom a major problem once the initial rights have been granted.

3. Revisions and Adaptations of the Script

If the property is a standard English-language play, it is unlikely that much work will need to be done on the script once the rights have been obtained. In certain cases, however, the script may need work by the director before rehearsals begin. It may be a novel that needs to be dramatized, a foreign play that must be translated, or a straight play to which the director wants to add songs or even turn into a full-scale musical. This work should be done before a producer is sought, and if the director is to be his own producer, it should be done well before the rehearsal period begins. Of course, some minor adaptations of the script will always take place throughout the period in which the director and actors work on the play.

4. Choosing a Theatre and an Audience

We emphasize once again that the sequence of stages in the model we are hypothesizing could be changed for any number of reasons. Frequently the theatre or the audience will be givens which may determine the choice of script, rather than the other way around. Given the script, however, the director must remember that no matter how much it may be adapted to contemporary circumstances, no play will do equally well in all situations. A comedy of manners might be well received in an elegant suburban community but rejected in a ghetto street theatre. Shakespearean tragedy might succeed in a university area but fail in the adjacent town.

Obviously the director does not simply pander to theatrical prejudices, but he will do well to consider his potential audience. Part of the reason for the disastrous reception of Beckett's *Waiting for Godot* in the United States was that it premiered in Miami Beach before an audience that lacked the theatrical sophistication to appreciate the merits of the play.

After he has a sense of the audience he feels will best appreciate his play, the director can select a suitable theatre. This choice has been fully discussed in Chapter 3, but essentially the director will be interested in the physical nature of the theatre: size (2,000 seats, 600, 150), type (outdoor, proscenium, thrust, arena), location (suburban, city, hip, university). In addition, the cost to him of the theatre, its availability, and equipment are important factors.

5. ESTABLISHMENT OF A TENTATIVE BUDGET

Theatre productions unavoidably require money. College students, who are used to assuming the availability of theatres, equipment, and a large pool of actors, frequently forget that they are blessed in the use of facilities and personnel that would cost dearly in the "outside" world. Every proposal must take into consideration the potential costs of production, which can be as high as the $1,000,000 reportedly spent on the Broadway musical *Coco*.

Budget items to be considered include the following:

1. Theatre building rental, rehearsal space rental, air conditioning, maintenance and janitorial service, heat, electricity, utilities
2. Royalties for the play, and for the translation or adaptation
3. Salaries for director, actors, designers, technicians, business staff, ushers, and box office personnel (in professional situations it is not unusual for the director, the leading actor, and the designers to take a royalty in addition to a salary)
4. Scenery, costumes, and props (ordinarily the major expense in an amateur production, but a fairly minor one in professional theatre)
5. Equipment for lighting and sound
6. Publicity and business expenses (programs, posters, tickets, advertising; all items of expenditure; huge in most professional situations)

Valid estimates should be made for all budget items including heating, lighting, and cleaning—expenses likely to be hidden in amateur productions, and which the director will not have to deal with because they are part of someone else's investment in the production. A new director will find that any theatre with a history of play production has model budgets available for consultation. The final budget figure should be realistic for all the areas of the director's proposal.

6. A PROPOSAL AND A PRODUCER

The director is now in a position to approach a producer with a formal or informal proposal. The producer, be he a college dean, a professional fund-raiser, or a community board of trustees, will guarantee the funding of the production.

The proposal may vary from a two-minute telephone call to a ninety-page written analysis. A written proposal usually includes the name of the property and why the director wishes to mount it (see 1 above); a copy of the script and statement of its availability, possibly supported by a tape of some of the musical elements, songs, or a scene from the play (see 3); the name of the theatre the director wants to use, and the anticipated audience (see 4); and an itemized budget (see 5). Additionally, the director may include in his proposal any pertinent material he feels will help clarify his ideas and make a stronger impact on the producer.

We feel that it is not out of place, in a book about directing, to mention the practical difficulties of attaining directorial positions. Since the director of a play can be the artistic leader of a massive, expensive enterprise, directing jobs are naturally difficult to come by. No one would walk into a major corporation and ask to be interviewed for the position of corporate president, but young directing students seem to feel no diffidence about walking straight from the classroom to a directorial chair. It is splendid that this should be the case; some of the best young directors in America have come almost straight from drama school to Broadway (Arvin Brown and Jeff Bleckner, for example), but such rapid career acceleration is unusual. For most directors it is a long, hard climb in which interim positions as stage manager, actor, designer, or lighting designer furnish experience and exposure. Most directors write many formal and informal proposals—most of which land in the producer's wastebasket—while honing their creative talents during the long wait.

The Preproduction Phase

At last the director's proposal is accepted, and he finds that he has the funds and assistance a producer can command. Or perhaps he has found the financial contacts or so reduced the cost that he can afford to produce the play himself. At this stage decisions are made firmly; once made, they cannot easily be revoked.

7. ORGANIZATION OF THE PRODUCTION PERIOD

Of first importance at this time is the establishment of firm dates, particularly of "opening night." Once a date has been established for the play's first performance, the rest of the scheduling can be arrived at by working backward from that crucial date.

Scheduling production dates is an intricate business. Time must be allotted for the construction of scenery and costumes even before the scenery and costumes have been designed, and frequently before the designers have been selected. Rehearsal time must include ample time for the actors to be on stage, or else a stage simulation must be built to duplicate the features of the eventual setting. The technical staff will need much time in the theatre itself to position scenery, hang and focus the lights, and make the machinery operable.

In professional productions, where actors' salaries are paid during rehearsals as well as performances, rehearsal time is usually compressed into three or four forty-hour weeks. In college and community situations rehearsal time is spread over four to ten weeks, with rehearsals occurring mainly in the evenings for two-and-a-half to four hours each. No scheduling system is mandatory. Summer stock productions are frequently put together in a single week of daytime rehearsals, while the actors perform another play at night. Government-supported theatres whose actors are salaried year-round rather than on a weekly basis enjoy a rehearsal period far longer than normal commercial allotments.

Do not assume that the quality of a production correlates directly with the time spent in rehearsal. Plays can be overrehearsed, particularly with amateur actors whose interest and enthusiasm may wane over a protracted period, and performances grow stale long before opening night. Even professionals are not immune to creeping ennui resulting from overlong, unstimulating rehearsal schedules.

When the production dates have been set and the theatre hired for the run, the director can work backward to schedule the other crucial stages of production. The most important of these is the start of the rehearsal period, for by that time the casting and most of the work on the script must be complete. The director then needs to schedule his design completion dates, by which time approved designs will have gone to the scene shop, the costume shop, and the property room, and then the dates for technical and dress rehearsals. Normally a production manager helps the director coordinate and establish this part of the timetable, but the director is finally responsible for seeing that the schedule is adhered to, and he should keep an eye on the progress of technical areas if he wishes to exercise genuine control over the production.

Those critical dates once set, the director then proceeds to set other target dates: for auditions, casting, publicity releases and interviews, photographs, and specific rehearsal accomplishments. If he is doing a dialect play and wishes to engage his cast in a three-day "crash course" in Irish brogue, now is the time to set aside those days on a calendar. If the play requires juggling, dancing, fencing, or any other special effect that the actors may not be accomplished at, then periods of special coaching should be worked into the schedule. Finally, the director should allow some time for himself, before the production begins, in which he is free to perform the major creative "homework" that will determine the specific nature of his production.

8. Preparation of a Preliminary Promptbook

The director works throughout the preproduction and production stages with some sort of promptbook, even if it is simply his personal dog-eared copy of the script. Most directors like to prepare, as soon as a play is committed to production, a formal preliminary promptbook which may be one of several eventually used in the play's production. The preliminary promptbook is a copy of the play whose text is surrounded by large margins which can accommodate the director's written comments at various points within the dialogue. The most common form of production book is constructed by pasting pages from the published text onto large 8½-inch by 11-inch mimeograph paper which has been cut so that both sides of the text page show, and collecting the resulting pages into a looseleaf binder. The preliminary promptbook becomes the director's property, although he may give it to the stage manager for use in rehearsals or running the show. It is probably better, and certainly more professional, however, for the stage manager to prepare his own promptbook. Annotated promptbooks of this sort have a long history in the theatre; those surviving from the seventeenth and eighteenth centuries have enormous value for theatre historians.

The preliminary promptbook becomes the repository for all the director's ideas during his preproduction reading and research. Copies of articles or discussions he feels will be valuable for later reading (perhaps to the cast) can be added at the back of the looseleaf binder. Concepts of linereadings, stagings, interpretations, and background information may be noted in the margins and related to specific lines. Since the preliminary promptbook is the director's property, purely speculative suggestions, images, and ideas can be set down without becoming a formal part of the production at that point. A director's notes to himself can usually be extracted from a well-used preliminary promptbook.

9. Derivation of Intrinsic Interpretation

Much of the director's interpretative function (see pages 21 through 43) can best be carried out at the preproduction stage, when time pressures are minimal and no one yet wants immediate results. The most obvious way to derive that interpretation is to read and reread the play. Some directors read a play once for each major character, each time examining the play from that character's point of view. Some read the play impressionistically, to select images, speeches, ideas, and striking moments which seem to them extraordinarily important. Some read and analyze the play from a dramaturgical standpoint (pages 30 through 33) to isolate the rising conflicts, climaxes, and resolutions and to evaluate their relative intensities. Some directors research the period in which the play is set, the period in which it was written, biographical material by and about the author, criticism of the play, criticism of previous productions of the play, other plays by the same author, and the literary or historical material mentioned or alluded to in the play. Some directors actually visit the locale in which the play is set or where the author wrote, to steep themselves in the play's atmosphere. Some directors do all of these things to develop an intrinsic interpretation of the play's meaning.

10. DECISIONS CONCERNING EXTRINSIC INTERPRETATION

The director should make these decisions carefully (see pages 40 through 43) before he enters the pressurized environment of actual rehearsals, possibly even before the actors have been cast. Will the play make a definite personal statement, and if so, what? The director may wish to examine the play in light of current situations, or in terms of situations relevant to his audience. He may wish to pursue possible leads in psychology, philosophy, current political events, or current sociological studies which might help him in this reinterpretation. Of course, he should move gingerly in this direction, and with respect for the author's genius, but he should not feel compelled to produce his play without some reference to his audience's environment and attitudes.

11. ESTABLISHING A STYLE

For the most part, style is the theatrical implementation of interpretation. Having decided on a theatre, a play, and an interpretation, the director is now concerned with the stylistic nature of the production. How will the actors be directed? How will the design project the interpretation? Will a particular period be used? Greek, Elizabethan, Restoration, Neoclassic? Does expressionistic, Epic, or Artaudian theatre work? At this juncture only the general conception of style will be determined—the details will evolve with the production itself—but it is important that the director have a stylistic concept at a fairly early stage, as it will inform many of his preproduction decisions.

12. SELECTING THE PRODUCTION STAFF

The production staff may number from one to twenty. It can consist of a set designer, a costume designer, a property designer, a lighting designer, a production manager, a technical director, a stage manager, a makeup artist, a hair stylist, a musical director, a choreographer, a sound technician, a lighting console operator, and a host of assistants to any of these technicians. There are also box office personnel, ushers, publicity writers, business administrators, bookkeepers, and secretaries, under the supervision of the producer; the members of the orchestra, under the supervision of the conductor; and the actors.

The director selects his production staff in consultation with the producer in all cases, and sometimes by the direct order of the producer. In most cases these decisions are in fact made beforehand; most college, community, and resident company theatres have a permanent staff to handle most if not all of these functions. This is usually a blessing; a well-functioning production team is a valuable asset for a director, and an ad hoc "all-star" group of individually talented theatre artists can create disastrous production situations.

The production staff, if the director has any say, should be selected with an eye to its members' potential interest in the specific production: the play, its proposed interpretation, and the stylistic guidelines the director has set forth. Designers in particular can be approached like producers, and shown copies of the play proposal so that they can determine whether they are interested. Without general agreement on the specific nature of the proposed production, catastrophe might result. Conversely, the collaboration should not be a one-way affair; directors frequently have their most inspiring ideas during or immediately after consultations with designers and technicians at this point in the preproduction stage.

In a production staff, therefore, the director seeks people who are talented, interested in the specific goals of the production as planned, helpful in offering suggestions and creative ideas toward the successful realization of those goals, amenable to the director and each other, and available within the time schedule and financial budget of the production.

13. Auditioning and Casting the Actors

The auditioning of actors may be done early or late in the preproduction schedule (see pages 209 through 212); in some professional situations it is done months before the first rehearsal. This practice can facilitate rehearsals by allowing the actors a long period of time for learning lines before the cast assembles (if the director operates in that way), and it can provide time for extensive research by the actors which might prove impossible during the production phase. Casting should be completed before rehearsals begin, and the casting of understudies might be made at the same time—a casting decision that is frequently overlooked.

14. Preparation of the Script

Besides the general work the director may do on the script before presenting it to a producer or the designers, he may do more specific work on the scripts the actors finally receive. Even published scripts may need editing for specific circumstances, and many directors choose to do some rewriting—a somewhat questionable practice. (We should note here that the practice of photocopying published and copyrighted scripts is presently of debatable legality.)

Editing or cutting may be required so that the audience can get home at a reasonable hour. An uncut production of *Hamlet* could easily run five hours, and most of Shakespeare's other plays, if played from the standard library edition, would run longer than most modern audiences care to sit in a theatre. Whether that is lamentable or not is moot; the decision, in any case, is up to the director.[1]

Cutting should be accomplished carefully without violating the sense of the scene or eliminating the ethos of the character whose line has been excised. The difficulty in cutting dialogue is to do so without affecting the rhythm of the play, the poetry of the line, and the climaxes of the arguments. If time is of the essence, it may be preferable to cut an entire scene that is found unnecessary rather than to take an erratic editorial pen to various lines throughout the play. Sometimes, however, particularly with older plays like Shakespeare's, effective cutting can dramatically intensify the meaning of a play. Unless the director's goal is to please the half-dozen scholars in attendance, he is well advised at least to consider the elimination of Shakespearean allusions which have long since fallen into such total disuse as to be meaningless to modern audiences.

A final note about cutting: it is always desirable, when possible, to cut dialogue during the preproduction phase rather than in rehearsals. Dialogue cut after it has been memorized by an actor can tend to irritate him and disturb his sense of the rhythm of the play.

15. CONSULTATION AND AGREEMENT ON DESIGNS

The director's responsibility for design does not end with his approval of a designer (see Chapter 4). The collaboration between director and design staff determines in great measure the stylistic consistency of the production. Design consultation usually begins as soon as a designer has been selected, when the director explains his concept and receives a preliminary response from the designers. The designer then begins his research and creative projections. The director should by this time be able to point the designer toward various sources that are in keeping with his overall interpretation of the play and with the stylistic guidelines he has

---

[1] Shakespeare was not only familiar with the practice of cutting, he probably approved of it. Hamlet approves of it: when Polonius complains that a speech of the player is "too long," Hamlet responds, "It shall to the barber's, with your beard" (II. ii. 496–97).

in mind. It is equally vital that specific dates be agreed on, by which the director may expect to see preliminary sketches, final sketches, set models, and finished products. It is rarely desirable for the director to set these dates arbitrarily; in almost every situation the deadline is agreed on by all involved. They should then be written in a formal memorandum, copies of which are distributed to the entire technical and production staff.

The extent of the models and designs to be provided by the designers is also subject to agreement. Some directors can visualize a setting from only a ground plan and an elevation sketch; others require a scale model to get the "feel" of the set. Similarly, some directors feel satisfied with color renderings of costumes; others prefer exacting sketches accompanied by color swatches of material. The more work a designer is asked to do in presenting models of his designs, the less time he will have (or the shops will have) to execute the actual settings or costumes. Some designers are adept at making models and others at drafting plans and elevations; the choices should be fairly and reasonably worked out by the individuals involved.

Unfortunately, the lighting designer and the sound engineer are frequently not consulted until later stages of the production period. This is often a grave mistake. It is always desirable to involve these people at the preproduction stage along with the other designers, since their scope can be greatly enlarged and enhanced by approaches to the settings or costumes which can be made only at this time. A lighting designer cannot, however, draw up any but the most general lighting plot until the set design has been approved, and the director should not expect a final light plot until the scenery is constructed and the lighting designer has had ample opportunity to work on it.

During this stage the property master and makeup designer should also be consulted and prop and makeup lists compiled. The property list is one preproduction aspect that may change a great deal during rehearsals; it is wise, therefore, that props be acquired (and designed, if necessary) as far ahead of schedule as possible, to allow them to be tested in rehearsal and modified if need be. Makeup, by contrast, can be finalized shortly before technical rehearsals unless special circumstances require earlier attention.

At various stages during the preproduction planning the director must approve the designs. He is ruled by deadlines and does not have an indefinite time to respond to the designers' proposals or sketches. Ordinarily, once general concepts for settings, costumes, and lighting have been agreed on by director and designers and the designers have submitted sets of renderings, models, or draftings to the director, the director looks at each proposed design and approves them individually or sends single items back for revision. Eventually a complete scenery system will be approved, along with a set of costumes, props, and a lighting plan. Once final approval is given, the director is pretty much bound to it. Certainly he has the right to ask for or even to insist on last-minute changes in design, but these are accomplished only at great expense and at rising levels of frustration among co-workers. Directors who like to hold back their decisions to the last possible moment and reverse them after they see what happens in the rehearsals are courting disastrous cost overruns and staff alienation; they may do it, but they should be prepared for the results.

The Production Phase

Eventually the director can no longer work privately in his office, study, or bathtub; he can no longer make leisurely decisions by himself or in interviews and consultations with his staff associates. From here on his work is highly public, highly visible, and the pressure of opening night increases ineluctably with every hour. All his homework should have been done by this moment and all directorial decisions made. In practice this is rarely the case; few directors come to the first rehearsals feeling as prepared as they would like to be. Whether this is a case of practice denying an overly idealistic theory, or simply that few creative people ever feel satisfied with their efforts, is impossible to say. However, a small degree of uncertainty on the director's part at the beginning of rehearsals may be an asset in guarding against undue self-satisfaction and allowing for a better reception of other people's ideas. A good precept, however, is to do as much work as is profitable before meeting the actors.

16. INITIAL REHEARSALS

Initial rehearsals introduce the play to the actors, and the actors and staff to each other. Some directors avoid this step altogether and begin blocking immediately; others, notably the late, great Jean Vilar of France's Théâtre Nationale Populaire, spend more than half the rehearsal period sitting around a table reading the play aloud.

During early rehearsals the cast, staff, and director become acquainted. They examine the designs, and the director discusses his concept of the play and the supporting material with which he wishes the cast to become familiar. Occasionally this can take the form of a lecture or a formal discussion; it might also be a series of remarks interjected during a first reading aloud of the play.

The *first reading* of the play (a step some directors omit) is a chance to make certain all roles have been properly assigned (including "Offstage shout" and "A man in the crowd"), and that all the lines are properly attributed. It is also an opportunity to ensure that the actors understand any obscure words and references in the play, and to pinpoint any possibly controversial readings in cases where the director did not realize that variant possibilities exist. The first reading is almost always given by the actors playing their roles, though they are rarely encouraged to "act." Occasionally, however, the first reading is performed by the playwright, if he is in attendance at this gathering, or even by the director. The latter practice is extremely rare now. Somewhat more common is the relatively new practice of having the play read "around the room," with actors reading lines in rotation irrespective of which character says them. This has all the benefits of a first reading without making the actors in lesser roles excessively bored, and it discourages actors from trying to jump into an immediate interpretation of their parts.

During first rehearsals directors might also use games, exercises, or discussions to generate an ensemble spirit (see pages 196 through 204). Directors often conclude the first rehearsal period with a party, which can help create an ensemble as well as providing valuable recreation.

17. BLOCKING AND ACTING REHEARSALS

It would be futile to try to suggest an order for "blocking" versus "acting" rehearsals, for in practice about as many directors choose to block immediately as choose to postpone blocking until other acting points are made. Most directors, in fact, refuse to separate the two forms of rehearsals, and instead allow them to happen simultaneously. However, in keeping with the "model" nature of this section, we include at the end of this chapter a hypothetical timetable which might be followed during the rehearsal of a three-act play over a four-week period. While it is subject to infinite permutations, it may give the young director some idea of the pattern of a play's development.

Because we have devoted an entire chapter to blocking (Chapter 6), and another to acting (Chapter 9), we need say little more at this point except that blocking and acting goals must be pursued with relentless effort and enthusiasm during this middle (and largest) period of the rehearsal schedule. This is the most difficult part of rehearsals for both amateurs and professionals; no longer does the cast enjoy the excitement of discovering a new script and new fellow-workers, and not yet do they have the excitement of audiences, telegrams, reviews, and cast parties. During the middle period the director must not only be at the peak of his talents, he must also provide a catalytic spark of excitement that no one else can. In Tyrone Guthrie's words, "The all-important thing for a director is not to let rehearsals be a bore. The chief practical means to this end,"

Guthrie continues, "is to keep people busy, not to keep them waiting around with nothing to do. This is largely a matter of sensible planning . . . it is also a matter of seeing that work proceeds at a good brisk pace, not at that of the slowest wits. Better to rush the dullards off their feet than to bore and frustrate the brighter spirits."[2] As blocking and acting rehearsals progress, directorial work becomes more and more precise and subtle, aimed at polishing effects to a fine edge.

18. Preparation for Technical Rehearsals

The director is actually preparing himself for technical rehearsals throughout the production period. As soon as the designs are approved he will, if possible, visit the scene and costume shops to see how the designs are being realized. Such visits are not for the purpose of looking over anyone's shoulder; they help the director get the feel of the actual sets, costumes, and props his actors will be using. The director is also in regular contact with the production manager and/or the technical director to ensure that the technical departments will be ready on schedule; if changes or omissions are necessary because of time or financial considerations, the director must be the one to decide which set is cut and which costumes eliminated.

A week or two before the technical rehearsals begin, the director and his stage manager prepare the official promptbooks for use in running the show. These should be prepared similarly to the preliminary promptbook, with absolutely clean and uncluttered margins. If a three-ring binder is used the punched holes should be reinforced, because this book will see a lot of use.

The promptbook is then marked, in pencil (to be inked in only when final), with all the light cues, sound cues, and scene shift cues that the director feels the play requires—and all those he would like to consider using. Ordinarily this follows extensive discussion and agreement with the sound engineer, the lighting designer, and the technical director. Procedures for beginning the show should also be included: cues for checking with the house manager, lowering the houselights, pulling the main curtain, and so forth. A staff competent and sufficient in size to execute all the desired technical effects should be retained.

A list of props should be inserted in the promptbook, together with instructions on where each will be located at the beginning of the play, who will use each prop, where the prop user will finally return the prop, and what props will be used up in performance (for example, food props) and require replacement.

[2] Tyrone Guthrie, *A Life in the Theatre* (New York: McGraw-Hill Book Company, 1959), p. 153.

A complete list of costumes should also be inserted in the prompt-book, together with their offstage location throughout the show. Quick changes should be spotted early in the rehearsal period and planned for by setting up quick-change rooms directly off stage.

Special effects to be used in the production are best acquired before the technical rehearsals, so that the personnel who operate them have a chance to familiarize themselves with special effects equipment before the final rehearsals begin. The same opportunity should be given to all equipment operators working in the production.

19. TECHNICAL REHEARSALS

Technical rehearsals are laborious and absolutely necessary for the success of a complex production. They are frequently agony for inexperienced actors and less so for experienced ones only because they have grown accustomed to them. The point of technical rehearsals is to ensure that every technical effect—every shift of the lights, cue of the sound, movement of the scenery, and special effect emanating from the floor, wings, traps, or flies—works absolutely as it is intended all of the time.

The length and complexity of technical rehearsals varies with the production. A one-set realistic drama with no special music or lighting effects can probably be "teched" in little more time than it takes to run the play. A highly sophisticated musical, on the other hand, may have to be technically put together over several days. Whatever time it takes, we must emphasize that technical rehearsals are for perfecting technical effects, and they must be run and rerun until the technician is completely secure in what he is doing. Some directors try to do a run-through in conjunction with a tech rehearsal. In our experience this is disastrous. It is of no profit to the actors, whose rhythm is constantly being upset, and it wastes the technicians' time. Tech rehearsals are for technical effects; if a director feels his production needs a run-through at this juncture, then his schedule has probably been wrong, and this is no time for it.

For a highly complex production the following series of technical rehearsals could be hypothesized:

1. *First tech*: no actors. Set all light and sound cues: volumes, intensities, timings, and duration. This could take up to two days. At the end of this period the stage manager must have all cues listed in his book in running order.
2. *Second tech*: no actors. Rehearse all scene shifts as the stage manager calls them from the stage. Two to three hours.
3. *Third tech*: no actors. Run through all scene shifts, light, and sound cues. Stage manager calls cues from his console. About four hours.
4. *Fourth tech*: Run as for third tech but with actors. Four to five hours.

The director may now wish to do a complete run of the play with all props and special effects involving actors.

As we have suggested, technical rehearsals are not for the benefit of the actors and will normally be run on a cue-to-cue basis, cutting through the dialogue and picking up the action shortly before each desired effect. In the model above, during the first three rehearsals the assistant stage managers would stand in for actors where a physical body was needed for correct focusing and intensity. During the run with actors (fourth tech) it is very important that the actors perform the actions preceding the technical cues exactly as they will in performance, so that those responsible for the effects can gain a sense of the rhythm and timing, and the director can get some idea of how well his ideas will work in practice. Actors generally dislike technical rehearsals. Professionals treat them as all in a day's work; inexperienced actors must also understand that patience and good discipline at this time are as much a part of their job as the more glamorous and rewarding moments on stage during the run.

During technical rehearsals the director shifts his responsibilities gradually to his stage manager. At the first technical rehearsal, when actual intensities and volumes are being set, the director assumes full charge and responsibility in consultation with the designers involved. As the technical rehearsals proceed to the operational stage, and the problems become the precise working out of prearranged timings, the stage manager must take over the responsibility for conducting the technicians' work. When in the fourth tech the actors enter the rehearsal, the stage manager must be able to exercise his authority over them as well; once a production is in this stage, the stage manager must be given full control of the show. Many directors are unwilling to hand over "their" production to a less experienced stage manager, but only chaos will result if this is not done: the director will probably find himself forced to remain backstage for every performance if he cannot hand over the reins of the production during technical rehearsals. Avoid such a situation at all costs.

20. DRESS REHEARSALS

Dress rehearsals are run entirely by the stage manager, and all technical instructions to the cast are usually relayed by the director through the stage manager. In the dress rehearsal everything comes together: sound, lights, costumes, scenery, acting, props, special effects, and make-up. If the technical rehearsals have been thorough and well organized, the first dress rehearsal can be a nonstop run-through of the play, with few hitches. It seldom if ever is.

The first dress rehearsal is often a disaster. This is not entirely surprising. The newness of the final costumes throws the actors' timing off, even when rehearsal costumes have been used; the actors are suddenly more aware of "things"; the lighting changes all perspectives; dialogue and carefully rehearsed action suddenly become unfamiliar; and concentration is dissipated on the surroundings rather than focused on the action. The director must learn to accept this in the faith that the second dress rehearsal will bring the production back up to performance level. Of course, this will happen only if enough work has been put into the production before technical rehearsals, and the director must learn to distinguish between a performance which is down because of external technical factors, and one which is not sufficiently tight and cleanly rehearsed. While he is entangled in wires, headsets, light booths, and so on during the technical period, a director must keep his other eyes, ears, and hands on the specific needs of certain scenes and actors, to ensure that they remain at the necessary level or are finally brought up to it.

In professional situations the director will call daytime rehearsals between the evening dresses. Here he can revivify scenes deadened by techs and cure problems brought up by scenery and costumes. College and community theatre rarely affords itself this time but could profit from it. Second dress and all dresses following the first (there is frequently only one dress rehearsal, and rarely more than three) simply repeat the first and try to better its record. They undoubtedly will unless something unexpected goes wrong in the meantime. The director ordinarily takes notes during dress rehearsals and conveys his comments to the cast by a full meeting after the rehearsal or before the next rehearsal, by individual written notes, or by dressing-room aside comments.

21. OPENING NIGHT

No one is more helpless than a director on opening night. The stage manager has control of the show, and anticipation has control of the actors. Most directors feel utterly useless on this day, and most *are* utterly useless. If it has not been done by opening night, chances are that there is absolutely no way to get it except by that magical adrenalized luck that seems so infectious at this time. But don't count on it.

22. CONTINUING REHEARSALS

One of the unfortunate things about much amateur theatre is that it seems to be directed solely toward an opening night, after which serious work on the production is abandoned in favor of cast parties and mutual self-congratulation. This is especially unfortunate because some of the most useful artistic work on a production can be done only after opening night, when the production finally includes its missing ingredient: an audience. Certainly an audience is absolutely indispensable for the successful playing of a farce or comedy, because audience laughter is virtually written into the script. But even in a tragedy or serious drama the response of the audience, and the response to that response by the actors, are a fundamental part of the theatrical experience, and can be gauged only in performance.

It is unthinkable to premiere a professional play in New York without at least one or two weeks of paid preview performances, during which the show is "shaken down," its ineffective parts tightened or pruned out, its climaxes heightened, and timing honed to perfection. These previews are accompanied by regular daytime rehearsals to run over and improve the weaknesses which appeared the night before. In the case of a new play there is frequently a great deal of script revision at this point.

Similarly, it should be possible in amateur theatre to hold preview performances, or at least to have continuing rehearsals and criticism by the director during the actual performance run. A truly artistic director works on his show until he has the maximum result he can achieve, even if it does not come until closing night. It is the duty of the director, even after his production has come under the technical control of the stage manager, to supervise the run of the play, the morale of the company, and the consistency of the performances.

Rehearsal Timetable

The hypothetical model below is for a three-act play of average technical complexity, in rehearsal for a four-week period. The term *block* refers to a block of action. This may or may not be sequential scenes; the director breaks the play into convenient rehearsal blocks, which could mean that certain parts of the action involving the same actors are rehearsed at the same time, even though they are not in plot sequence. This often saves actors unnecessary calls and avoids their hanging around for three hours in the theatre for a ten-minute scene. This is especially important for amateur actors, but even with professionals who are being paid for their time it is much more profitable to allow them to work on their parts when not occupied on stage. Of course, it is possible to work in this manner only in early rehearsals; when the play is being put together its flow overrides all other considerations. Our hypothetical play has been split into six working blocks.

WEEK 1

Day 1. First reading. General concept; clarification of text.
Day 2. Second reading. Designers show renderings or models.

Day 3. Block 1.
Day 4. Block 2.
Day 5. Blocks 1 and 2.
Day 6. Block 3.

WEEK 2

Day 1. Block 4.
Day 2. Blocks 3 and 4.
Day 3. Blocks 1 and 2.
Day 4. Block 5.
Day 5. Block 6.
Day 6. Blocks 3 and 4, 5 and 6.

WEEK 3

Day 1. Run-through.
Day 2. Act I.
Day 3. Act II.
Day 4. Act III.
Day 5. Run-through.
Day 6. Work as necessary.

WEEK 4

Day 1. Run-through.
Day 2. Work as necessary, or run-through, or free.
Day 3. Tech.
Day 4. Tech.
Day 5. Tech or dress.
Day 6. Dress.
Day 7. Dress or free.

COMMENT

1. Rehearsals can be split into time blocks of concentration on different action blocks, depending on the time available at any rehearsal. Two to three hours' work on a block is probably the optimum at one time.
2. It is always useful to spend a few minutes on a warm-up before rehearsal.
3. Early rehearsals can include ensemble games and improvisations around the text (see Chapter 9).
4. In the model each block is given three rehearsal periods before polishing work begins on the acts. A possible use of these three periods is:
   First—loose structuring and exploration of the action;

Second—further exploration, selection, and solidifying of structure;
Third—smooth running of spatial structure, character interrelationships, and business. Here one should return to the text for subtleties that are now apparent, and to ensure that the action is revealed in the spatial structure.

5. Have a run-through some time during the first two weeks. This is important to keep the actors from losing sight of the play as a totality.

6. Do not allow any blocks to lie fallow for more than three days.

7. Act III should come together more quickly than the earlier acts, because the actors are becoming accustomed to each other's work, the working relationship is established between actors and director, and the actors have developed a sense of the play and character.

Bibliography

This bibliography is highly selective for two reasons. First, rather than providing a bald list of works in the area, we wish to give the neophyte director some indication of what he might find useful in the most influential works. Second, the possible sources the contemporary director might be referred to are as comprehensive as the spectrum of human activity itself. Our listing is, therefore, the nucleus of a library for the director, to which he may add books on theatre, sociology, art, politics, or psychology as his interest and capacity allow.

ANTOINE, ANDRÉ, *Memories of the Théâtre-Libre.* Miami, Fla.: University of Miami Press, 1964. Autobiographical work by the great exponent of naturalism. Interesting for its views on the theatre as a minute recapitulation of life, and on how this can be achieved.

ARTAUD, ANTONIN, *The Theatre and Its Double.* New York: Grove Press, Inc., 1958. The classic collection of the ideas and aesthetic of perhaps the most influential spiritual force behind the contemporary theatre.

BARRAULT, JEAN-LOUIS, *Reflections on the Theatre*. London: Rockliff Press, 1951. A highly personal autobiographical series of essays by France's leading actor-director of the mid-twentieth century.

BRECHT, BERTOLT, *The Messingkauf Dialogues*. London: Eyre Methuen, 1971. In Socratic form Brecht discusses the theatrical experience—what happens between actor and audience—from Shakespeare to the alienation effect.

BROOK, PETER, *The Empty Space: A Book About Theatre—Deadly, Holy, Rough, Immediate*. New York: Atheneum Publishers, 1968. A brilliant discussion by Britain's leading experimental director of how theatre can and must be a dynamic contemporary force.

BURRIS-MEYER, HAROLD, and EDWARD COLE, *Theatres and Auditoriums* (2nd ed.). New York: Van Nostrand Reinhold Company, 1964. The standard reference work on theatre buildings and stages.

CLURMAN, HAROLD, *On Directing*. New York: The Macmillan Company, 1972. The considered views and consolidated technique of forty years' experience in the American theatre. Important for an understanding of the basically naturalistic approach of the American director.

COLE, TOBY, and HELEN CHINOY (eds.), *Directors on Directing* (rev. ed.). Indianapolis: The Bobbs-Merrill Co., Inc., 1963. An excellent historical review of the emergence of the director, plus a brief selection of the ideas of the principal directors from Saxe-Meiningen to Elia Kazan.

GROTOWSKI, JERZY, *Towards a Poor Theatre*. New York: Simon & Schuster, Inc., 1969. Principles and techniques of acting described by the best-known practitioner of the theatrical spirit of Artaud.

GUTHRIE, SIR TYRONE, *A Life in the Theatre*. New York: McGraw-Hill Book Company, 1959. Anecdotes, attitudes, and achievements of the great director of classical theatre. Interesting because of Guthrie's dynamic and innovative approach to Shakespeare.

HETHMON, ROBERT (ed.), *Strasberg at the Actors Studio*. New York: The Viking Press, Inc., 1965. Transcribed tape recordings of Strasberg's teaching, with comment by Hethmon. Does much to set the record straight about what the "Method" actually is.

HODGSON, JOHN, and ERNEST RICHARDS, *Improvisation: Discovery and Creativity in Drama*. London: Eyre Methuen, 1966. Excellent practical discussion of how a director can employ improvisational methods in any production.

HOUGHTON, NORRIS, *Moscow Rehearsals*. New York: Harcourt Brace Jovanovich, Inc., 1936. The classic work on the methods of the great Russian directors in the period of Russian theatrical supremacy and experimentation.

KIRBY, E. T. (ed.), *Total Theatre: A Critical Anthology*. New York: E. P. Dutton & Co., Inc., 1969. A collection of essays on the roots and aesthetic of media incorporation in theatre, from Wagner to McLuhan.

KIRBY, MICHAEL, *The Art of Time: Essays on the Avant-Garde*. New York: E. P. Dutton & Co., Inc., 1969. A discussion of the ideas behind the relativity, subjectivity, and immediacy of the contemporary avant-garde in all areas of art. Discussion of the aesthetic of environmental theatre.

—— (ed.), *Happenings: An Illustrated Anthology*. New York: E. P. Dutton & Co., Inc., 1969. An examination of happenings, the theatrical phenomenon of the 1960s, and their relationship to Dada, expressionism, and collage painting. Contains scenarios and performance details.

LEWIS, ROBERT, *Method—or Madness*. New York: French & European Publications, Inc., 1958. Fine common sense discussion of some of the virtues and shortcomings of the Strasberg system.

McLUHAN, H. MARSHALL, *Understanding Media: The Extensions of Man*. New York: McGraw-Hill Book Company, 1964. Classic examination of the effect of technological advances in communication on how man now looks at his world.

MUNK, ERIKA (ed.), *Stanislavski and America*. New York: Fawcett World Library, 1966. A collection of the important commentaries on the influence of the great Russian actor and director on the American theatre.

PILBROW, RICHARD, *Stage Lighting*. New York: Van Nostrand Reinhold Company, 1970. A new approach to stage lighting by the successful British designer.

SCHECHNER, RICHARD (ed.), *Dionysus in 69*. New York: Farrar, Straus & Giroux, Inc., 1970. A pictorial edition of The Performance Group's environmental production of *The Bacchae*.

SPOLIN, VIOLA, *Improvisation for the Theatre: A Handbook of Teaching and Directing Techniques*. Evanston, Ill.: Northwestern University Press, 1963. The classic handbook of games and exercises for actor training and play improvisation.

ST. DENIS, MICHEL, *The Rediscovery of Style*. New York: Theatre Arts Books, 1960. An examination of style seen as the distillation of the spirit of a text. Also includes a brief discussion of actor training methods.

STANISLAVSKI, KONSTANTIN, *My Life in Art*. New York: Theatre Arts Books, n.d. Personal memoirs including discussions of Stanislavski's approach to acting and directing.

Index